1 MONTH OF
FREE
READING

at

www.ForgottenBooks.com

By purchasing this book you are
eligible for one month membership to
ForgottenBooks.com, giving you
unlimited access to our entire
collection of over 1,000,000 titles via
our web site and mobile apps.

To claim your free month visit:
www.forgottenbooks.com/free448909

ISBN 978-0-428-78988-6
PIBN 10448909

Clarendon Press Series

CHAUCER

E PROLOGUE, THE KNIGHTES TALE,

THE NONNE PRESTES TALE

FROM

THE CANTERBURY TALES

EDITED BY

R. MORRIS

Author of 'Specimens of Early English.'
Editor of Hampole's 'Pricke of Conscience,' 'Early English Alliterative Poems,'
'The Story of Genesis and Exodus,' 'The Ayenbite of Inwyt,' &c.
Member of the Council of the Philological Society.

Oxford

AT THE CLARENDON PRESS

MDCCCLXVII

INTRODUCTION.

EVENTFUL as the early life of Chaucer must have been, we have no sources of information from which we can gather even the simplest *facts* concerning his birth, birthplace, parentage and education, which are thus involved in much obscurity and uncertainty. If the Testament of Love be allowed to have any weight as an authentic autobiography, London [a] may claim the honour of being the place of the poet's birth. The name Chaucer, though not belonging to any noble or distinguished family, was of some antiquity, and seems to have been borne by persons of respectability and wealth, some of whom were connected with the city of London; and in the local records of the period (23rd year of Edward III), mention is made of a certain Richard Chaucer, a vintner of London, 'who,' says Speght, 'might well be Geoffrey Chaucer's father [b].'

For want of historical evidence to settle the exact year of the poet's birth, we are obliged to follow the ordinary traditionary account which places it at the commencement of the reign of Edward III, somewhere about the year 1328, a date which is perhaps not far wrong, inasmuch as it agrees with many better-known periods of his life. According to the inscription on his tomb, erected to his memory in 1556 by Nicholas Brigham, Chaucer died in the year 1400, and, having attained to the ripe age of three score and ten, would justly be entitled to the epithets *old*

---

[a] 'Also the citye of London, that is to me so dere and swete, in which I was forthgrowen; and more kindly (natural) love have I to that place than to any other in yerth (earth), as every kindly creture hath full appetite to that place of his kindely engendrure and to wilne reste and peace in that stede to abyde.' (Test of Love, Book I. § 5.)

[b] See Morley's English Writers, vol. ii. p. 142.

and *reverent,* applied to him by his contemporaries Gower and Occleve [c].

Whether Chaucer studied at Oxford or at Cambridge [d], whether he was educated for the Bar or the Church, we have now no means of determining. Nor do we even know when or what he studied, or how long his education was carried on; but it is quite certain that he was a diligent student, and a man of the most extensive learning. 'The acquaintance he possessed with the classics, with divinity, with astronomy, with so much as was then known of chemistry, and indeed with every other branch of the scholastic learning of the age, proves that his education had been particularly attended to; and his attainments render it impossible to believe that he quitted college at the early period at which persons destined for a military life usually began their career. It was not then the custom for men to pursue learning for its own sake; and the most natural manner of accounting for the extent of Chaucer's acquirements is to suppose that he was educated for a learned profession. The knowledge he displays of divinity would make it more likely that he was intended for the Church than for the Bar, were it not that the writings of the Fathers were generally read by all classes of students [e].'

For what is known of the latter half of Chaucer's life we are indebted to public records still in existence [f], in which the poet appears in close connection with the court, and as the recipient of royal favours.

---

[c] Leland says that Chaucer 'lived to the period of grey hairs, and at length found old age his greatest disease.' In Occleve's portrait of the poet he is represented with grey hair and beard.

[d] In one of his early poems, The Court of Love, Chaucer is supposed to make reference to his residence at Cambridge—

'My name ?
Philogenet I cald am, fer and nere,
Of Cambrige clerke.'

Leland thinks that Chaucer studied at both Universities.

[e] Life of Chaucer by Sir H. Nicolas.

[f] Issue Rolls of the Exchequer and the Tower Rolls. The details here are from Sir H. Nicolas' life of Chaucer, prefixed to Chaucer's poetical works in the Aldine series of the Poets.

The first important record of Chaucer is his own statement, in a deposition made by him at Westminster in October 1386, at the famous trial between Richard Lord Scrope and Sir Robert Grosvenor, when we find that the poet had already borne arms for twenty-seven years. His military career therefore did not commence until the year 1359, at which time he must have joined Edward the Third's army, which invaded France in the beginning of November of that year. After ineffectually besieging Rheims the English army laid siege to Paris (1360), when at length, suffering from famine and fatigue, Edward made peace at Bretigny near Chartres. This treaty, called the 'Great Peace,' was ratified in the following October, and King John was set at liberty. In this expedition Chaucer was made prisoner, and most probably obtained his release after the ratification of the treaty.

We have no means of ascertaining how he spent the next six years of his life, as we have no further record of his history until 1367. In this year the first notice of the poet occurs on the Issue Rolls of the Exchequer, where a pension of twenty marks[g] for life was granted by the king to Chaucer as one of the 'valets of the king's chamber;' or, as the office was sometimes called, 'valet of the king's household,' in consideration of former and future services.

About the same time, or perhaps a little earlier, he married Philippa[h], daughter of Sir Paon de Roet (a native of Hainault and King of Arms of Guienne) and sister to Katherine, widow of Sir Hugh Swynford, successively governess, mistress, and wife to John of Gaunt, Duke of Lancaster.

---

[g] A mark was 13s. 4d. of our money, but the buying power of money was nearly ten times greater than at present. In 1350 the average price of a horse was 18s. 4d.; of an ox 1l. 4s. 6d.; of a cow 17s. 2d.; of a sheep 2s. 6d.; of a goose 9d.; of a hen 2d.; of a day's labour in husbandry 3d. In Oxford, in 1310, wheat was 10s. a quarter; in December 7s. 8d., and in October 1311, 4s. 10d.

[h] Philippa was one of the ladies in attendance on Queen Philippa, and in 1366 a pension of ten marks was granted to her. After the death of the queen she appears to have been attached to the court of Constance of Castile, second wife of John of Gaunt.

During the years 1368 and 1369, Chaucer was in London, and received his pension in person.

In 1369 the death of Queen Philippa took place, and two or three months later Blanche, the wife of John of Gaunt, died at the age of twenty-nine. Chaucer did honour to the memory of his patron's wife in a funeral poem entitled the Boke of the Duchesse [i].

In the course of the next ten years (1370—1380) the poet was attached to the court and employed in no less than seven diplomatic services. In 1370 he was abroad in the king's service, and received letters of protection, to be in force from June till Michaelmas. Two years after this (Nov. 12, 1372) Chaucer was joined in a commission with two citizens of Genoa to treat with the doge, citizens and merchants of Genoa, for the choice of an English port where the Genoese might form a commercial establishment. He appears to have left England before the end of the year, having on the 1st of December received the sum of 63*l.* 13*s.* 4*d.* in aid of his expenses. He remained in Italy near twelve months and went on the king's service to Florence as well as to Genoa. His return to England must have taken place before the 22nd of Nov. 1373, as on this day he received his pension in person [k].

This was Chaucer's first important mission. It was no doubt skilfully executed, and gave entire satisfaction to the king, who on the 23rd of April, 1374, on the celebration of the feast of St. George at Windsor, made him a grant of a pitcher of wine

---

[i] ' And goodë fairë white she hete (was called),
That was my lady name righte.
She was therto bothe faire and bryghte,
She haddë not hir namë wronge.'
(Boke of the Duchesse, ll. 947—950.)

[k] In this embassy Chaucer is supposed to have made acquaintanceship with Petrarch, who was at Arqua, two miles from Padua, in 1373, from January till September, and to have learned from him the tale of the patient Griselda. But the old biographers of Chaucer are not to be trusted in this matter. Petrarch did not translate this tale from Boccaccio's Decameron into Latin until the end of Sept. 1373, after Chaucer's return, and his death occurred the next year (July 1374). It is the Clerk of Oxenford, and not Chaucer, that asserts that he learned the tale of ' a worthy clerk' at Padua, ' Fraunces Petrarch, the laureate poete.'

daily, to be received in the port of London from the hands of the king's butler[1]. About six weeks later, on the 8th of June, he was appointed Comptroller of the Customs and Subsidy of Wools, Skins and Leather, in the Port of London [m], and on the 13th of the same month he received a pension of 10*l.* for life from the Duke of Lancaster.

In 1375 Chaucer's income was augmented by receiving from the crown (Nov. 8) the custody of the lands and person of Edmond Staplegate of Kent, which he retained for three years, during which time he received as wardship and marriage fee the sum of 104*l.*; and (on Dec. 8) the custody of five 'solidates' of rent [n] in Soles in Kent. Toward the end of 1376 Sir John Burley and Chaucer were employed in some secret service, the nature of which is not known. On the 23rd of the same month the poet received 6*l.* 13*s.* 4*d.* and Burley twice that sum for the work upon which they had been employed.

In February 1377, the last year of Edward's reign, the poet was associated with Sir Thomas Percy (afterward Earl of Worcester) in a secret mission to Flanders [o], and was shortly afterwards (April) joined with Sir Guichard d'Angle (afterwards Earl of Huntingdon) and Sir Richard Sturry to treat of peace with Charles V, and to negotiate a secret treaty for the marriage of Richard, Prince of Wales, with Mary, daughter of the king of France [p]. In 1378 Richard II succeeded to the throne, and Chaucer appears to have been reappointed one of the king's esquires. In the middle of January he was again sent to France to treat for a marriage of Richard with the daughter of the King of France. On his return he was employed in a new mission to Lombardy, along with Sir Edward Berkeley, to treat with Bernard Visconti, Lord

[1] This was commuted in 1378 for a yearly payment of 20 marks.

[m] In July 1376 Chaucer, as Comptroller of Wool Customs, received from the king the sum of 71*l.* 4*s.* 6*d.*, being the fine paid by John Kent of London for shipping wool to Dordrecht without having paid the duty thereon.

[n] A *solidate* of land was as much land (probably an acre) as was worth 1*s.*

[o] Chaucer received for this service 10*l.* on Feb. 17, and 20*l.* on the 11th of April.

[p] Chaucer received 26*l.* 13*s.* 4*d.* on April 30, as part payment for this service, and in 1381 (March) he was paid an additional sum of 22*l.*

of Milan, and Sir John Hawkwood, 'on certain affairs touching the expediting the king's war ꝙ.' When Chaucer set out on this embassy he appointed Gower as one of his trustees to appear for him in the courts in case of any legal proceedings being instituted against him during his absence ʳ.

During the next three years Chaucer received his pension as usual. On the 8th of May, 1382, he was made Comptroller of the Petty Customs, retaining at the same time his office of Comptroller of the Wool Customs. These emoluments he continued to hold for the next four years, and was allowed the privilege of nominating a deputy, so that he had leisure to devote himself to his great work, the Canterbury Tales, which was not written till after 1386.

In 1386 Chaucer was elected a knight of the shire for Kent, in the Parliament held at Westminster. John of Gaunt was abroad at this time; and the Duke of Gloucester, at the head of the government, was most likely not well disposed towards the relative and *protégé* of his brother, with whom he was now

ꝙ Chaucer was absent on this service until the end of the year, but was not paid till 1380, when he received 56*l.* 13s. 4*d.*

ʳ This circumstance proves the existence of an intimate friendship between the two poets. Chaucer dedicated his Troilus and Criseyde to Gower; and the latter poet, in the Confessio Amantis (Book vii.), makes Venus speak of Chaucer as follows :—

> 'And grete wel Chaucer, when ye mete,
> As my disciple and my poete,
> For in the floures of his youthe,
> In sondry wyse, as he wel couthe,
> Of dytees and of songes glade,
> The whiche he for my sake made,
> The land fulfylled is over alle ;
> Whereof to him in specyalle
> Above alle other, I am most holde (beholden).
> Forthy nowe in his dayes olde
> Thou shalt him telle this message,
> That he uppon his latter age,
> To sette an end of al his werke,
> As he whiche is myn owne clerke,
> Do make his Testament of Love,
> As thou hast done thy shrift above,
> So that my courte yt may recorde.'

on ill terms. On the 1st of December Chaucer was dismissed from his offices of Comptroller of Wool, Woolfells, and Leather, and of Comptroller of Petty Customs, and others were appointed in his place[s]. The loss of his emoluments reduced the poet from affluence to poverty, and we find him raising money upon his two pensions of 20 marks, which on the 1st of May, 1388, were cancelled and assigned to John Scalby. To add to his trouble his wife died in 1389. Richard, in 1387, dismissed his council and took the reins of government into his own hands; the Lancastrian party were restored to power, and Chaucer was appointed Clerk of the King's Works at Westminster, at a salary of 2s. a-day, about 1l. of our money. The next year he was made Clerk of the King's Works for repairing St. George's Chapel at Windsor. But these appointments were of short duration. In another year he either retired or was superseded, and for the next three years his only income was his annuity of 10l. from the Duke of Lancaster, and an allowance of 40s., payable half-yearly, for robes as the king's esquire.

On the 28th of July, 1394, Chaucer obtained a grant from the king of 20l. a-year for life, payable half-yearly at Easter and Michaelmas; but at this time the poet appears to have been in very distressed circumstances, for we find him making application for advances from the Exchequer on account of his annuity, and as these were not always made to him personally during the next few years, it is supposed that he was labouring under sickness or infirmity, for it does not appear that he was absent from London[t].

---

[s] The Parliament of 1386 compelled Richard to appoint a commission to enquire into the state of the subsidies and customs. The commissioners began their duties in November, and the removal of certain officers may be attributed to their investigations.

[t] Chaucer appears to allude to his pecuniary difficulties in the following verses 'To his Empty Purse:'—

> 'To yow, my Purse, and to noon other wight,
> Complayn I, for ye be my lady dere;
> I am so sory now that ye been lyght,
> For, certes, but yf ye make me hevy chere,
> Me were as leef be layd upon my bere.

In 1398 (May 4) letters of protection were issued to Chaucer, forbidding any one, for the term of two years, to sue or arrest him on any plea except it were connected with land. Five months later (Oct. 18) the king made him a grant of a tun of wine a-year for life. Next year Henry Bolingbroke, son of John of Gaunt, supplanted his cousin Richard, and within four days after he came to the throne Chaucer's pension of 20 marks was doubled, in addition to the annuity of 20*l.* which had been given him by Richard II.

On Christmas Eve, 1399, the poet covenanted for the lease, for 53 years (a curious agreement for a man in his 71st year to make), of a house in the garden of the Chapel of St. Mary, Westminster, where it is probable that he ended his days. The date (Oct. 25, 1400) assigned to his death by Nicholas Brigham is corroborated by the entries in the Issue Rolls, no note of payment being found after March 1st, 1400.

Chaucer had two sons, Lewis, who died young, to whom he addressed his treatise on the Astrolabe, and Thomas, who attained to immense wealth, and whose great-grandson, John de la Pole (Earl of Lincoln), was declared by Richard III heir-apparent to the throne.

In the Prologue to the Rime of Sir Thopas", we have pro-

> For whiche unto your mércy thus I crye,
> Beeth hevy ayeyne or elles moote I dye,
> Now voucheth sauf this day or hyt be nyhte,
> That I of yow the blissful soune may here,
> Or see your colour lyke the sonne bryghte,
> That of yelownesse hadde never pere ;
> Ye be my lyfe, ye be myn hertys stere.
> Quene of comfort and good companye
> Beth hevy ayeyne, or elles moote I dye.
> Now Purse, that art to me my lyves lyghte,
> And saveour, as doun in this worlde here,
> Oute of this toune help me thurgh your myghte,
> Syn that ye wole nat bene my tresorere,
> For I am shave as nye as is a frere,
> But I pray unto your curtesye
> Beth hevy ayeyne, or elles moote I dye.'

> " 'Oure host to japen he began,
> And than at erst he loked upon me
> And saydë thus, "What man art thou?" quod he;

bably a faithful picture of Chaucer's personal appearance, agreeing in many points with his portrait by Occleve[x]. In person he was corpulent, and, like his host of the Tabard, 'a large man' and no 'poppet' to embrace, but his face was small, fair and intelligent; his eye downcast and meditative, but dazed by age and study. Altogether he had an 'elvish' or weird[y] expression of countenance which attracted the attention of those who came into contact with him for the first time, and with whom he seems to have been reserved and reticent. His extensive acquirements and voluminous writings show that he was a hard-working student; from incidental allusions in the House of Fame, we learn that when his labours and 'reckonings' at the Custom House were over, and he returned home, instead of rest and novelties he sat and pored over his books until his eyes were 'dased' and dull; and often at night an aching head followed the making of 'books, songs, and ditties.' So absorbed was he in his studies, that for the time neither foreign affairs, his neighbours' gossip, 'nor anything else that God had made,' had any interest for him. Hermit-like though he lived, Chaucer was not naturally a recluse, and still less an ascetic; given more to observe than to talk, he loved good and pleasant society, and to sit at the festive board; for, as he himself tells us, 'his abstinence was but little.'

But the personality of Chaucer is obscured by the essentially dramatic spirit which pervades nearly the whole of his works; and consequently we have but few opportunities of judging correctly of the poet's peculiar views, feelings, and tastes. His ardent love of Nature, finely apostrophised by the poet as 'the vicar of the

> " Thou lokest as thou woldest fynde an hare,
> For ever upon the ground I se the stare;
> Approche ner, and loke merily.
> Now ware you, sires, and let this man have space,
> He in the waste is schape as wel as I;
> This were a popet in an arme to embrace
> For any womman, smal and fair of face.
> He semeth elvisch by his countenaunce,
> For unto no wight doth he daliaunce." '

[x] This is a coloured portrait found in the margin of Occleve's work 'De Regimine Principum' in Harl. MS. 4866.

[y] Tyrwhitt renders *elvish* by 'shy.'

Almighty Lord,' is everywhere apparent.   What is more sponta-
neous and characteristic of the poet than such joyous outbursts
as the following :—

> ' Herknith these blisful briddes how they synge,
>   And seth these freissche floures how they springe ;
>   Ful is myn hert of revel and solaas.'

Even his love and reverence for books gave way before an eager
desire to enjoy the beauties of nature in that season of the year
when all around him was manifesting life and loveliness [z].

Not less evident is Chaucer's high estimation of woman and his
' perception of a sacred bond, spiritual and indestructible, in true
marriage between man and woman [a].'   Of all the flowers in the
mead the daisy, 'the emperice and floure of floures alle,' was
Chaucer's favourite, because to him it was the fit representative of
the ' trouthe of womanhede.'

As Mr. Morley has well remarked, ' Ditties in praise of the
Marguerite, or daisy, were popular with the French fashionable
poets; but none of them, like Chaucer, among all their allegorical
dreamings, ever dreamed of celebrating in that flower an emblem
of womanly truth and purity, wearing its crown as a gentle, inno-
cent, devoted wife.'

Though Chaucer was so intimately connected with the court,
and enjoyed no small share of courtly favours, he protested nobly
and fearlessly against the popular opinion that churls or villains, in
the legal sense of the term, that is, persons of plebeian rank, were
necessarily prone to be guilty of base and unworthy actions ; and

---

[z]   ' And as for me, though that I konne but lyte (little),
      On bokes for to rede I me delyte,
      And to hem yive (give) I feyth and ful credence,
      And in myn herte have hem in reverence
      So hertely that there is game noon,
      That for my bokes maketh me to goon,
      But yt be seldom on the holy day,
      Save, certeynly, whan that the monethe of May
      Is comen, and that I here the foules synge,
      And that the floures gynnen for to sprynge,
      Farwel my boke, and my devocioun !'
                          (Legende of Goode Women, ll. 29 —39.)
[a] See Morley's English Writers, vol. ii. pp. 135, 256, 286.

at the present day we can hardly appreciate the boldness which made him assert more than once that the true test of gentility is nobleness of life and courtesy of manners, and not mere ancestral rank[b].

As we have already said, Chaucer's great work, the Canterbury Tales, was not written till after the year 1386. His earlier literary productions were mostly translations, or imitations from foreign sources, chiefly Latin and French, and have therefore but little claim to originality, except so far as he altered or added to his originals; but even in these efforts there are many excellences and traces of the poet's genius, especially of his great power over language, which made his ability as a translator known and highly appreciated by his literary contemporaries. Francis Eustace Deschamps, in a ' Ballade à Geoffroi Chaucer,' speaks of him in the warmest terms of praise as ' grant translator, noble Geoffroy Chaucier !' But it is to the Canterbury Tales [c] that Chaucer

[b] ' But undirstonde in thyn entente
That this is not myn entendement,
To clepe no wight in noo ages
Oonly gentille for his lynages.
But whoso is vertuous,
And in his post nought outrageous,
Whanne sich oon thou seest thee biforn,
Though he be not gentille born,
Thou mayst wel seyn, this is in soth,
That he is gentil, bycause he doth
As longeth to a gentilman ;
Of hem noon other deme I can,
For certeynly withouten drede (doubt),
A cherle is demed by his dede,
Of hie or lowe, as ye may see,
Or of what kynrede that he bee.'
(Romaunt of the Rose, ll. 2187—2202.)

' Lok who that is most vertous alway,
Prive and pert (open), and most entendith aye
To do the gentil dedes that he can,
Tak him for the grettest gentilman.
Crist wol we clayme of him oure gentilesse,
Nought of our eldres for her olde richesse.'
(The Wife of Bath's Tale.)

[c] The chief minor works of Chaucer are :—The Court of Love; The Romaunt of the Rose (a translation of the Roman de la Rose), a work in

owes his fame and rank as the first poet of modern English litera-
ture, and in this work—the result of years of labour and study—
the genius and power of the poet are most strongly expressed.

The Canterbury Tales are a collection of stories related by
certain pilgrims who rode together in true English fellowship to
worship and pay their vows at the shrine of the 'holy and blisful
(blessed) martyr Thomas à Becket.'

The first hint of thus joining together a number of stories by
one common bond was probably borrowed from Boccaccio's De-
cameron [d]; 'but Chaucer's plan was far better than that of the
Decameron, and looked to a much greater result. . . . Boccaccio,
who died twenty-five years before Chaucer, placed the scene of
his Decameron in a garden, to which seven fashionable ladies had
retired with three fashionable gentlemen, during the plague that
devastated Florence in 1348. The persons were all of the same
class, young and rich, with no concern in life beyond the bandying
of compliments. They shut themselves up in a delicious garden
of the sort common in courtly inventions of the middle ages, and
were occupied in sitting about idly, telling stories to each other.
The tales were usually dissolute, often witty, sometimes ex-
quisitely poetical, and always told in simple charming prose. The
purpose of the story-tellers was to help each other to forget the
duties on which they had turned their backs, and stifle any sym-
pathies they might have had for the terrible griefs of their friends
and neighbours who were dying a few miles away. Chaucer

---

two parts, the first part of 4,070 lines by Guillaume de Louis (1200—1230),
and the Sequel of 18,002 lines by Jean de Meung, written nearly half a
century later; The Assembly of Fowls, or the Parliament of Birds (1358);
The Complaint of the Black Knight (about 1359); Chaucer's A B C trans-
lated out of Guillaume de Guileville's 'Pelerinage de l'Homme' written
about 1330; Chaucer's Dream (about 1359); The Book of the Duchess
(1369); Troylus and Criseyde, an enlarged version of Boccaccio's Filo-
strato written 1347-8; The Complaint of Marsand Venus, translated from
Granss on; The Flower and the Leaf (1387); The House of Fame; The
Legend of Good Woman; The Tale of Palamon and Arcite; The Cuckoo
and the Nightingale; The Testament of Love (1388); and A Treatise on
the Astrolabe (1391).

[d] Mr. Wright thinks that the widespread Romance of the 'Seven Sages,' of
which there are several English versions, gave Chaucer the idea of his plot.

substituted for the courtly Italian ladies and gentlemen who with-
drew from fellowship with the world, as large a group as he could
form of English people, of rank widely differing, in hearty human
fellowship together.. Instead of setting them down to lounge in
a garden, he mounted them on horseback, set them on the high
road, and gave them somewhere to go and something to do. The
bond of fellowship was not fashionable acquaintance and a com-
mon selfishness. It was religion; not indeed in a form so solemn
as to make laughter and jest unseemly, yet according to the cus-
tom of the day, a popular form of religion, the pilgrimage to the
shrine of Thomas à Becket, into which men entered with much
heartiness. It happened to be a custom which had one of the
best uses of religion, in serving as a bond of fellowship in which
conventional divisions of rank were for a time disregarded;
partly because of the sense, more or less joined to religious exer-
cise of any sort, that men are equal before God, and also, in no
slight degree, because men of all ranks trotting upon the high-road
with chance companions whom they might never see again, have
been in all generations disposed to put off restraint, and enjoy
such intercourse as might relieve the tediousness of travel ᵉ.'

It would take up too much space to enter upon any analysis of
the several stories which make up this wonderful collection. It
will suffice to consider briefly such portions of the Canterbury
Tales as are included in this volume of Selections; and first in
order and importance comes the **Prologue,** in which we have
laid before us the general plan, and the several characters of the
whole work.

In the pleasant season of April ᶠ, as Chaucer lay at the Tabard,
one of the chief houses of public entertainment, situated in the
High Street of Southwark, nine-and-twenty pilgrims on their way
to Canterbury arrived at the 'hostelry.' The poet being on the
same errand as themselves, joined them, and in a short time was
on intimate and friendly terms with each member of the company.

ᵉ Morley's English Writers, from Chaucer to Dunbar, vol. ii. pp. 287,
288.

ᶠ Elsewhere a date is given, the 28th of April, corresponding to the 7th
of May.

The host of the inn, 'Harry Bailly,' made one more, and presided over this 'merry company' during their journey to and from Canterbury. At his suggestion it was agreed that each pilgrim should tell two tales on their road to Becket's shrine, and two other tales on the way home; but as the number of the pilgrims was thirty-two g, and there are only twenty-four stories, it is evident that more than half the tales are wanting, which may be accounted for by supposing that Chaucer died before the completion of his work, or even before he had settled upon the exact arrangement of the several tales.

'After a brief introduction, filled with the most cheerful images of spring, the season of the pilgrimage, the poet commences the narrative with a description of the person and the character of each member of the party. This description extends to about seven hundred lines, and of course affords space for a very spirited and graphic portrayal of the physical aspect, and an outline of the moral features of each. This latter part of the description is generally more rapidly sketched, because it was a part of the author's plan to allow his personages to bring out their special traits of character, and thus to depict and individualize themselves, in the interludes between the tales. The selection of the pilgrims is evidently made with reference to this object of development in action, and therefore constitutes an essential feature of the plot. We have persons of all the ranks not too far removed from each other by artificial distinctions to be supposed capable of associating upon that footing of temporary equality which is the law of good fellowship, among travellers bound on the same journey and accidentally brought together. All the great classes of English humanity are thus represented, and opportunity is given for the display of the harmonies and the jealousies which now united, now divided the interests of the different orders and different vocations in the commonwealth. The clerical pilgrims, it will be observed, are proportionately very numerous. The exposure of the corruptions of the Church was doubtless

g The canon and his yeoman joined them at Boughton-under-Blean, seven miles on the London side of Canterbury; but the master's doings being exposed by his servant, he was glad to ride away 'for very sorrow and shame.'

a leading aim with the poet; and if the whole series, which was designed to extend to at least fifty-eight tales, had been completed, criminations and recriminations of the jealous ecclesiastics would have exhibited the whole profession in an unenviable light.

'But Chaucer could be just as well as severe. His portrait of the prioress, though it does not spare the affectations of the lady, is complimentary; and his "good man of religion," the "pore Persoun of a toun," of whom it is said that—

> " Cristes lore, and his apostles twelve
> He taught, and ferst he folwed it himselve,"

has been hundreds of times quoted as one of the most beautiful pictures of charity, humility, and generous, conscientious, intelligent devotion to the duties of the clerical calling, which can be found in the whole range of English literature.

'None of these sketches, I believe, has ever been traced to a foreign source, and they are so thoroughly national that it is hardly possible to suppose that any imagination but that of an Englishman could have conceived them. In the first introduction of the individuals described in the prologues to the several stories, and in the dialogues which occur at the pauses between the tales, wherever, in short, the narrators appear in their own persons, the characters are as well marked and discriminated, and as harmonious and consistent in action, as in the best comedies of modern times. Although, therefore, there is in the plan of the composition nothing of technical dramatic form or incident, yet the admirable conception of character, the consummate skill with which each is sustained and developed, and the nature, life, and spirit of the dialogue, abundantly prove that if the drama had been known in Chaucer's time as a branch of living literature, he might have attained to as high excellence in comedy as an English or Continental writer. The story of a comedy is but a contrivance to bring the characters into contact and relation with each other, and the invention of a suitable plot is a matter altogether too simple to have created the slightest difficulty to a mind like Chaucer's. He is essentially a dramatist; and if his great work does not appear in the conventional dramatic form, it is an accident of the time, and by no means proves a want of power of original conception or of artistic skill in the author.

' This is a point of interest in the history of modern literature, because it is probably the first instance of the exhibition of unquestionable dramatic genius in either the Gothic or the Romance languages. I do not mean that there had previously existed in modern Europe nothing like histrionic representation of real or imaginary events; but neither the Decameron of Boccaccio, to which the Canterbury Tales have been compared, nor any of the Mysteries and Moralities, or other imaginative works of the middle ages, in which several personages are introduced, show any such power of conceiving and sustaining individual character as to prove that its author could have furnished the *personnel* of a respectable play. Chaucer therefore may fairly be said to be not only the earliest dramatic genius of modern Europe, but to have been a dramatist before that which is technically known as the existing drama was invented [h].'

The Knightes Tale, or at least a poem upon the same subject, was originally composed by Chaucer as a separate work. As such it is mentioned by him, among some of his other works, in the Legende of Goode Women (ll. 420, 1), under the title of ' Al the Love of Palamon and Arcite of Thebes, thogh the storye ys knowen lyte;' and the last words seem to imply that it had not made itself very popular. It is not impossible that at first it was a mere translation of the Teseide of Boccaccio, and that its present form was given it when Chaucer determined to assign it the first place among his Canterbury Tales [i].

It may not be unpleasing to the reader to see a short summary

---

[h] Marsh, Origin and History of the English Language, pp. 417–419.

[i] ' The Knight's Tale is an abridged translation of a part of Boccaccio's Teseide, but with considerable change in the plan, which is, perhaps, not much improved, and with important additions in the descriptive and the more imaginative portions of the story. These additions are not inferior to the finest parts of Boccaccio's work ; and one of them, the description of the temple of Mars, is particularly interesting, as proving that Chaucer possessed a power of treating the grand and terrible, of which no modern poet but Dante had yet given an example.' (Marsh, Origin and History of the English Language, pp. 423, 424.)

of it, which will show with what skill Chaucer has proceeded in reducing a poem of about ten thousand lines to a little more than two thousand without omitting any material circumstance.

The Teseide is distributed into twelve Books or Cantos.

Bk. i. Contains the war of Theseus with the Amazons, their submission to him, and his marriage with Hippolyta.

Bk. ii. Theseus, having spent two years in Scythia, is reproached by Perithous in a vision, and immediately returns to Athens with Hippolyta and her sister Emilia. He enters the city in triumph; finds the Grecian ladies in the temple of Clemenzia; marches to Thebes; kills Creon, &c., and brings home Palemone and Arcita, who are

> 'Damnati—ad eterna presone.'

Bk. iii. Emilia, walking in a garden and singing, is heard and seen first by Arcita [k], who calls Palemone. They are both equally enamoured of her, but without any jealousy or rivalship. Emilia is supposed to see them at the window, and to be not displeased with their admiration. Arcita is released at the request of Perithous; takes his leave of Palemone, with embraces, &c.

Bk. iv. Arcita, having changed his name to *Pentheo*, goes into the service of Menelaus at Mycenae, and afterwards of Peleus at Aegina. From thence he returns to Athens and becomes a favourite servant of Theseus, being known to Emilia, though to nobody else; till after some time he is overheard making his complaint in a wood, to which he usually resorted for that purpose, by Pamphilo, a servant of Palemone.

Bk. v. Upon the report of Pamphilo, Palemone *begins* to be jealous of Arcita, and is desirous to get out of prison in order to

---

[k] In describing the commencement of this amour, which is to be the subject of the remainder of the poem, Chaucer has entirely departed from his author in three principal circumstances, and, I think, in each with very good reason: 1. By supposing Emilia to be seen first by Palamon, he gives him an advantage over his rival which makes the catastrophe more consonant to poetical justice; 2. The picture which Boccaccio has exhibited of two young princes violently enamoured of the same object, without jealousy or rivalship, if not absolutely unnatural, is certainly very insipid and unpoetical; 3. As no consequence is to follow from their being seen by Emilia at this time, it is better, I think, to suppose, as Chaucer has done, that they are not seen by her.

fight with him. This he accomplishes with the assistance of Pamphilo, by changing clothes with Alimeto, a physician. He goes armed to the wood in quest of Arcita, whom he finds sleeping. At first they are very civil and friendly to each other. Then Palemone calls upon Arcita to renounce his pretensions to Emilia, or to fight with him. After many long expostulations on the part of Arcita, they fight, and are discovered first by Emilia, who sends for Theseus. When he finds who they are, and the cause of their difference, he forgives them, and proposes the method of deciding their claim to Emilia by a combat of a hundred on each side, to which they gladly agree.

Bk. vi. Palemone and Arcita live splendidly at Athens, and send out messengers to summon their friends, who arrive; and the principal of them are severally described, viz. Lycurgus, Peleus, Phocus, Telamon, &c.; Agamemnon, Menelaus, Castor, and Pollux, &c.; Nestor, Evander, Perithous, Ulysses, Diomedes, Pygmalion, Minos, &c., with a great display of ancient history and mythology.

Bk. vii. Theseus declares the laws of the combat, and the two parties of a hundred on each side are formed. The day before the combat, Arcita, after having visited the temples of all the gods, makes a formal prayer to Mars. The prayer, *being. personified*, is said to go and find Mars in his temple in Thrace, which is described; and Mars, upon understanding the message, causes favourable signs to be given to Arcita. In the same manner Palemone closes his religious observances with a prayer to Venus. His prayer, *being also personified*, sets out for the temple of Venus on Mount Citherone, which is also described; and the petition is granted. Then the sacrifice of Emilia to Diana is described; her prayer; the appearance of the goddess, and the signs of the two fires. In the morning they proceed to the theatre with their respective troops, and prepare for the action. Arcita puts up a private prayer to Emilia, and harangues his troop publicly, and Palemone does the same.

Bk. viii. Contains a description of the battle, in which Palemone is taken prisoner.

Bk. ix. The horse of Arcita, being frighted by a Fury, sent from Hell at the desire of Venus, throws him. However, he is carried to Athens in a triumphal chariot with Emilia by his side; is put to bed dangerously ill; and there by his own desire espouses Emilia.

Bk. x. The funeral of the persons killed in the combat. Arcita, being given over by his physicians, makes his will, in discourse with Theseus, and desires that Palemone may inherit all his possessions and also Emilia. He then takes leave of Palemone and Emilia, to whom he repeats the same request. Their lamentations. Arcita orders a sacrifice to Mercury, which Palemone performs for him, and dies.

Bk. xi. Opens with the passage of Arcita's soul to heaven, imitated from the Ninth Book of Lucan. The funeral of Arcita. Description of the wood felled takes up six stanzas. Palemone builds a temple in honour of him, in which his whole history is painted. The description of this painting is an abridgment of the preceding part of the poem.

Bk. xii. Theseus proposes to carry into execution Arcita's will by the marriage of Palemone and Emilia. This they both decline for some time in formal speeches, but at last are persuaded and married. The kings, &c., take their leave, and Palemone remains—'in gioia e in diporto con la sua dona nobile e cortese [1].'

The Nonne Prest his Tale is so characteristic of Chaucer's genius that Dryden, who modernized it as the fable of the 'Cock and Fox,' thought it to be of the poet's own invention; but it is probably taken from a fable of about forty lines, 'Dou coc et dou Werpil,' in the poems of Marie of France, which again is borrowed from the fifth chapter of the old French metrical Roman de Renart, entitled 'Se conme Renart prist Chantecler le Coc.'

Chaucer's English, like that of the present day, is an uninflected or analytic language, and in this respect it differed from the language of many earlier authors, and especially from that oldest form of English usually termed Anglo-Saxon, which was originally inflected or synthetic, that is to say it expressed

---

[1] Tyrwhitt, Introductory Discourse to the Canterbury Tales.

grammatical relation by a change in the *form* of words, instead of employing auxiliary words. The circumstances which led to this conversion are well known, forming as they do a part of the history of the English people. The first in order of time is the invasion, settlement, and conquest of the country by the Danes, extending over a period of nearly a century and a half (A.D. 867—1013). The Danish influence upon the language seems to have affected chiefly the dialects of the north and east parts of the island, in consequence of which their inflections and syntactical structure were much simplified, and assumed a more modern appearance than the speech prevailing in other districts. Doubtless it caused the language generally to be in a very unsettled state, and the revolution thus commenced was accelerated by the Norman Conquest, which followed in the year 1066. Norman rule introduced a new civilisation of a far higher order than had ever before existed in England, and of this the Normans were fully sensible, and utterly despised both the language and literature of the Saxons as only fit for churls and villains. In a certain sense English ceased to be the language of literature [m], and for about two hundred years Norman-French was the language of the Court, the Church, the Courts of Law, and of the upper and middle classes of society, and divided literature with the Latin tongue. But though the English were thus made to feel their position as a subject people, they clung most pertinaciously to the speech of their forefathers, and after a long and continuous struggle English regained its supremacy as the language of literature and the common tongue of all who claimed the name of Englishmen, while Norman-French was reduced to a mere provincial dialect. This was brought about by the fusion of the Saxon and Norman races, about the time of Henry II; by the severance of Normandy from England and its annexation to France, in the time of John; by the wars of Edward III, which did much to promote re-

---

[m] It is altogether erroneous to suppose that immediately after the Norman Conquest English ceased to be written, for from Aelfric to Chaucer we have an almost unbroken series of vernacular literature by which we are able to determine with tolerable exactness the various changes in grammar and vocabulary which occurred during this interval.

ligious and political liberty, and by the adoption of English as the household speech by that part of the nation that had previously spoken French, which happened about the middle of the fourteenth century.

The Norman Conquest wrought a twofold revolution in the language: the first, which extended over nearly the whole of the twelfth century, affected the grammatical forms of the language; final vowels were changed, some consonants became softened, and many of the older inflexions of nouns, adjectives and verbs went out of use, their place being supplied by prepositions and auxiliary words. This was a period of great grammatical confusion, but the vocabulary remained unchanged. At the beginning of the thirteenth century, we find the grammatical forms more settled; but many provincial elements unknown to the oldest English had crept in, and about the middle of this period we have to note a further change in the *substance* of the language, caused by the infusion of the Norman-French element. The additions to the vocabulary were at first small, but they gradually increased, and about the middle of the fourteenth century they formed no inconsiderable part of the *written* language. In Chaucer's works these loans are so numerous that he has been accused of corrupting the English language by a large and unnecessary admixture of Norman-French terms. But Chaucer, with few exceptions, employed only such terms as were in use in the *spoken* language, and stamped them with the impress of his genius, so that they became current coin of the literary realm.

The period in which Chaucer lived was one of great literary activity, and such names as Richard Rolle of Hampole, Minot, Mandeville, Langland, Wicliffe, and Gower, prove that the English language was in a healthy and vigorous condition, and really deserving of the importance into which it was rising. But as yet there was no *national language*, and consequently no *national literature;* the English of the fourteenth century diverged into many dialects, each having its own literature intelligible only to a comparatively small circle of readers, and no one form of English can be considered as the type of the language of the period.

Of these dialects the East Midland, spoken, with some variation, from the Humber to the Thames, was perhaps the simplest in its grammatical structure, the most free from those broad provincialisms which particularized the speech of other districts, and presented the nearest approach in form and substance to the language of the present day as spoken and written by educated Englishmen. In the works of Orm and Robert of Brunne we have evidence of its great capacity for literary purposes. Wicliffe and Gower added considerably to its importance, but in the hands of Chaucer it attained to the dignity of a national language". He represented, and identified himself with, that new life which the English people at this time were just commencing, and his works reflect not only his own inimitable genius, but the spirit, tastes, and feelings of his age. It was this, combined with his thorough mastery over the English language, that caused Chaucer to become to others (what no one had been before) a standard of literary excellence; and for two hundred years after he had no equal, but was regarded as the father of English poetry, the Homer of his country, and the well of English undefiled.

With the Canterbury Tales commences the modern period of English literature. Our earlier authors are usually studied for their philological importance, and most of them require the aid of a grammar and a glossary, but Chaucer is as easily understood as Spenser and Shakespeare. Not many of his terms are wholly obsolete, and but few of his inflections have gone wholly out of use. But as some special acquaintance with Chaucer's English will be of great service in mastering the poet's system of versification, an outline of his grammatical forms is subjoined, which will be found useful should the young student feel disposed to make himself acquainted with the works of earlier English writers.

n ʻFrom this Babylonish comparison of speech [i. e. the numerous local dialects of the English language in the fourteenth century] the influence and example of Chaucer did more to rescue his native tongue than any other single cause; and if we compare his dialect with that of any writer of an earlier date, we shall find that in compass, flexibility, expressiveness, grace, and of all the higher qualities of poetical diction, he gave it at once the utmost perfection which the materials at his hand would admit of.ʼ (Marsh, The Origin and History of the English Language, p. 381.)

NOUNS.

Number.—The nominative plural for the most part terminates in -*ës* :—

> ' And with his *strëmes* dryeth in the *grevës*
> The silver *dropés* hongyng on the *leevës.*'
>
> (Knightes Tale, ll. 637–8.)

1. -*s* is frequently added—1. To nouns terminating in a liquid or dental, as *bargayns, naciouns, palmers, pilgryms,* &c.; 2. To most words of more than one syllable.

-*is*, -*us*, for -*es*—as *bestis* (beasts), *leggus* (legs), *othus* (oaths)—is a dialectical variety, and probably due to the scribe who copied the MS.

2. Some few nouns (originally forming the plural in -*an*) have -*en*, -*n*; as *asschen* (ashes); *assen* (asses); *been* (bees); *eyen, yen* (eyes); *fleen* (fleas); *flon* (arrows); *oxen*; *ton, toon* (toes); *schoon* (shoes).

The following have -*n*, which has been added to older forms—(1) in -*e* (originally in -*u*); (2) in *a* or *y*.

(1) *Bretheren* (A. S. *brothru*, O. E. *brothre, brethre*), brothers. *Doughteren* (A. S. *dohtru*, O. E. *dohtere*), daughters. *Sistren, sustren* (A. S. *sweostru*, O. E. *swustre*), sisters. *Children* (A. S. *cildru*, O. E. *childere*), children [o].

(2) *Fon, foon* (A. S. *fá*), foes; *kyn* (A. S. *cy*) kine [p].

3. The following nouns, originally neuter, have no termination in the plural: *deer, folk, good, hors, neet, scheep, swin, thing, yer, yeer*; as in the older stages of the language *night, winter, freond* (A. S. *frynd*) are used as plurals.

4. *Feet, gees, men, teeth,* are examples of the plural by vowel-change.

Case.—The genitive case singular ends in -*ës* ; as—

> ' Ful worthi was he in his *lordës* werre.' (Prol. l. 47.)

---

[o] In some of the O. E. Northern and Midland dialects we find *brether* (brothers), *childer* (children), *deghter* (daughters).
[p] In some of the Northern and Midland dialects we find *kye* (cows).

1. In Anglo-Saxon *fader, brother, doughter*, took no inflexion in the genitive singular: this explains such phrases as '*fader* day,' '*fader* soule,' '*brother* sone,' '*doughter* name.'

2. The following phrases contain remnants of feminine nouns which originally formed the genitive in *-an* (1st declension of A.S. nouns):—'*Lady* (= *ladyë*) grace;' '*lady* veyl;' '*cherchë* blood;' '*hertë* blood;' '*widow* (= *widewë*) sone;' '*sonnë* upriste' (up-rising).

3. The dative case singular terminates in *-e*; as *beddë, holtë*, &c.

4. The genitive plural is much the same as in modern English; as '*foxës* tales;' '*mennës* wittes.' Forms in *-en* (= *-ene*) are not common in Chaucer's works: 'his *eyghen* (of eyes) sight' occurs in Canterbury Tales, l. 10134 (Wright's Text).

ADJECTIVES.

Adjectives, like the modern German, have two forms—Definite and Indefinite. The definite form preceded by the definite article, a demonstrative adjective, or a possessive pronoun, terminates in *-ë* in all cases of the singular; as 'the *yonge* sone,' 'his *halfe* cours,' &c. Words of more than one syllable nearly always omit the final *-e*.

The vocative case of the adjective takes this *-e*; as '*leeve* bro-ther' (l. 326, p. 38); 'O *stronge* God' (l. 155, p. 74).

Degrees of Comparison.—The Comparative degree is formed by adding *-er* (*-ere*) to the Positive; as *lever, farrer* (*farrere*), *gretter* (*grettere*).

We have some few abbreviated forms remaining; as *derre* (dearer); *ferre* (further); *herre* (higher); *ner, nerre* (nearer); *sore* (sorer). *Leng, lenger* (*lengere*), *strenger*, are examples of vowel-change; as in modern English *elder*, the comparative of *old*.

The Superlative degree terminates in *-est* (*-este*): *nest* or *next*, and *hext* (highest) are abbreviated forms.

Number.—The plural of adjectives is denoted by the final *-e* :—

'And *smalë* fowles maken melodie.' (Prol. l. 9.)

Adjectives of more than one syllable, and adjectives used pre-
dicatively, mostly drop the -*e* in the plural. Some few adjectives
of Romance origin form the plural in -*es*; as '*places delitables.*'

DEMONSTRATIVES.

1. **Definite Article.**—*The* (pl. *tho* = A.S. *tha*).

In the phrases 'that oon,' 'that other'—which in some dia-
lects became *toon* (*ton*), and *tother*—*that* is the old form of the
neuter article; but Chaucer never uses *that* except as a demon-
strative adjective, as in the present stage of the language.

2. *Atte* = at the (A.S. *at tham*; O.E. *at than, attan, atta*).

3. *Tho* must be rendered *those*, as well as *the*; as '*tho* wordes,'
'and *tho* were bent.' It is occasionally used pronominally, as
'oon of *tho* that' = one of those that.

4. *This* has for its plural *this, thise, thes, these* (A.S. *thás, thæs*).

5. *Som* . . . *som* = one . . . another.

> ' He moot ben deed, the kyng as schal a page;
>   *Sum* in his bed, *som* in the deepë see,
>   *Som* in the largë feelde, as men may se.'
>   (Knightes Tale, ll. 2162-4.)

PRONOUNS.

	SING.	PLURAL.
Nom.	I, Ich, Ik,	we.
Gen.	min (myn), mi (my),	our, oure.
Dat. Acc.	me,	us.
Nom.	thou, thow,	ye.
Gen.	thin (thyn), thi (thy),	your, youre.
Dat. Acc.	the, thee,	yow.

	SING.			PLURAL.
	Mas.	*Fem.*	*Neut.*	
Nom.	he,	she,	hit, it,	thei, they.
Gen.	his,	hir, hire,	his,	here, her, hire, hir.
Dat. Acc.	him,	hir, hire, here,	hit, it,	hem.

1. The Independent, or more properly speaking, the Predicative forms of the pronouns are *min* (pl. *mine*); *oure, oures,* ours; *thin* (pl. *thine*); *youre, youres,* yours; *hire, heres,* hers; *here, heres,* theirs.

2. The Midland dialect seems to have borrowed the forms *oures, youres,* &c., from the Northern dialect in which *oure, youre,* &c., are not used.

3. The dative case of the pronouns are used after *wel, wo, loth, leef* (lief), with impersonal verbs, as '*me* mette;' '*him* thoughte;' and with some verbs of motion, as 'goth *him;*' 'he rydeth *him.*'

4. The pronoun *thow* is sometimes joined to the verb, as *schaltow, wiltow.*

5. The Interrogative pronouns are *who* (gen. *whos;* dat. and acc. *whom*), *which* and *what.*

    a. Which has often the sense of *what, what sort of:*—

       '*Which a* miracle ther befel anoon.'
              (Knightes Tale, 1809; see Prol. l. 40.)

It is not used exactly as a relative, as in modern English, but is joined with *that;* as 'Hem *whiche that* wepith;' 'His love *the which that* he oweth.'

    b. What is occasionally used for *why* (cp. Lat. *quid,* Ger. *was*):—

       '*What* schulde he studie and make himselven wood?
              (Prol. l. 184.)

       '*What* schulde I alway of his woe endite?'
              (Knightes Tale, l. 522.)

6. *That* is a relative pronoun, but it is often used with the personal pronouns, in the following manner:—

    a. That he = who.
       'A knight ther was, and that a worthy man,
       That from the tymë that he first began
       To ryden out, *he* lovede chyvalrye.' (Prol. ll. 43–45.)

    b. That his = whose.
       'Al were they sorë hurt, and namely oon,
       That with a spere was thirled *his* brest boon.'
              (Knightes Tale, ll. 1843–44.)

c. That him = whom.

> ' I saugh to-day a corps yborn to chirche
> *That* now on Monday last I saugh *him* wirche.'
>
> (Milleres Tale.)

7. The words *who* and *whoso* are used indefinitely; as, ' As who seith' = as *one* says; ' Who so that can him rede' = if that *any one* can read him.

8. *Me* and *men* are used like the French *on*, English *one*.

VERBS.

I. REGULAR OR WEAK VERBS.

INDICATIVE MOOD.

Present Tense.

Singular.	Plural.
1. I lov-ë,	We lov-en, lov-ë.
2. Thou lov-est,	Ye lov-en, lov-ë.
3. He lov-eth,	They lov-en, lov-ë.

Past Tense.

Singular.	Plural.
1. I lov-edë,	We lov-eden, lov-edë.
2. Thou lov-edest,	Ye lov-eden, lov-edë.
3. He lov-edë,	They lov-eden, lov-edë.

1. In the 2nd person, *t* is often dropped, as *dos* = dost, *has* = hast, &c. This has been considered by some as a mere clerical error; but in the East Midland dialects, there was a tendency to drop the *t*, probably arising from the circumstance of the 2nd person of the verb in the Northumbrian dialects terminating always in *-es*.

2. Verbs of Saxon origin, which have *d* or *t* for the last letter of the root (and one or two that have *s*), form the 3rd sing. in *t*, as *sit* = sitteth, sits; *writ* = writeth, writes; *fint* = findeth, finds; *halt* = holdeth, holds; *rist* = riseth, rises.

3. We often find *-th* instead of *-eth*, as *spekth* = speaketh.

4. The plural of the present indicative occasionally ends in *-eth* (*-th*), which was the ordinary inflexion for all persons in the Old English Southern dialects.

> 'And over his heed ther *schyneth* two figures.'
>
> (Knightes Tale, l. 1185.)

5. There are two other classes of the weak conjugation which form the past tense by *-dë* or *-të*. To the first class belong—

PRES.	PAST.
Heren, to hear,	herde.
Hiden, to hide,	hidde.
Kepen, to keep,	kepte.

Some few verbs have a change of vowel in the past tense; as,—

PRES.	PAST.
Delen, to deal,	dalte.
Leden, to lead,	ladde.
Leven, to leave,	lafte.

If the root ends in *d* or *t*, preceded by another consonant, *ë* only is added, as—

PRES.	PAST.
Wenden, to turn,	wende (=wend-de).
Sterten, to start,	sterte (=stert-te).
Letten, to hinder,	lette (=lett-te).

To the second class belong

PRES.	PAST.
Tellen, to tell,	tolde.
Sellen, to sell,	solde.
Seche, to seek,	soughte.

II. IRREGULAR OR STRONG VERBS.

1. These verbs have a change of vowel in the past tense, and the past participle ends in *en* or *-ë*; as *sterven*, to die; pret. *starf*; pp. *storven* or *storve*. (See Participles, p. xxxiv. 3.)

2. Some few strong verbs take the inflexions of the weak verbs, so that we have double forms for the past tense, as—

Sleep and slep-te.
Creep and crep-te.
Weep and wep-te.

3. The 1st and 3rd persons of the past indicative of strong verbs do *not* take an -*e* in the singular number; the addition of this syllable turns them into plurals.

4. The East Midland dialect, in the Early English period, drops the -*e* in the 2nd person past indicative; and we find in Chaucer 'thou *bar*,' 'thou *spak*,' 'thou *dronk*' (O.E. thou *ber-e*, thou *spek-e*, thou *drunk-e*),=thou barest, thou spakest, thou drankest.

Occasionally we find -*est*, as in modern English; as *bygonnest, highlest, knewest*, &c.

5. The plural of the past indicative ends in -*en* or -*e*.

6. Some few verbs, as in the older stages of the language, have a change of vowel in the past tense plural, as—

INFINITIVE.	PRET. SING.	PAST PL.
Riden, to ride,	rood, rod,	riden.
Smiten, to smite,	smoot,	smiten.
Sterven, to die,	starf,	storven.

SUBJUNCTIVE MOOD.

1. The present subjunctive, singular number, terminates in -*e*, the plural in -*en*; the past in -*ede*, -*de*, -*te*, the plural in -*eden*, -*den*, -*ten*, through all persons.

2. Such forms as *speke we, go we*, = let us speak, let us go.

IMPERATIVE MOOD.

1. Verbs conjugated like *loven* and *tellen*, have the 2nd person sing. imperative in -*e*; as *love* thou, *telle* thou. All other verbs have properly no final *e*, as '*her* thou' =hear thou, '*ches* thou' =choose thou.

2. The plural terminates usually in -*eth*, but sometimes the -*th* is dropped.

INFINITIVE MOOD.

The infinitive ends in -*en* or -*e*: as *speken, speke*, to speak. The -*n* was dropped at a very early period in the Southern English dialect of the fourteenth century, and -*e* is preferred to -*en*.

The gerundial infinitive, or dative case of the infinitive (preceded by *to*), occasionally occurs, as *to doon-e* (=*to don-ne*), *to seen-e* (=*to seen-ne*), to do, to see.

PARTICIPLES.

1. The present participle ends usually in *-yng*. The A. S. suffix was *-ende*, which is used by Gower; but in the Southern dialect of Early English we find *-inde*⁹, which has evidently given rise to *-inge; -yng* is a shorter form, and the longer *-ynge* is occasionally employed by Chaucer, to rhyme with an infinitive verb in *-e*.

The suffix *-ing*, of nouns like *morning*, was *-ung* in the older stages of the language.

2. The past participle of weak verbs terminates in *-ed*, *-d*, and occasionally in *-et*, *-t;* those of strong verbs in *-en* or *-e*.

3. The prefix *y-* or *i-* (A.S. *ge-*) occurs frequently before the past participle, as *i-ronne* (run), *i-falle* (fallen), &c.

ANOMALOUS VERBS.

1. *Ben, been,* to be:—1st sing. pres. indic. *am;* 2nd *art;* 3rd *beth, is;* pl. *beon, aren, are:*—1st and 3rd past. *was;* 2nd *were.* Imperative pl. *beth;* pp. *ben, been.*

2. *Conne,* to know, be able :—pres. indic., 1st. and 3rd *can;* 2nd *can, canst;* pl. *connen, conne;* past, 1st and 3rd *couthe, cowthe, cowde;* pp. *couth, coud.*

3. *Daren, dare:*—pres. indic. sing., 1st and 3rd *dar;* 2nd *darst;* pl. *dar, dorre;* past *dorste, durste.*

4. *May:*—pres. indic. sing., 1st and 3rd *mow, may;* 2nd *mayst, maist, might;* pl. *mowen;* pres. subjunctive *mowe;* past tense, 1st and 3rd *mighte, moghte.*

5. *Mot,* must, may:—indic. pres. sing., 1st and 3rd *mot, moot;* 2nd *must, most;* pl. *mooten, moste;* past *moste.*

6. *Owen,* to owe (*debeo*):—pres. *oweth:* past *oughte, aughte;* pl. *oughten, oughte.*

---

⁹ The Northern form of the participle was *-ande*, *-and*, which occasionally occurs in Chaucer, as *lepand*, leaping; *touchand*, touching. The East Midland dialect had the double forms *-end* and *-and*.

7· *Schal*, shall :—pres. indic. sing., 1st and 3rd *schal;* 2nd *schalt;* pl. *schullen, schuln, schul;* past *schulde, scholde.*

8. *Thar*, need :—pres. indic. sing., 1st and 3rd *thar;* past *thurte;* subjunctive 3rd, *ther.*

9. *Witen*, to know :—pres. indic. sing., 1st and 3rd *wat, wot;* 2nd *wost;* pl. *witen, wite, woote;* past *wiste.*

10. *Wil*, will :—pres. indic. sing., 1st *wil, wol = wille, wolle;* 2nd *wilt, wolt;* 3rd *wile, wole, wol;* pl. *woln, wille, willen;* past *wolde.*

. NEGATIVE VERBS.

Nam, nys, = am not, is not ; *nas, nere,* = was not, were not ; *nath* = hath not ; *nadde, nad,* = had not ; *nylle, nyl,* = will not ; *nolde* = would not ; *nat, not, noot,* = knows not ; *nost* = knowest not ; *nyste, nysten,* = knew not.

ADVERBS.

1. Adverbs are formed from adjectives by adding *-e* to the positive degree ; as *brighte*, brightly ; *deepe*, deeply ; *lowe*, lowly.

2. Some few adverbs have *e* before *ly*, as *boldely, needely, softely, semely, trewely.*

3. Adverbs in *-en* and *-e:—abouen, aboue; abouten, aboute; biforn, bifore; siththen, siththe* (since); *withouten, withoute;* many have dropped the form in *-n;* as *asondre, behynde, bynethe, bytwene, biyonde; henne* (hence), *thenne* (thence).

4. Adverbs in *-e:—ofte, selde* (seldom), *soone, twie* (twice), *thrie* (thrice).

5. Adverbs in *-es:—needes* (A.S. *neáde*), needs; *ones* (A.S. *ǽne*), once; *twies* (A.S. *twiwa*), twice; *thries* (A.S. *thriwa*), thrice.

   (*a*) *-es* for *-e, -an* or *-a:—unnethes* (A.S. *uneáthe*), scarcely ; *whiles* (A.S. *hwile*), whilst; *bysides* (A.S. *besidan*); *togideres* (A.S. *to-gædere*).

   (*b*) *-es* for *-e* or *-en:—hennes* (A.S. *heonnan*); *thennes* (A.S. *thanan*); *whennes* (A.S. *hwanon*), hence, thence, whence.

   (*c*) *-es* = *-st:—agaynes, ayens* (A.S. *agean*), against; *amonges* (A.S. *gemang*), amongst; *amyddes* (A.S. *amiddan, amiddes*), amidst.

6. *Of-newe*, newly, recently; *as-now*, at present; *on slepe*, asleep; *on honting*, a hunting.

7. Negative Adverbs. Two negatives (more common than one in Chaucer) do *not* make an affirmative.

> ' He *never* yit *no* viloyne *ne* sayde,
>   In al his lyf unto no maner wight.'   (Prol. ll. 70, 71.)

But (only) takes a negative *before* it; as, ' I *nam but* deed.' (Knightes Tale, l. 416.)

8. *As* is used before *in, to, for, by,* = considering, with respect to, so far as concerns. See Prol. l. 87.

It is used before the imperative mood in supplicatory phrases. See Knightes Tale, l. 1444.

9. *There, then,* occasionally signify *where, when.*

PREPOSITIONS.

Occasionally *til* = to; *unto* = until; *up* = upon; *uppon* = on.

CONJUNCTIONS.

Ne ... *ne* = neither ... nor; *other* = or; *other* ... *other* = either ... or.

METRE AND VERSIFICATION.

1. Except the Tale of Melibeus and the Persounes Tale, the Canterbury Tales are written in rhyming verse; but this system of versification did not come into general use in England until after the Norman Conquest. The poetry of the Anglo-Saxons, like that of the Scandinavian and old Germanic races, was rhythmical and alliterative. Their poems are written in couplets, in such a manner that in each couplet there are three emphatic words, two in the first and one in the second, commencing with the same letter; and this letter is also the initial of the first emphatic, or accented word, in the second line.

' Rathe wæs gefylled	Rathe (quickly) was fulfilled
*b*eah-cininges *b*æs	the *b*igh king's be*b*est;
him wæs *b*alig leoht	for him was *b*oly light
ofer wéstenne.'	over the wild waste [r].

Langland's Vision of Piers Ploughman, written in 1362, presents all the peculiarities of this form of verse:—

' I was *w*eori of *w*andringe,
And *w*ent me to reste
Undur a *b*rod *b*anke
Bi a *b*ourne syde ;
And as I *l*ay and *l*eonede
And *l*okede on the watres,
I *s*lumberde in a *s*lepynge
Hit *s*ownede so murie.' (ll. 13-20.)

In the North and West of England alliteration was employed as late as the end of the fifteenth century, but it appears to have gone out of use in the Southern and Eastern parts of the country, which early in the thirteenth century adopted the classical and Romance forms of versification.

2. The greater part of the Canterbury Tales are written in heroic couplets, or lines containing five accents. In this metre we have ten syllables; but we often find eleven, and occasionally nine. Of these variations the former is obtained by the addition of an unaccented syllable at the end of a line [s].

' Him wolde | he snyb | bë scharp] ly for | the nones.
A bet | trë preest | I trowe | ther no | wher non is.'

(Prol. ll. 523-4.)

' The answer | of this | I le | të to | divinis.'
But wel | I woot | that in | this world | gret pyne is.'

(Knightes Tale, ll. 465-6.)

So in lines 1 and 2, of the Prologue :—

'Whan that | April | lë with | his schow | res swootë
The drought | of Marche | hath per | ced to | the rootë.'

---

[r] Cædmon, p. 8, ll. 13-16.

[s] For fuller information the reader is referred to an essay on the Metres of Chaucer, by the Rev. W. W. Skeat, in the Introduction to Chaucer's Poetical Works (Aldine Series), ed. Morris, 1867.

In the second variation, the first foot consists of a single accented syllable :—

'*In* | a gowne of faldyng to the kne.'   (Prol. l. 393.)

'*Til* | that deeth departë schal us twayne.'   (Knightes Tale, l. 276.)

'*Now* | it schyneth, now it reyneth faste.'   (Ib. l. 677.)

3. Chaucer frequently contracts two syllables into one ; as *nam, nis, nath, nadde,* = *ne am, ne is, ne hath, ne hadde,* am not, is not, hath not, had not; *thasse, theffect, tabide* = the asse, the effect, to abide, &c.   In Troylus and Criseyde we find *ny* = *ne I,* not I, nor I ; *mathinketh* = *me athinketh,* it seems to me.   But this contraction is not always so expressed in writing, though observed in reading :—

'And cer | tus lord | *to abi* | *den* your | presence.'
(Knightes Tale, l. 69.)

'But to | *the effect* | it hap | ped on | a day.'   (Ib. l. 331.)

'*By eter* | *ne* word | to dey | en in | prisoun.'   (Ib. l. 251.)

4. The syllable -*en,* -*er,* -*eth,* -*el,* -*ow* (-*owe,* -*ewe*), are often said to be contracted, but properly speaking they are *slurred* over and nearly, but not quite, absorbed by the syllable preceding :—

'*Weren* of | his bit | ter sal | të te | res wete.'
(Knightes Tale, l. 422.)

'And ye | *schullen* bothe | anon | unto | me swere,
That ne | ver ye | *schullen* my | corow | ne dere.'
(Ib. ll. 963-4.)

With this compare the following :—

'Ful lon | ge *wern* | his leg | gus, and | ful lene.'   (Prol. l. 591.)

'*Schuln* the | decla | ren, or | that thou | go henne.'
(Knightes Tale, l. 1498.)

'And forth | we *riden* | a li | tel more | than paas.'   (Prol. l. 819.)

'And won | durly | *delyver,* | and gret | of strengthe.'   (Ib. l. 84.)

'He was | the bes | të *begger* | in al | his hous.'   (Ib. l. 252.)

'As a | ny ra | ven *fether* | it schon | for blak.'
(Knightes Tale, l. 1286.)

' I wot | *whether* [t] sche | be wom | man or | goddesse.' (Ib. l. 243.)

' And· *thenketh* | here *cometh* | my mor | tel e | nemy.' (Ib. l. 785.)

' Sche ga | *dereth* floures | par | ty white | and rede.' (Ib. l. 195.)

' Thus hath | this *widow* | hir li | tel child | i-taught.'
(Spec. of Early Eng., p. 361, l. 497.)

' A man | to light | a *candel* | at his | lanterne.'
(Cant. Tales, l. 5961, Wright's edition.)

5. Many words of French origin ending in *-ance* (*-aunce, -ence*), *-oun, -ie* (*-ye*), *-er* (*-ere*), *-age, -une, -ure,* are often accented on the final syllable (not counting the final *-e*), but at other times the accent is thrown further back, as in modern English: e. g. *batáille* and *bátaille*; *fortúne* and *fórtune,* &c.

So also many nouns of A. S. origin, in *-ing* (*inge, ynge* [u]), as *hóntyng* and *huntýng.* (See Knightes Tale, ll. 821, 1450.)

6. Many nouns (of French origin) ending in *-le, -re,* are written, and probably pronounced, as in modern French; e. g. *table, temple, miracle, obstacle, propre* = *tabl', templ', miracl',* &c.

7. Final *es* is a distinct syllable in—

  a. The genitive case singular of nouns; as, ' *souwës* eeres' (Prol. l. 556); ' *kingës* court' (Knightes Tale, l. 323).

  b. The plural of nouns (see Prol. ll. 1, 5, 9, &c.).

  c. Adverbs; as *nonës, ellës, twiës.*

8. The *-ed* (*-ud*) of past participles is generally sounded; as *percëd, entunëd, i-pynchëd* (Prol. ll. 2, 123, 151); *bathud, enspirud* (Prol. ll. 3, 6):

9. The past tense of weak verbs ends in *-dë* or *-të*; as *wentë, cowdë, woldë, bleddë, feddë, weptë* (Prol. ll. 78, 94, 145, 146, 148).

  -edë seems to have been pronounced as *-dë*; as *lovede* = *lovdë* (Prol. l. 97): so *wypude* in l. 133 of Prologue must be pronounced *wyptë*; and in l. 107 *drowpud* = *drowpude* = *drowptë.* In Troylus and Criseyde we often find *shrightë* and *sightë* written for *shrikedë* and *sighedë.*

---

[t] *Whether* was pronounced and often written *wher.*
[u] The forms of the present participle in O. E. ended in *-inde* (*-ende, -ande*), and many verbal nouns ended in *-ung.* These were gradually changed into the affix *-ing.*

10. Final *-en* is for the most part a distinct syllable in—

    a. The infinitive mood; as, to *seekën, wendën, yevën, standën* (Prol. ll. 13, 21, 489, 772).

    b. Past participles of strong verbs; as *holpën, spokën* (Prol. ll. 18, 31).

    c. Present and past tenses plural of verbs; as *makën, slepën, longën, werën* (Prol. ll. 9, 10, 12, 29); *besekën, makën, lestën* (Knightes Tale, ll. 60, 77, 78).

    d. Adverbs (originally ending in *-on* or *-an*); as *withoutën, siththën.*

11. Final *-e.* As the manuscripts of the Canterbury Tales are not always grammatically correct, an attention to the final *e* is of great importance. The following remarks will enable the reader to understand when and why it is employed.

    a. In nouns and adjectives (of A. S. origin) the final *e* represents one of the final vowels *a, u, e;* as *asse, bane, cuppe* = A. S. *assa, bana, cuppa. Herte, mare* = A. S. *herte, mare. Bale, care, wode* = A. S. *bealu, caru, wudu. Dere, drye* = A. S. *deore, dryge,* &c.

    b. The final *e* (unaccented) in words of French origin is sounded as in French verse (but it is also frequently silent); as—

        ‘Who spryngeth up for joyë but Arcite.’
                        (Knightes Tale, l. 1013.)

        ‘Ne wette hire fingres in hire *saucë* depe.’ (Prol. l. 129.)

        ‘In *curtesië* was set al hire leste.’ (Ib. l. 132.)

    c. Final *-e* is a remnant of various grammatical inflexions:—

        (1) It is a sign of the dative case in nouns; as *roote, breethe, heethe* (Prol. ll. 2, 5, 6).

        f is often changed into *v* before *e*, as nom. *wif, lif;* dat. *wive, live.*

        bedde[1], *brigge* (bridge), &c., are the datives of *bed, brig,* &c.

---

[1] See note, page 150, on line 182 of the Nonne Prest his Tale, and compare Knightes Tale, l. 818.

(2) In adjectives it marks—

    (*a*) The definite form of the adjective; as 'the *yongë* sonne' (Prol. l. 7).

    (*b*) The plural of adjectives; as '*smalë* fowles' (Prol. l. 9).

    (*c*) The vocative case of adjectives; as 'O *strongë* god' (Knightes Tale, l. 1515).

(3) In verbs the final -*e* is a sign—

    (*a*) Of the infinitive mood; as, to *seekë, tellë* (Prol. ll. 17, 38).

    (*b*) Of the gerundial infinitive. See Infinitive Mood, pp. xxxiii. xxxiv.

    (*c*) Of the past participles of strong verbs; as *ironnë, ifallë* (Prol. ll. 8, 25); *dronkë, brokë* (Knightes Tale, ll. 404, 406, 877).

    (*d*) Of the past tense (attached to -*ed*, -*d* or -*t*). See p. xxxix. 9.

    (*e*) Of the subjunctive and optative moods. See Prol., ll. 102, 764.

    (*f*) Of the imperative mood 3rd person (properly the 3rd person of the subjunctive mood). See Subjunctive Mood, p. xxxiii.

(4) In adverbs the *e* is very common :—

    (*a*) It represents an older vowel-ending; as *sone* (soon), *twie, thrie*. See xxxv. 4, 5.

    (*b*) It distinguishes adverbs from adjectives ; as *fairë, rightë* = fairly, rightly.

    (*c*) It represents an -*en* ; as *aboutë, abovë* = O. E. *abouten, aboven* = A. S. *abutan, abufan.*

    (*d*) -*e* is a distinct syllable in adverbs ending in -*ëly* ; as *lustëly, needëly, seemëly, trewëly.*

On the other hand the final *e* is often silent—

    1. In the personal pronouns; as *oure, youre, hire, here.*

    2. In many words of more than one syllable, and in words of Romance origin.

It is elided—

1. Before a word commencing with a vowel:

'For I mot wep*e* and weylë whil I lvye.' (Knightes Tale, l. 437.)

'And in the grove at tyme and place ̓isette.' (Ib. l. 777.)

2. Often before some few words beginning with *h*; as *he, his, him, hem, hire, hath, hadde, have, how, her, heer* (here):

'Wel cowd*e* he dress*e* his takel yomanly.' (Prol. l. 106.)

'Then wold*e* he wep*e* he myghtë nought be stent.'
(Knightes Tale, l. 510.

'That in that grove he wold*e* him hyd*e* al day.' (Ib. l. 623.)

In all other cases *h* is regarded as a consonant; as 'to fernë halwes' (Prol. l. 14); 'of smalë houndes' (Ibid. l. 146); 'the fairë hardy quyen' (Knightes Tale, l. 24).

The following metrical analysis of the opening lines of the Prologue will enable the reader to apply the rules already given. The mark ◡ represents an unaccented, and ─ an accented syllable.

'Whăn thāt | Ăpril | lĕ wĭth | hĭs schōw | rĕs swoōte
Thĕ droūght | ŏf Mārche | hăth pēr | cĕd tō | thĕ roōte,
Ănd bā | thŭd ēve | rў vēyne | ĭn swĭch | lĭcoūr,
Ŏf whĭch | vĕrtue | ēngēn | drĕd ĭs | thĕ floūr;
Whăn Zē | phĭrūs | ĕek wĭth | hĭs swē | tĕ breēthe
Ĕnspī | rŭd hāth | ĭn ēve | rў hōlte | ănd heēthe
Thĕ tēn | drĕ crōp | pĕs, ānd | thĕ yōn | gĕ sōnne
Hăth ĭn | thĕ Rām | hĭs hal | fĕ coūrs | ī-rōnne,
Ănd smā | lĕ fōw | lĕs mā | kĕn mē | lŏdïë,
Thăt slē | pĕn āl | thĕ nĭght | wĭth ̔ō | pĕn ȳhë,
Sŏ prī | kĕth hēm | nătūre | ĭn hēre | cŏrāges:—
Thănne lŏn | gĕn fōlk | tŏ gŏn | ŏn pīl | grĭmāges,
Ănd pāl | mĕrs fŏr | tŏ seē | kĕn straūn | gĕ strōndes,
Tŏ fer | nĕ hāl | wĕs, koūthe | ĭn sŏn | drў lōndes;
Ănd spē | cĭallў, | frŏm ēve | rў schī | rĕs ēnde
Ŏf Eñ | gĕlōnd, | tŏ Cānt | tŭrbūry | thĕy wēnde,
Thĕ hō | lў blĭs | fŭi mār | tĭr fŏr | tŏ seēke,
Thăt hēm | hăth hōlpen | whăn thăt | thĕy wē | re seēke.'

1. The final *e* in *Aprille, melodie*, is sounded; but is silent in *Marche, veyne, vertue, nature*; because in these cases it is followed by a word commencing with a vowel or with the letter *h*.

2. The final *e* in *swoote, smale, straunge, ferne, seeke*, is sounded, as the sign of the plural number.

3. The final *e* in *roote, breethe, heethe*, is sounded, as the sign of the dative case.

4. The final *e* in *sweete, yonge, halfe*, is sounded, as the sign of the definite form of the adjective.

5. The final *e* in *sonne, yhe, ende*, is sounded, and represents the older A.S. vowel-endings.

6. The final *e* in *ironne* is sounded, as the sign of the past participle representing the fuller form *ironen*.

7. The final *e* in *wende* and *were* is sounded, and represents the fuller form *-en* of the past tense plural in *wenden* and *weren*.

8. The final *e* in *to seeke* is sounded, as the sign of the infinitive mood, representing the fuller form *to seeken*.

9. The final *en* is sounded in *slepen, maken, longen*, as the sign of the present plural indicative.

10. The final *en* is sounded in *to seeken*, as the sign of the infinitive mood.

11. The final *en*, the ending of the past participle, is *slurred over* in *holpen;* more frequently it is sounded fully.

12. The final *es* in *schowres, croppes, fowles, halwes, strondes, londes*, is sounded, as the inflexion of the plural number.

13. The final *es* is sounded in *schires*, as the inflexion of the genitive case.

14. *Vertue, licour, nature*, and *corages*, are accented on the last syllable of the root, as in French.

The text of the present selection from the Canterbury Tales is taken from the best-known MS. Harl. 7334, which, however, is by no means free from clerical errors. It has, therefore, been collated throughout with Lansdowne MS. 851; and such collations as seemed to furnish better readings (metrical or grammatical) than those in the text have been inserted in their proper place in the Notes.

As the Old English character þ (th) is not uniformly or constantly employed in the Harleian MS., and ð does not occur at all, the modern form of the letter has been substituted for it. An initial ȝ (A.S. *g*) is represented in the text by 'y'; in all other cases, whether medial or final, by 'gh': but in order that the reader may know where the older character is used, its modern representatives *y* and *gh* have been printed in Italics.

No other deviations from the original copy have been allowed; so that the reader has before him a text which, notwithstanding its manifest errors, is that of a MS. not later perhaps than the year of Chaucer's death.

The outlines of grammar and versification which form part of the present Introduction will enable the reader to perceive for himself in most instances where the copyist has blundered[y]. It must be recollected that even during Chaucer's lifetime the language was in a transition state, and many changes from old to modern forms were going on; so that some licence was permissible in the use of such grammatical inflexions as were gradually becoming obsolete. Chaucer himself had great fear lest his language should be corrupted through subsequent transcription, and he cautions his copyists to be careful not to 'mismetre' his lines through 'default of tongue.'

As we have already said, the appearance of the Canterbury Tales marks the commencement of the period of modern English; and though Chaucer's orthography may appear to us somewhat antiquated, yet his language presents but few difficulties even to an ordinary reader[z]. Some few of his words have become obsolete, while those that no longer form part of the literary language still live on in our provincial dialects.

All verbal and grammatical difficulties in the text are explained in the Notes and Glossary, which, it is hoped, will afford young students all the help that they may require in studying the present selection.

R. M.

Tottenham,
October, 1867.

---

[y] See Knightes Tale, ll. 429, 656, where *werrë* and *grovë* show that *so* and *ful* have been inserted by the old copyist.

[z] 'I cannot in the least allow any necessity for Chaucer's poetry, especially the Canterbury Tales, being considered obsolete.' (Coleridge—Table Talk.)

To face page xliv.

By an oversight I have omitted any reference to Professor Child's admirable Essay on Chaucer's Grammatical Forms, of which I have made frequent use in the compilation of the Grammatical Introduction. I regret that this was not done in its proper place in the Notes.

R. M.

TABLE OF HISTORICAL EVENTS.

AT HOME.	A.D.	ABROAD.	A.D.
Edward III crowned	1327		
Birth of Chaucer	1328	Nicholas V	1328
		Philip VI (Valois) King of France	,,
Death of Robert Bruce and accession of David II	1329		
		Germany under papal interdict	1330
		Order of Teutonic Knights settled in Prussia	1331
Edward Baliol crowned at Scone	1332		
Battle of Halidon Hill	1333		
		Benedict XII	1334
Freedom of trading guaranteed by the Legislature to foreign merchants	1335		
Exports of Wool prohibited; Foreign cloth-makers allowed to settle in England	1337	Sir John Froissart born	1337
		Simon Boccanegra (first Doge of Genoa)	1339
One weight and measure established for the whole kingdom (14 Edward III, c. 12)	1340	The Black Death	1340
Defeat of the French off Sluys	,,		
The Ayenbite of Inwyt, by Dan Michel of Northgate, Kent	,,		
Death of Robert of Brunne	,,		
		Petrarch crowned at Rome on Easter Day	1341
		Brittany the seat of civil war	,,

AT HOME.	A.D.	ABROAD.	A.D.
		Clement VI . . .	1342
		Boccaccio crowned in the Capitol by Robert the Good	,,
		Settlement of Turks in Europe	1343
		jacob van Arteveldt (Edward the Third's partisan in Flanders) killed . .	1345
Battle of Neville's Cross .	1346		
Battle of Creçy . .	,,		
		Charles IV of Germany .	1347
Death of Richard Rolle of Hampole, author of *The Pricke of Conscience* .	1349	The Plague of Florence .	1348–9
The First Great Pestilence	,,		
Order of the Garter instituted	,,		
		John II King of France .	1350
Papal Provisions forbidden	1351		
Poems on the Wars of Edward III, by Lawrence Minot . . .	1352	Innocent VI . . .	1352
Polychronicon, by Ralph Higden . . .	,,		
Sir John Mandeville .	1354	Death of Rienzi . .	1354
Death of Baliol . .	1355		
Battle of Poictiers . .	1356		
Last Age of the Church, by Wycliffe . . .	,,		
		La Jacquerie in France .	1358
Edward III invades France	1359	Charles the Bad claims the crown of France .	1359
Chaucer commences his military career; is taken prisoner by the French .	,,		
		Peace between the English and French at Bretigny	1360
The Second Great Pestilence	1361		
Law pleadings, &c., in English (36 Edward III, c. 15)	1362	Urban V . . .	1362
The Vision of Piers Ploughman, by Langlande .	,,	War between Florence and Pisa; English auxiliaries employed by the Pisans	,,

AT HOME.	A.D.	ABROAD.	A.D.
Diet and Apparel of each class of the community regulated by Statute	1363		
		Charles V of France	1364
Chaucer receives an annual pension of 20 marks	1367		
The Brus, by Barbour	„		
The Third Great Pestilence	1369	War re-commenced between France and England	1370
		Gregory XI	„
Robert II (the first of the Stuart family in Scotland)	1371		
Chaucer employed on a mission to Florence and Genoa	1372		
Death of Sir John Mandeville	„		
A pension of a pitcher of wine daily granted to Chaucer	1374	Truce between England and France	1374
Chaucer appointed Comptroller of the Customs, and Subsidy of Wools, &c.	„	Death of Petrarch	„
		Death of Boccaccio	1375
Death of Edward the Black Prince	1376		
Chaucer sent on a mission to France	1377	Gregory I returns to Rome	1377
Death of Edward III, and accession of Richard II	„		
Wycliffe condemned by papal bull	1378		
		Clement VII	1379
Bible translated into English by Wycliffe	1380	Charles VI of France	1380
Poll-tax of 12 pence levied upon all persons above fifteen years of age	„		
Wat Tyler's Rebellion	1381		
Chaucer is appointed Comptroller of the Petty Customs	1382		
		John I of Portugal	1383
Death of Wycliffe	1384		
Chaucer dismissed from his offices of Comptroller of Wool and Petty Customs	1386		

AT HOME.	A.D.	ABROAD.	A. D.
The Polychronicon translated into English by John Trevisa	1387	Conversion of the Lithuanians	1387
Chaucer writes his Canterbury Tales . . .	„		
Chaucer is appointed Clerk of the King's Works at Windsor . . .	„		
And at Westminster .	1388		
Battle of Otterbourne .	„	Victory of the Swiss over the Austrians at Näfels .	1389
		Ottoman Victory over Christians at Kossova . .	„
Robert III of Scotland .	1390	Boniface IX . . .	1390
		Restoration of the Greek Language in Italy by Manuel Chrysolaras .	„
Gower's *Confessio Amantis*	1393		
A pension of 20l. a-year for life granted to Chaucer	1394	Benedict XIII . .	1394
Persecution of Lollards .	1395		
Death of Barbour . .	„	Battle of Nicopolis .	1396
		Union of Calmar . .	1397
A grant of a tun of wine a-year made to Chaucer	1398		
Chaucer's pension doubled	1399		
Death of John of Gaunt .	„		
Henry IV . . .	„		
Death of Chaucer . .	1400		

CHAUCER.

THE PROLOGUE.

WHAN that Aprille with his schowres swoote
The drought of Marche hath perced to the roote,
And bathud every veyne in swich licour,
Of which vertue engendred is the flour;
Whan Zephirus eek with his swete breeth[e]   5
Enspirud hath in every holte and heeth[e]
The tendre croppes, and the yonge sonne
Hath in the Ram his halfe cours i-ronne,
And smale fowles maken melodie,
That slepen al the night with open yhe,   10
So priketh hem nature in here corages :—
Thanne longen folk to gon on pilgrimages,
And palmers for to seeken straunge strondes,
To ferne halwes, kouthe in sondry londes;
And specially, from every schires ende   15
Of Engelond, to Canturbury they wende,
The holy blisful martir for to seeke,
That hem hath holpen whan that they were seeke.
   Byfel that, in that sesoun on a day,
In Southwerk at the Tabbard as I lay,   20

B

Redy to wenden on my pilgrimage
To Canturbury with ful devout corage,
At night was come into that hostelrie
Wel nyne and twenty in a companye,
Of sondry folk, by aventure i-falle   25
In felawschipe, and pilgryms were thei alle,
That toward Canturbury wolden ryde.
The chambres and the stables weren wyde,
And wel we weren esud atte beste.
And schortly, whan the sonne was to reste,   30
So hadde I spoken with hem everychon,
That I was of here felawschipe anon,
And made forward erly to aryse,
To take oure weye ther as I yow devyse.
But natheles, whiles I have tyme and space,   35
Or that I ferthere in this tale pace,
Me thinketh it acordant to resoun,
To telle yow alle the condicioun
Of eche of hem, so as it semed[e] me,
And which they weren, and of what degre;   40
And eek in what array that they were inne:
And at a knight than wol I first bygynne.

   A KNIGHT ther was, and that a worthy man,
That from the tyme that he ferst bigan
To ryden out, he lovede chyvalrye,   45
Trouthe and honour, fredom and curtesie.
Ful worthi was he in his lordes werre,
And therto hadde he riden, noman ferre,
As wel in Cristendom as [in] hethenesse,
And evere honoured for his worthinesse.   50
At Alisandre he was whan it was wonne,
Ful ofte tyme he badde the bord bygonne
Aboven alle naciouns in Pruce.

In Lettowe badde reyced and in Ruce,
No cristen man so ofte of his degre. 55
In Gernade atte siege hadde he be
Of Algesir, and riden in Belmarie.
At Lieys was he, and at Satalie,
Whan thei were wonne; and in the Greete see
At many a noble arive badde he be. 60
At mortal batailles badde he ben fiftene,
And foughten for our feith at Tramassene
In lystes thries, and ay slayn his foo.
This ilke worthi knight hadde ben also
Somtyme with the lord of Palatye, 65
Ageyn another hethene in Turkye :
And everemore he badde a sovereyn prys.
And though that he was worthy he was wys,
And of his port as meke as [is] a mayde.
He never yit no vilonye ne sayde 70
In al his lyf unto no maner wight.
He was a verray perfig*h*t gentil knight.
But for to telle you of his array,
His hors was good, but he ne was noug*h*t gay.
Of fustyan he wered a gepoun 75
Al by-smoterud with his haburgeoun.
For he was late comen from his viage,
And wente for to doon his pilgrimage.
  With him ther was his sone, a *y*ong SQUYER,
A lovyer, and a lusty bacheler, 80
With lokkes crulle as they were layde in presse.
Of twenty *y*eer he was of age I gesse.
Of his stature he was of evene lengthe,
And wondurly delyver, and gret of strengthe.
And he hadde ben somtyme in chivachie, 85
In Flaundres, in Artoys, and in Picardie,

And born him wel, as in so litel space,
In hope to stonden in his lady grace.
Embrowdid was he, as it were a mede
Al ful of fresshe floures, white and reede.　　　　90
Syngynge he was, or flowtynge, al the day;
He was as fressh as is the moneth of May.
Schort was his goune, with sleeves long and wyde.
Wel cowde he sitte on hors, and faire ryde.
He cowde songes make and wel endite,　　　　95
Justne and eek daunce, and wel purtray and write.
So hote he lovede, that by nightertale
He sleep nomore than doth a nightyngale.
Curteys he was, lowly, and servysable,
And carf byforn his fadur at the table.　　　　100

　A Yeman had he, and servantes nomoo
At that tyme, for him lust ryde soo;
And he was clad in coote and hood of grene.
A shef of pocok arwes bright and kene
Under his belte he bar ful thriftily.　　　　105
Wel cowde he dresse his takel yomanly;
His arwes drowpud nought with fetheres lowe.
And in his hond he bar a mighty bowe.
A not-heed badde he with a broun visage.
Of woode-craft cowde he wel al the usage.　　　　110
Upon his arme he bar a gay bracer,
And by his side a swerd and a bokeler,
And on that ofher side a gay daggere,
Harneysed wel, and scharp as poynt of spere;
A Cristofre on his brest of silver schene.　　　　115
An horn he bar, the bawdrik was of grene;
A forster was he sothely, as I gesse.
　Ther was also a Nonne, a PRIORESSE,
That of hire smylyng was ful symple and coy;

Hire grettest ooth[e] nas but by seynt Loy; 120
And sche was clept madame Engle[n]tyne.
Ful wel sche sang the servise devyne,
Entuned in hire nose ful semyly;
And Frensch sche spak ful faire and fetysly,
Aftur the scole of Stratford atte Bowe, 125
For Frensch of Parys was to hire unknowe.
At mete wel i-taught was sche withalle;
Sche leet no morsel from hire lippes falle,
Ne wette hire fyngres in hire sauce deepe.
Wel cowde sche carie a morsel, and wel keepe, 130
That no drope [ne] fil uppon hire brest[e].
In curtesie was sett al hire lest[e].
Hire overlippe wypud[e] sche so clene,
That in hire cuppe was no ferthing sene
Of grees, whan sche hadde dronken hire draught. 135
Ful semely aftur hire mete sche raught.
And sikurly sche was of gret disport,
And ful plesant, and amyable of port,
And peyned hire to counterfete cheere
Of court, and ben estatlich of manere, 140
And to ben holden digne of reverence.
But for to speken of hire conscience,
Sche was so charitable and so pitous,
Sche wolde weepe if that sche sawe a mous
Caught in a trappe, if it were deed or bledde. 145
Of smale houndes hadde sche, that sche fedde
With rostud fleissh, or mylk and wastel breed.
But sore wepte sche if oon of hem were deed,
Or if men smot it with a ȝerde smerte:
And al was conscience and tendre herte. 150
Ful semely hire wymple i-pynched was;
Hire nose streight; hire eyen grey as glas;

Hire mouth ful smal, and therto softe and reed;
But sikurly sche badde a fair forheed.
It was almost a spanne brood, I trowe,   155
For hardily sche was not undurgrowe.
Ful fetys was hire cloke, as I was waar.
Of smal coral aboute hire arme sche baar
A peire of bedes gaudid al with grene;
And theron heng a broch of gold ful schene,   160
On which was first i-writen a crowned A,
And after that, *Amor vincit omnia.*
Anothur NONNE also with hire badde sche,
That was hire chapelleyn, and PRESTES thre.

A MONK ther was, a fair for the maistrie,   165
An out-rydere, that loved[e] venerye;
A manly man, to ben an abbot able.
Ful many a deynté hors badde he in stable:
And when he rood, men might his bridel heere
Gyngle in a whistlyng wynd so cleere,   170
And eek as lowde as doth the chapel belle.
Ther as this lord was keper of the selle,
The reule of seynt Maure or of seint Beneyt,
Bycause that it was old and somdel streyt,
This ilke monk leet [him] forby hem pace,.   175
And held aftur the newe world the space.
He *y*af nat of that text a pulled hen,
That seith, that hunters been noon holy men;
Ne that a monk, whan he is cloysterles,
Is likned to a fissche that is watirles,   180
This is to seyn, a monk out of his cloystre.
But thilke text hild he not worth an oystre.
And I seide his opinioun was good.
What schulde he studie, and make himselven wood,
Uppon a book in cloystre alway to powre,   185

Or swynke with his handes, and laboure,
As Austyn byt? How schal the world be served?
Lat Austyn have his swynk. to him reserved.
Therfore he was a pricasour aright;
Greyhoundes he hadde as swifte as fowel in flight;
Of prikyng and of huntyng for the hare   191
Was al his lust, for no cost wolde he spare.
I saugh his sleves purfiled atte hond[e]
With grys, and that the fynest of a lond[e].
And for to festne his hood undur his chyn[ne]   195
He badde of gold y-wrought a curious pyn[ne]:
A love-knotte in the gretter ende ther was.
His heed was ballid, and schon as eny glas,
And eek his face as he badde be anoynt.
He was a lord ful fat and in good poynt;   200
His eyen steep, and rollyng in his heed[e],
That stemed as a forneys of a leed[e];
His bootes souple, his hors in gret estat.
Now certeinly he was a fair prelat;
He was not pale as a for-pyned goost.   205
A fat swan loved he best of eny roost.
His palfray was as broun as eny berye.

     A FRERE ther was, a wantoun and a merye,
A lymytour, a ful solempne man.
In alle the ordres foure is noon that can   210
So moche of daliaunce and fair langage.
He badde i-mad many a fair mariage
Of yonge wymmen, at his owne cost.
Unto his ordre he was a noble post.
Ful wel biloved and famulier was he   215
With frankeleyns overal in his cuntre,
And eek with worthi wommen of the toun:
For he badde power of confessioun,

As seyde himself, more than a curat,
For of his ordre he was licenciat.   220
Ful sweet[e]ly herde he confessioun,
And plesaunt was his absolucioun;
He was an esy man to yeve penance
Ther as he wiste han a good pitance;
For unto a povre ordre for to yeve   225
Is signe that a man is wel i-schreve.
For if he yaf, he dorste make avaunt,
He wiste that a man was repentaunt.
For many a man so hard is of his herte,
He may not wepe though him sore smerte.   230
Therfore in stede of wepyng and prayeres,
Men mooten yiven silver to the pore freres.
His typet was ay farsud ful of knyfes
And pynnes, for to yive faire wyfes.
And certayn[li] he hadde a mery noote.   235
Wel couthe he synge and pleye[n] on a rote.
Of yeddynges he bar utturly the prys.
His nekke whit was as the flour-de-lys.
Therto he strong was as a champioun.
He knew wel the tavernes in every toun,   240
And every ostiller or gay tapstere,
Bet than a lazer, or a beggere,
For unto such a worthi man as he
Acorded not, as by his faculté,
To have with sike lazars aqueyntaunce.   245
It is not honest, it may not avaunce,
For to delen with such poraile,
But al with riche and sellers of vitaille.
And overal, ther eny profyt schulde arise,
Curteys he was, and lowe[ly] of servyse.   250
Ther was no man nowher so vertuous.

He was the beste begger in al his bous,
[And yaf a certeyn ferme for the graunte
Non of his bretheren cam in his haunte]
For though a widewe badde but oo schoo,   255
So plesaunt was his *In principio*,
Yet wolde he have a ferthing or he wente.
His purchace was bettur than his rente.
And rage he couthe and pleye[n] as a whelpe,
In love-days ther couthe he mochil helpe.   260
For ther was he not like a cloysterer,
With a thredbare cope as a pore scoler,
But he was like a maister or a pope.
Of double worstede was his semy-cope,
That rounded was as a belle out of presse.   265
Somwhat he lipsede, for [his] wantounesse,
To make his Englissch swete upon his tunge;
And in his harpyng, whan that he badde sunge,
His eyghen twynkeled in his heed aright,
As don the sterres in the frosty night.   270
This worthi lymytour was called Huberd.
    A MARCHAUNT was ther with a forked berd,
In motteleye, and high on horse he sat,
Uppon his heed a Flaundrisch bever hat;
His botus clapsud faire and fetously.   275
His resons he spak ful solempnely,
Sownynge alway the encres of his wynnynge.
He wolde the see were kepud for eny thinge.
Bitwixe Middulburgh and Orewelle.
Wel couthe he in eschange scheeldes selle.   280
This worthi man ful wel his witte bisette;
Ther wiste no man that he was in dette;
So estately was he of governaunce,
With his bargayns, and with his chevysaunce.

For sothe he was a worthi man withalle, 285
But soth to say, I not what men him calle.
  A CLERK ther was of Oxenford also,
That unto logik badde longe i-go.
Al-so lene was his hors as is a rake,
And he was not right fat, I undertake; 290
But lokede holwe, and therto soburly.
Ful thredbare was his overest courtepy,
For he badde nought geten him yit a benefice,
Ne was not worthy to haven an office.
For him was lever have at his beddes heed 295
Twenty bookes, clothed in blak and reed,
Of Aristotil, and of his philosophie,
Then robus riche, or fithul, or [gay] sawtrie.
But al-though he were a philosophre,
Yet badde he but litul gold in cofre; 300
But al that he might[e] gete, and his frendes sende
On bookes and his lernyng he it spende,
And busily gan for the soules pray[e]
Of hem that yaf him wherwith to scolay[e]
Of studie took he most[e] cure and heede. 305
Not oo word spak he more than was neede;
Al that he spak it was of heye prudence,
And schort and quyk, and ful of gret sentence.
Sownynge in moral manere was his speche,
And gladly wolde he lerne, and gladly teche. 310
  A SERGEANT OF LAWE, war and wys,
That often badde ben atte parvys,
Ther was also, ful riche of excellence.
Discret he was, and of gret reverence:
He semed[e] such, his wordes were so wise, 315
Justice he was ful often in assise,
By patent, and by pleyn commissioun;

For his science, and for his heih renoun,
Of fees and robes had he many oon.
So gret a purchasour was ther nowher noon.   320
Al was fee symple to him in effecte,
His purchasyng might[e] nought ben to him suspecte.
Nowher so besy a man as he ther nas,
And yit he semed[e] besier than he was.
In termes badde [he] caas and domes alle, *judgment* 325
That fro the tyme of kyng [Will] were falle.
Therto he couthe endite, and make a thing,
Ther couthe no man pynche at his writyng.
And every statute couthe he pleyn by roote.
He rood but hoomly in a medled coote,   330
Gird with a seynt of silk, with barres smale ;
Of his array telle I no lenger tale.

A FRANKELEYN ther was in his companye ;
Whit was his berde, as [is] the dayesye.
Of his complexioun he was sangwyn.   335
Wel loved he in the morn a sop in wyn.
To lyve[n] in delite was al his wone,
For he was Epicurius owne sone,
That heeld opynyoun that pleyn delyt
Was verraily felicité perfyt.   340
An househaldere, and that a gret, was he ;
Seynt Julian he was in his countré.
His breed, his ale, was alway after oon ;
A bettre envyned man was nowher noon.
Withoute bake mete was never his hous,   345
Of fleissch ánd fissch, and that so plentyvous,
It snewed in his hous of mete and drynk[e],
Of alle deyntees that men cowde thynk[e].
Aftur the sondry sesouns of the yeer,
He chaunged hem at mete and at soper.   350

Ful many a fat partrich had he in mewe,
And many a brem and many a luce in stewe.
Woo was his cook, but-if his sauce were
Poynant and scharp, and redy al his gere.
His table dormant in his halle alway   355
Stood redy covered al the longe day.
At sessions ther was he lord and sire.
Ful ofte. tyme he was knight of the schire.
An anlas and a gipser al of silk
Heng at his gerdul, whit as morne mylk.   360
A schirreve badde he ben, and a counter;
Was nowher such a worthi vavaser.

    An HABURDASSHER and a CARPENTER,
A WEBBE, a DEYER, and a TAPICER,
Weren with us eeke, clothed in oo lyveré,   365
Of a solempne and gret fraternité.
Ful freissh and newe here gere piked was;
Here knyfes were i-chapud nat with bras,
But al with silver wrought ful clene and wel,
Here gurdles and here pouches every del.   370
Wel semed eche of hem a fair burgeys,
To sitten in a yeldehalle on the deys.
Every man for the wisdom that he can,
Was schaply for to ben an aldurman.
For catel badde they inough and rente,   375
And eek here wyfes wolde it wel assente;
And elles certeyn hadde thei ben to blame.
It is right fair for to be clept *madame,*
And for to go to vigilies al byfore,
And han a mantel rially i-bore.   380

    A COOK thei badde with hem for the nones,
To boyle chiknes and the mary bones,
And poudre marchaunt, tart, and galyngale.

Wel cowde he knowe a drau*gh*t of Londone ale.
He cowde roste, sethe, broille, and frie,   385
Make mortreux, and wel bake a pye.
But gret harm was it, as it semedè me,
That on his schyne a mormal badde he;
For blankmanger he made with the beste.

A SCHIPMAN was ther, wonyng fer by weste: 390
For ought I woot, he was of Dertemouthe.
He rood upon a rouncy, as he couthe,
In a gowne of faldyng to the kne.
A dagger hangyng on a laas hadde he
Aboute his nekke under his arm adoun.   395
The hoote somer had[de] maad his hew al broun;
And certeinly he was a good felawe.
Ful many a draught of wyn had he [y-]drawe
From Burdeux-ward, whil that the chapman sleep.
Of nyce conscience took he no keep.   400
If that he foughte, and badde the heig*h*er hand,
By water, he sente hem hoom to every land.
But of his craft to rikne wel the tydes,
His stremes and his dangers him bisides,
His herbergh and his mone, his lodemenage,   405
Ther was non such from Hulle to Cartage.
Hardy he was, and wys to undertake;
With many a tempest badde his berd ben schake.
He knew wel alle the havenes, as thei were,
From Scotlond to the cape of Fynestere,   410
And every cryk in Bretayne and in Spayne;
His barge y-clepud was the Magdelayne.

Ther was also a DOCTOUR OF PHISIK,
In al this world ne was ther non him lyk
To speke of phisik and of surgerye;   415
For he was groundud in astronomye.

He kepte his pacient wondurly wel
In houres by his magik naturel.
Wel cowde he fortune the ascendent
Of his ymages for his pacient.   420
He knew the cause of every maladye,
Were it of cold, or hete, or moyst, or drye,
And where thei engendrid, and of what humour;
He was a verrey perfight practisour.
The cause i-knowe, and of his harm the roote,   425
Anon he yaf the syke man his boote.
Ful redy badde he his apotecaries,
To sende him dragges, and his letuaries,
For eche of hem made othur [for] to wynne;
Here frendschipe was not newe to begynne.   430
Wel knew he the olde Esculapius,
And Deiscorides, and eeke Rufus;
Old Ypocras, Haly, and Galien;
Serapyon, Razis, and Avycen;
Averrois, Damescen, and Constantyn;   435
Bernard, and Gatisden, and Gilbertyn.
Of his diete mesurable was he,
For it was of no superfluité,
But of gret norisching and digestible.
His studie was but litel on the Bible.   440
In sangwin and in pers he clad was al,
Lined with taffata and with sendal.
And yit he was but esy in dispence;
He kepte that he wan in pestilence.
For gold in phisik is a cordial,   445
Therfore he lovede gold in special.
    A good WIF was ther of byside BATHE,
But sche was somdel deef, and that was skathe.
Of cloth makyng she hadde such an haunt,

Sche passed hem of Ypris and of Gaunt.   450
In al the parisshe wyf ne was ther noon
That to the offryng byforn hire schulde goon,
And if ther dide, certeyn so wroth was sche,
That sche was thanne out of alle charité.
Hire keverchefs weren ful fyne of grounde;   455
I durste swere they weyghede ten pounde
That on a Sonday were upon hire heed.
Hire hosen were of fyn[e] scarlètt reed,
Ful streyte y-teyed, and schoos ful moyste and newe.
Bold was hir face, and fair, and reed of hewe.   460
Sche was a worthy womman al hire lyfe,
Housbondes atte chirche dore hadde sche fyfe,
Withouten othur companye in youthe;
But thereof needeth nought to speke as nouthe.
And thries hadde sche ben at Jerusalem;   465
Sche hadde passud many a straunge streem;
At Rome sche hadde ben, and at Boloyne,
In Galice at seynt Jame, and at Coloyne.
Sche cowde moche of wandryng by the weye.
Gattothud was sche, sothly for to seye.   470
Uppon an amblere esely sche sat,
Wymplid ful wel, and on hire heed an hat
As brood as is a bocler or a targe;
A foot-mantel aboute hire hupes large,
And on hire feet a paire of spores scharpe.   475
In felawschipe wel cowde [sche] lawghe and carpe.
Of remedyes of love sche knew perchaunce,
For of that art sche knew the olde daunce.
   A good man was ther of religioun,
And was a pore PERSOUN of a toun;   480
But riche he was of holy thought and werk.
He was also a lerned man, a clerk

That Cristes gospel gladly wolde preche;
His parischens devoutly wold he teche.
Benigne he was, and wondur diligent,   485
And in adversité ful pacient;
And such he was i-proved ofte sithes.
Ful loth were him to curse for his tythes,
But rather wolde he *y*even out of dowte,
Unto his pore parisschens aboute,   490
Of his offrynge, and eek of his substaunce.
He cowde in litel thing han suffisance.
Wyd was his parisch, and houses fer asondur,
But he ne lafte not for reyne ne thondur,
In siknesse ne in meschief to visite   495
The ferrest in his parissche, moche and lite,
Uppon his feet, and in his hond a staf.
This noble ensample unto his scheep he *y*af,
That ferst he wroughte, and after that he taughte,
Out of the gospel he tho wordes caughte,   500
And this figure he addid[e] *y*it therto,
That if gold ruste, what schulde yren doo?
For if a prest be foul, on whom we truste,
No wondur is a lewid man to ruste;

                *   *   *   *   *

Wel oughte a prest ensample for to *y*ive,   505
By his clennesse, how that his scheep schulde lyve.
He sette not his benefice to huyre,
And lefte his scheep encombred in the myre,
And ran to Londone, unto seynte Poules,
To seeken him a chaunterie for soules,   510
Or with a brethurhede be withholde;
But dwelte at hoom, and kepte wel his folde,
So that the wolf ne made it not myscarye.
He was a schepperde and no mercenarie;

And though he holy were, and vertuous,   515
He was to senful man nought dispitous,
Ne of his speche daungerous ne digne,
But in his teching discret and benigne.
To drawe folk to heven by fairnesse,
By good ensample, [this] was his busynesse: 520
But it were eny persone obstinat,
What so he were of high or lowe estat,
Him wolde he snybbe scharply for the nones.
A bettre preest I trowe ther nowher non is.
He waytud after no pompe ne reverence,   525
Ne maked him a spiced conscience,
But Cristes lore, and his apostles twelve,
He taught, and ferst he followed it himselve.

With him ther was a PLOUGHMAN, his brothur,
That hadde i-lad of dong ful many a fothur.   530
A trewe swynker and a good was hee,
Lyvynge in pees and perfight charitee.
God loved he best with al his trewe herte
At alle tymes, though him gamed or smerte,
And thanne his neighebour right as himselve.   535
He wolde threisshe, and therto dyke and delve,
For Cristes sake, with every pore wight,
Withouten huyre, if it laye in his might.
His tythes payede he ful faire and wel,
Bathe of his owne swynk and his catel.   540
In a tabbard [he] rood upon a mere.

Ther was also a reeve and a mellere,
A sompnour and a pardoner also,
.A maunciple, and my self, ther was no mo.
The MELLERE was a stout carl for the nones,   545
Ful big he was of braun, and eek of boones;
That prevede wel, for overal ther he cam,

At wrastlynge he wolde bere awey the ram.
He was schort schuldred, broode, a thikke knarre,
Ther nas no dore that he nolde heve of harre,　550
Or breke it at a rennyng with his heed.
His berd as ony sowe or fox was reed,
And therto brood, as though it were a spade.
Upon the cop right of his nose he hade
A werte, and theron stood a tuft of heres,　555
Reede as the berstles of a souwes eeres.
His nose-thurles blake were and wyde.
A swerd and a bocler baar he by his side,
His mouth as wyde was as a gret forneys.
He was a jangler, and a golyardeys,　560
And that was most of synne and harlotries
Wel cowde he stele corn, and tollen thries;
And yet he had a thombe of gold pardé.
A whit cote and [a] blewe hood wered he.
A baggepipe cowde he blowe and sowne,　565
And therwithal he brought us out of towne.
　　A gentil MAUNCIPLE was ther of a temple,
Of which achatours mighten take exemple
For to be wys in beyying of vitaille.
For whethur that he payde, or took by taille,　570
Algate he wayted[e] so in his acate,
That he was ay biforn and in good state.
Now is not that of God a ful fair grace,
That such a lewed mannes wit schal pace
The wisdom of an heep of lernede men?　575
Of maystres badde [he] moo than thries ten,
That were of lawe expert and curious;
Of which ther were a doseyn in an house
Worthi to be stiwardz of rente and lond
Of any lord that is in Engelond,　580

To make him lyve by his propre good,
In honour detteles, but-if he were wood,
Or lyve as scarsly as he can desire;
And able for to helpen al a schire
In any caas that mighte falle or happe;   585
And *y*it this maunciple sette here a*ii*er cappe.

 The REEVE was a sklendre colerik man,
His berd was schave as neigh as ever he can.
His heer was by his eres neighe i-schorn.
His top was dockud lyk a preest biforn.   590
Ful longe wern his leggus, and ful lene,
Al like a staff, ther was no calf y-sene.
Wel cowde he kepe a gerner and a bynne;
Ther was non auditour cowde on him wynne.
Wel wiste he by the drought, and by the reyn,   595
The *y*eeldyng of his seed, and of his greyn.
His lordes scheep, his nete, [and] his dayerie,
His swyn, his hors, his stoor, and his pultrie,
Was holly in this reeves governynge,
And by his covenaunt *y*af the rekenynge,   600
Syn that his lord was twenti *y*eer of age;
Ther couthe noman bringe him in arrerage.
Ther nas ballif, ne herde, ne other hyne,
That they ne knewe his sleight and his covyne;
They were adrad of him, as of the deth[e].   605
His wonyng was ful fair upon an heth[e],
With grene trees i-schadewed was his place.
He cowde bettre than his lord purchace.
Ful riche he was i-stored prively,
His lord wel couthe he plese subtilly,   610
To *y*eve and lene him of his owne good,
And have a thank, a cote, and eek an hood.
In *y*outhe he lerned hadde a good mester;

He was a wel good wright, a carpenter.

This reeve sat upon a wel good stot,   615

That was a pomely gray, and highte Scot.

A long surcote of pers uppon he hadde,

And by his side he bar a rusty bladde.

Of Northfolk was this reeve of which I telle,

Byside a toun men callen Baldeswelle.   620

Tukkud he was, as is a frere, aboute,

And ever he rood the hynderest of the route.

    A Sompnour was ther with us in that place,

That badde a fyr-reed cherubyn[e]s face,

For sawceflem he was, with eyg*h*en narwe.   625

       *   *   *   *   *

With skalled browes blak, and piled berd;

Of his visage children weren [sore] aferd.

Ther nas quýksilver, litarge, ne bremstone,

Boras, ceruce, ne oille of tartre noon,

Ne oynement that wolde clense and byte,   630

That him might helpen of his whelkes white,

Ne of the knobbes sittyng on his cheekes.

Wel loved he garleek, oynouns, and ek leekes,

And for to drinke strong wyn reed as blood.

Thanne wolde he speke, and crye as he were wood.

And whan that he wel dronken badde the wyn, 636

Than wolde he speke no word but Latyn.

A fewe termes badde he, tuo or thre,

That he hadde lerned out of som decree;

No wondur is, he herde it al the day;   640

And eek ye knowe wel, how that a jay

Can clepe Watte, as wel as can the pope.

But who-so wolde in othur thing him grope,

Thanne badde he spent al his philosophie,

Ay, *Questio quid juris*, wolde he crye.   645

He was a gentil harlot and a kynde;
A bettre felaw schulde men nowher fynde.

*   *   *   *   *

And if he fond owher a good felawe,
He wolde teche him to have non awe
In such a caas of the archedeknes curs,   650
But if a mannes soule were in his purs;
For in his purs he scholde punyssched be.
'Purs is the ercedeknes helle,' quod he.
But wel I woot he lyeth right in dede;
Of cursyng oweth ech gulty man to drede;   655
For curs wol slee right as assoillyng saveth;
And also ware of him a *significavit.*
In daunger badde he at his own assise
The *y*onge gurles of the diocise,
And knew here counseil, and was here aller red. 660
A garland had he set up on his heed,   a lwr
As gret as it were for an ale-stake;
A bokeler had he maad him of a cake.

  With him ther rood a gentil PARDONER
Of Rouncival, his frend and his comper,   665
That streyt was comen from the court of Rome.
Ful lowde he sang, Com hider, love, to me.
This sompnour bar to him a stif burdoun,
Was nevere trompe of half so gret a soun.
This pardoner badde heer as *y*elwe as wex,   670
But smothe it heng, as doth a strike of flex;
By unces hynge his lokkes that he badde,
And therwith he his schuldres overspradde.
Ful thinne it lay, by culpons on and oon,
But hood, for jolitee, ne wered he noon,   675
For it was trussud up in his walet.
Him thought he rood al of the newe get,

Dischevele, sauf his cappe, he rood al bare.
Suche glaryng eyghen badde he as an hare.
A vernicle badde he sowed on his cappe.   680
His walet lay byforn him in his lappe,
Bret-ful of pardoun come from Rome al hoot.
A voys he badde as smale as eny goot.
No berd ne badde he, ne never scholde have,
As smothe it was as it were late i-schave;   685

* * * * *

But of his craft, fro Berwyk unto Ware,
Ne was ther such another pardoner.
For in his malè he hadde a pilwebeer,
Which, that he saide, was oure lady veyl:
He seide, he badde a gobet of the seyl   690
That seynt Petur badde, whan that he wente
Uppon the see, til Jhesu Crist him hente.
He hadde a cros of latoun ful of stones,
And in a glas he badde pigges bones.
But with thise reliq[u]es, whanne that he fand   695
A pore persoun dwellyng uppon land,
Upon a day he gat him more moneye
Than that the persoun gat in monthes tweye.
And thus with feyned flaterie and japes,
He made the persoun and the people his apes.   700
But trewely to tellen atte laste,
He was in churche a noble ecclesiaste.
Wel cowde he rede a lessoun or a storye,
But altherbest he sang an offertorie;
For wel he wyst[e] whan that song was songe,   705
He moste preche, and wel affyle his tunge,
To wynne silver, as he right wel cowde;
Therfore he sang ful meriely and lowde.
 Now have I told you schortly in a clause

Thestat, tharray, the nombre, and eek the cause 710
Why that assembled was this companye
In Southwerk at this gentil ostelrie,
That highte the Tabbard, faste by the Belle.
But now is tyme to yow for to telle
How that we bare us in that ilke night, 715
Whan we were in that ostelrie alight;
And aftur wol I telle of oure viage,
And al the remenaunt of oure pilgrimage.
But ferst I pray you of your curtesie,
That ye ne rette it nat my vilanye, 720
Though that I speke al pleyn in this matere,
To telle you here wordes and here cheere;
Ne though I speke here wordes propurly.
For this ye knowen also wel as I,
Who-so schal telle a tale aftur a man, 725
He moste reherce, as neigh as ever he can,
Every word, if it be in his charge,
Al speke he never so rudely ne large;
Or elles he moot telle his tale untrewe,
Or feyne thing, or fynde wordes newe. 730
He may not spare, though he were his brothur;
He moste as wel sey oo word as anothur.
Crist spak himself ful broode in holy writ,
And wel ye woot no vilanye is it.
Eke Plato seith, who so that can him rede, 735
The wordes mot be cosyn to the dede.
Also I pray you to foryeve it me,
Al have I folk nat set in here degre
Here in this tale, as that thei schulde stonde;
My witt is thynne, ye may wel undurstonde. 740
  Greet cheere made oure ost us everichon,
And to the souper sette he us anon;

And served us with vitaille atte beste.
Strong was the wyn, and wel to drynke us leste.
A semely man our ooste was withalle   745
For to han been a marchal in an halle;
A large man was he with eyghen stepe,
A fairere burgeys is ther noon in Chepe:
Bold of his speche, and wys and wel i-taught,
And of manhede lakkede he right naught.   750
Eke therto he was right a mery man,
And after soper playen he bygan,
And spak of myrthe among othur thinges,
Whan that we hadde maad our rekenynges;
And sayde thus: 'Lo, lordynges, trewely   755
Ye ben to me right welcome hertily:
For by my trouthe, if that I schal not lye,
I ne saugh this yeer so mery a companye
At oones in this herbergh as is now.
Fayn wold I do yow merthe, wiste I how,   760
And of a merthe I am right now bythought,
To doon you eese, and it schal coste nought.
Ye goon to Caunturbury; God you speede,
The blisful martir quyte you youre meede!
And wel I woot, as ye gon by the weye,   765
Ye schapen yow to talken and to pleye;
For trewely comfort ne merthe is noon
To ryde by the weye domb as a stoon;
And therfore wol I make you disport,
As I seyde erst, and do you som confort.   770
And if yow liketh alle by oon assent
Now for to standen at my juggement,
And for to werken as I schal you seye,
To morwe, whan ye riden by the weye,
Now by my fadres soule that is deed,| 775

But ye be merye, smyteth of myn heed.
Hold up youre hond withoute more speche.'
Oure counseil was not longe for to seche;
Us thoughte it nas nat worth to make it wys,
And graunted him withoute more avys,   780
And bad him seie his verdite, as him leste.
'Lordynges,' quoth he, 'now herkeneth for the beste;
But taketh not, I pray you, in disdayn;
This is the poynt, to speken schort and playn,
That ech of yow to schorte with youre weie,   785
In this viage, schal telle tales tweye,
To Caunturburi-ward, I mene it so,
And hom-ward he schal tellen othur tuo,
Of aventures that ther han bifalle.
And which of yow that bereth him best of alle,   790
That is to seye, that telleth in this caas
Tales of best sentence and of solas,
Schal han a soper at your alther cost
Here in this place sittynge by this post,
Whan that we comen ageyn from Canturbery.   795
And for to make you the more mery,
I wol myselven gladly with you ryde,
Right at myn owen cost, and be youre gyde.
And whoso wole my juggement withseie
Schal paye for al we spenden by the weye.   800
And if ye vouche sauf that it be so,
Telle me anoon, withouten wordes moo,
And I wole erely schappe me therfore.'
This thing was graunted, and oure othus swore
With ful glad herte, and prayden him also   805
That he wolde vouche sauf for to doon so,
And that he wolde ben oure governour,
And of our tales jugge and reportour,

And sette a souper at a certeyn prys;
And we wolde rewled be at his devys,   810
In heygh and lowe; and thus by oon assent
We been accorded to his juggement.
And therupon the wyn was fet anoon;
We dronken, and to reste wente echoon,
Withouten eny lengere taryinge.   815
A morwe whan that the day bigan to sprynge,
Up roos oure ost, and was oure althur cok,
And gaderud us togidur alle in a flok,
And forth we riden a litel more than paas,
Unto the waterynge of seint Thomas.   820
And there oure ost bigan his hors areste,
And seyde; 'Lordus, herkeneth if yow leste.
Ye woot youre forward, and I it you recorde.
If eve-song and morwe-song accorde,
Let se now who schal telle ferst a tale.   825
As evere I moote drynke wyn or ale,
Who so be rebel to my juggement
Schal paye for al that by the weye is spent.
Now draweth cut, er that we forther twynne;
Which that hath the schortest schal bygynne.'   830
'Sire knight,' quoth he, '[my] maister and my lord,
Now draweth cut, for that is myn acord.
Cometh ner,' quoth he, 'my lady prioresse;
And ye, sir clerk, lat be your schamfastnesse,
Ne studieth nat; ley hand to, every man.'   835
    Anon to drawen every wight bigan,
And schortly for to tellen as it was,
Were it by aventure, or sort, or cas,
The soth is this, the cut fil to the knight,
Of which ful glad and blithe was every wight;   840
And telle he moste his tale as was resoun,

By forward and by composicioun,
As ye han herd; what needeth wordes moo?
And whan this goode man seigh that it was so,
As he that wys was and obedient   845
To kepe his forward by his fre assent,
He seyde: 'Syn I schal bygynne the game,
What, welcome be thou cut, a Goddus name!
Now lat us ryde, and herkneth what I seye.'

And with that word we ridden forth oure weye;
And he bigan with right a merie chere   851
His tale, and seide right in this manere.

THE KNIGHTES TALE.

WHILOM, as olde stories tellen us,
Ther was a duk that highte Theseus;
Of Athenes he was lord and governour,
And in his tyme swich a conquerour,
That gretter was ther non under the sonne.   5
Ful many a riche contré badde he wonne;
That with his wisdam and his chivalrie
He conquered al the regne of Femynye,
That whilom was i-cleped Cithea;
And weddede the queen Ipolita,   10
And brought hire hoom with him in his contré,
With moche glorie and gret solempnité,
And eek hire yonge suster Emelye.
And thus with victorie and with melodye
Lete I this noble duk to Athenes ryde,   15
And al his ost, in armes him biside.
And certes, if it nere to long to heere,
I wolde han told yow fully the manere,
How wonnen was the regne of Femenye
By Theseus, and by his chivalrye;   20

And of the grete bataille for the nones
Bytwix Athenes and [the] Amazones;
And how asegid was Ypolita,
The faire hardy quyen of Cithea;
And of the feste that was at hire weddynge,   25
And of the tempest at hire hoom comynge;
But al that thing I most as now forbere.
I have, God wot, a large feeld to ere,
And wayke ben the oxen in my plough,
The remenaunt of the tale is long inough;   30
I wol not lette eek non of al this rowte
Lat every felawe telle his tale aboute,
And lat see now who schal the soper wynne,
And ther I lafte, I wolde agayn begynne.
    This duk, of whom I make mencioun,   35
Whan he was comen almost unto the toun,
In al his wele and in his moste pryde,
He was war, as he cast his eyghe aside,
Wher that ther kneled in the hye weye
A companye of ladies, tweye and tweye,   40
Ech after other, clad in clothes blake;
But such a cry and such a woo they make,
That in this world nys creature lyvynge,
That herde such another weymentynge,
And of that cry ne wolde they never stenten,   45
Til they the reynes of his bridel henten.
'What folk be ye that at myn hom comynge
Pertourben so my feste with cryenge?'
Quod Theseus, 'have ye so gret envye
Of myn honour, that thus compleyne and crie?   50
Or who hath yow misboden, or offendid?
And telleth me if it may ben amendid;
And why that ye ben clad thus al in blak?'

The oldest lady of hem alle spak,
When sche bad[de] swowned with a dedly chere,   55
That it was routhe for to seen or heere;
And seyde: 'Lord, to whom Fortune hath yeven
Victorie, and as a conquerour to lyven,
Nought greveth us youre glorie and honour,
But we beseken mercy and socour.   60
Have mercy on oure woo and oure distresse.
Som drope of pitee, thurgh youre gentilnesse,
Uppon us wrecchede wommen lat thou falle.
For certus, lord, ther nys noon of us alle,
That sche nath ben a duchesse or a queene;   65
Now be we caytifs, as it is wel seene;
Thanked be Fortune, and hire false wheel,
That noon estat assureth to ben weel.
And certus, lord, to abiden youre presence
Here in the temple of the goddesse Clemence   70
We han ben waytynge al this fourtenight;
Now help us, lord, syn it is in thy might.
I wrecche, which that wepe and waylle thus,
Was whilom wyf to kyng Capaneus,
That starf at Thebes, cursed be that day!   75
And alle we that ben in this array,
And maken alle this lamentacioun!
We lesten alle oure housbondes at the toun,
Whil that the sege ther aboute lay.
And yet the olde Creon, welaway!   80
That lord is now of Thebes the citee,
Fulfild of ire and of iniquité,
He for despyt, and for his tyrannye,
To do the deede bodyes vilonye
Of alle oure lordes, which that ben i-slawe,   85
Hath alle the bodies on an heep y-drawe,

And wol not suffren hem by noon assent
Nother to ben y-buried nor i-brent,
But maketh houndes ete hem in despite.'
And with that word, withoute more respite, 90
They fillen gruf, and criden pitously,
'Have on us wrecched wommen som mercy,
And lat oure sorwe synken in thyn herte.'
This gentil duke doun from his courser sterte
With herte pitous, whan he herde hem speke. 95
Him thoughte that his herte wolde breke,
Whan he seyh hem so pitous and so maat,
That whilom weren of so gret estat.
And in his armes he hem alle up hente,
And hem conforteth in ful good entente; 100
And swor his oth, as he was trewe knight,
He wolde do so ferforthly his might
Upon the tyraunt Creon hem to wreke,
That al the poeple of Grece scholde speke
How Creon was of Theseus y-served, 105
As he that hath his deth right wel deserved.
And right anoon, withoute eny abood
His baner he desplayeth, and forth rood
To Thebes-ward, and al his oost bysyde;
No ner Athenes wolde he go ne ryde, 110
Ne take his eese fully half a day,
But onward on his way that nyght he lay;
And sente anoon Ypolita the queene,
And Emelye hir yonge suster schene,
Unto the toun of Athenes to dwelle; 115
And forth he ryt; ther is no more to telle.
 The reede statue of Mars with spere and targe
So schyneth in his white baner large,
That alle the feeldes gliteren up and doun;

And by his baner was born his pynoun   120
Of gold ful riche, in which ther was i-bete
The Minatour which that he slough in Crete.
Thus ryt this duk, thus ryt this conquerour,
And in his oost of chevalrie the flour,
Til that he cam to Thebes, and alighte   125
Faire in a feeld wher as he thoughte to fighte.
But schortly for to speken of this thing,
With Creon, which that was of Thebes kyng,
He faught, and slough him manly as a knight
In pleyn bataille, and putte his folk to flight;   130
And by assaut he wan the cité aftur,
And rente doun bothe wal, and sparre, and raftur;
And to the ladies he restored agayn
The bones of here housbondes that were slayn,
To do exequies, as was tho the gyse.   135
But it were al to long for to devyse
The grete clamour and the waymentynge
Which that the ladies made at the brennynge
Of the bodyes, and the grete honour
That Theseus the noble conquerour   140
Doth to the ladyes, whan they from him wente;
But schortly for to telle is myn entente.
Whan that this worthy duk, this Theseus,
Hath Creon slayn, and Thebes wonne thus,
Stille in the feelde he took al night his reste,   145
And dide with al the contré as him leste.
      To ransake in the cas of bodyes dede
Hem for to streepe of herneys and of wede,
The pilours diden businesse and cure,
After the bataile and discomfiture.   150
And so byfil, that in the cas thei founde,
Thurgh girt with many a grevous blody wounde,

Two *y*onge knighte[s] liggyng by and by,
Bothe in oon armes clad ful richely;
Of whiche two, Arcite hight that oon,　　　　155
And that othur knight hight Palamon.
Nat fully quyk, ne fully deed they were,
But by her[e] coote armure, and by here gere,
Heraudes knewe hem wel in special,
As they that weren of the blood real　　　　160
Of Thebes, and of sistren tuo i-born.
Out of the chaas the pilours han hem torn,
And han hem caried softe unto the tente
Of Theseüs, and ful sone he hem sente
Tathenes, for to dwellen in prisoun　　　　165
Perpetuelly, he wolde no raunceoun.
And this duk whan he badde thus i-doon,
He took his host, and hom he ryt anoon
With laurer crowned as a conquerour;
And there he lyveth in joye and in honour　　　　170
Terme of his lyf; what wolle ye wordes moo?
And in a tour, in angwische and in woo,
This Palamon, and his felawe Arcite,
For evermo, ther may no gold hem quyte.
This passeth *y*eer by *y*eer, and day by day,　　　　175
Til it fel oones in a morwe of May
That Emelie, that fairer was to seene
Than is the lilie on hire stalkes grene,
And fresscher than the May with floures newe—
For with the rose colour strof hire hewe,　　　　180
I not which was the fairer of hem two—
Er it was day, as sche was wont to do,
Sche was arisen, and al redy dight;
For May wole have no sloggardye a nyght.
The sesoun priketh every gentil herte,　　　　185

And maketh him out of his sleepe sterte,
And seith, 'Arys, and do thin observance.'
This maked Emelye han remembrance
To do honour to May, and for to ryse.
I-clothed was sche fressh for to devyse.   190
Hire yolwe heer was browdid in a tresse,
Byhynde hire bak, a yerde long I gesse.
And in the gardyn at the sonne upriste
Sche walketh up and doun wher as hire liste.
Sche gadereth floures, party whyte and reede,   195
To make a sotil gerland for hire heede,
And as an aungel hevenly sche song.
The grete tour, that was so thikke and strong,
Which of the castel was the cheef dongeoun,
(Ther as this knightes weren in prisoun,   200
Of which I tolde yow, and telle schal)
Was evene joynyng to the gardeyn wal,
Ther as this Emely badde hire pleyynge.
Bright was the sonne, and cleer that morwenynge,
And Palamon, this woful prisoner,   205
As was his wone, by leve of his gayler
Was risen, and romed in a chambre on heigh,
In which he al the noble cité seigh,
And eek the gardeyn, ful of braunches grene,
Ther as the fresshe Emelye the scheene   210
Was in hire walk, and romed up and doun.
This sorweful prisoner, this Palamon,
Gooth in the chambre romyng to and fro,
And to himself compleynyng of his woo;
That he was born, ful ofte he seyd, alas!   215
And so byfel, by aventure or cas,
That thurgh a wyndow thikke and many a barre
Of iren greet and squar as eny sparre,

He cast his eyen upon Emelya,
And therwithal he bleynte and cryed, a!　　　220
As that he stongen were unto the herte.
And with that crye Arcite anon up sterte,
And seyde, 'Cosyn myn, what eyleth the,
That art so pale and deedly for to see?
Why crydestow? who hath the doon offence?　　225
For Goddes love, tak al in pacience
Oure prisoun, for it may non othir be;
Fortune hath *y*even us this adversité.
Som wikke aspect or disposicioun
Of Saturne, by sum constellacioun,　　　230
Hath *y*even us this, although we badde it sworn;
So stood the heven whan that we were born;
We moste endure it: this is the schort and pleyn.'

　　This Palamon answered, and seyde ageyn,
'Cosyn, for-sothe of this opynyoun　　　235
Thou hast a veyn ymaginacioun.
This prisoun caused[e] me not for to crye.
But I was hurt right now thurgh[out] myn yhe
Into myn herte, that wol my bane be.
The fairnesse of the lady that I see　　　240
Yonde in the gardyn rome to and fro,
Is cause of [al] my cryying and my wo.
I not whethur sche be womman or goddesse;
But Venus is it, sothly as I gesse.'
And therwithal on knees adoun he fil,　　　245
And seyde: 'Venus, if it be youre wil
Yow in this gardyn thus to transfigure,
Biforn me sorwful wrecched creature,
Out of this prisoun help that we may scape.
And if so be oure destyné be schape,　　　250
By eterne word to deyen in prisoun,

Of oure lynage haveth sum compassioun,
That is so lowe y-brought by tyrannye.'
And with that word Arcite gan espye
Wher as this lady romed[e] to and fro.   255
And with that sight hire beauté hurt him so,
That if that Palamon was wounded sore,
Arcite is hurt as moche as he, or more.
And with a sigh he seyde pitously :
'The freissche beauté sleeth me sodeynly   260
Of hir that rometh yonder in the place;
And but I have hir mercy and hir grace
That I may see hir atte leste weye,
I nam but deed; ther nys no more to seye.'
This Palamon, whan he tho wordes herde,   265
Dispitously he loked, and answerde :
'Whether seistow in ernest or in pley?'
'Nay,' quoth Arcite, 'in ernest in good fey.
God help me so, me lust ful evele pleye.'
This Palamon gan knytte his browes tweye :   270
'Hit nere,' quod he, 'to the no gret honour,
For to be fals, ne for to be traytour
To me, that am thy cosyn and thy brother.
I-swore ful deepe, and ech of us to other,
That never for to deyen in the payne,   275
Til that deeth departe schal us twayne,
Neyther of us in love to hynder other,
Ne in non other cas, my leeve brother ;
But [that] thou schuldest trew[e]ly forther me
In every caas, and I schal forther the.   280
This was thyn oth, and myn eek certayn ;
I wot right wel, thou darst it nat withsayn.
Thus art thou of my counseil out of doute.
And now thou woldest falsly ben aboute

To love my lady, whom I love and serve,   285
And evere schal, unto myn herte sterve.
Now certes, fals Arcite, thou schal[t] not so.
I loved hir first, and tolde the my woo
As to my counseil, and to brother sworn
To forthere me, as I have told biforn.   290
For which thou art i-bounden as a knight
To helpe me, if it lay in thi might,
Or elles art thou fals, I dar wel sayn.'
This Arcite ful proudly spak agayn.
'Thou schalt,' quoth he, 'be rather fals than I. 295
But thou art fals, I telle the uttirly.
For par amour I loved hir first then thow.
What wolt thou sayn? thou wost it not yit now
Whether sche be a womman or goddesse.
Thyn is affeccioun of holynesse,   300
And myn is love, as of a creature;
For which I tolde the myn adventure
As to my cosyn, and my brother sworn.
I pose, that thou lovedest hire biforn;
Wost thou nat wel the olde clerkes sawe,   305
That who schal yeve a lover eny lawe,
Love is a grettere lawe, by my pan,
Then may be yeve to eny erthly man?
Therfore posityf lawe, and such decré,
Is broke alway for love in ech degree,   310
A man moot needes love maugre his heed.
He may nought fle it, though he schulde be deed,
Al be sche mayde, or be sche widewe or wyf.
And [eke it] is nat likly al thy lyf
To stonden in hire grace, no more schal I;   315
For wel thou wost thyselven verrily,
That thou and I been dampned to prisoun

Perpetuelly, us gayneth no raunsoun.
We stryve, as doth the houndes for the boon,
They foughte al day, and yit here part was noon;   320
Ther com a kyte, whil that they were wrothe,
And bar awey the boon bitwixe hem bothe.
And therfore at the kynges court, my brother,
Eche man for himself, ther is non other.
Love if the list; for I love and ay schal;   325
And sothly, leeve brother, this is al.
Here in this prisoun moote we endure,
And every of us take his aventure.'
Gret was the stryf and long bytwixe hem tweye,
If that I hadde leysir for to seye;   330
But to the effect. It happed on a day,
(To telle it yow as schortly as I may)
A worthy duk that highte Perotheus,
That felaw was to the duk Theseus
Syn thilke day that they were children lyte,   335
Was come to Athenes, his felawe to visite,
And for to pley, as he was wont to do,
For in this world he loved[e] noman so:
And he loved him as tendurly agayn.
So wel they loved, as olde bookes sayn,   340
That whan [that] oon was deed, sothly to telle,
His felawe wente and sought him doun in helle:
But of that story lyst me nought to write.
Duk Perotheus loved[e] wel Arcite,
And hadde him knowe at Thebes yeer by yeer: 345
And fynally at requeste and prayer
Of Perotheus, withoute any raunsoun
Duk Theseus him leet out of prisoun,
Frely to go wher him lust overal,
In such a gyse, as I you telle schal.   350

This was the forward, playnly to endite,
Bitwixe Theseus and him Arcite:
That if so were, that Arcite were founde
Evere in his lyf, by daye, [or] night, o stounde
In eny contré of this Theseus,   355
And he were caught, it was acorded thus,
That with a swerd he scholde lese his heed;
Ther nas noon other remedy ne reed,
But took his leeve, and homward he him spedde;
Let him be war, his nekke lith to wedde.   360
      How gret' a sorwe suffreth now Arcite!
The deth he feleth thorugh his herte smyte;
He weepeth, weyleth, and cryeth pitously;
To slen himself he wayteth pryvyly.
He seyde, 'Allas the day that I was born!   365
Now is my prisoun werse than was biforn;
Now is me schape eternally to dwelle
Nought in purgatorie, but in helle.
Allas! that ever knewe I Perotheus!
For elles had I dweld with Theseus   370
I-fetered in his prisoun for evere moo.
Than had I ben in blis, and nat in woo.
Oonly the sight of hir, whom that I serve,
Though that I [never] hir grace may nat deserve,
Wold han sufficed right ynough for me.   375
O dere cosyn Palamon,' quod he,
'Thyn is the victoire of this aventure,
Ful blisfully in prisoun to endure;
In prisoun? nay, certes but in paradys!
Wel hath fortune y-torned the [the] dys,   380
That hath the sight of hir, and I the absence.
For possible is, syn thou hast hir presence,
And art a knight, a worthi and an able,

That by som cas, syn fortune is chaungable,
Thou maist to thy desir somtyme atteyne.   385
But I that am exiled, and bareyne
Of alle grace, and in so gret despeir,
That ther nys water, erthe, fyr, ne eyr,
Ne creature, that of hem maked is,
That may me helpe ne comfort in this.   390
Wel ought I sterve in wanhope and distresse;
Farwel my lyf and al my jolynesse.
Allas! why playnen folk so in comune
Of purveance of God, or of fortune,
That yeveth hem ful ofte in many a gyse   395
Wel better than thei can hemself devyse?
Som man desireth for to have richesse,
That cause is of his morthre or gret seeknesse.
And som man wolde out of his prisoun fayn,
That in his bous is of his mayné slayn.   400
Infinite barmes ben in this mateere;
We wote nevere what thing we prayen heere.
We faren as he that dronke is as a mows.
A dronke man wot wel he hath an hous,
But he not nat which the righte wey is thider,   405
And to a dronke man the wey is slider,
And certes in this world so faren we,
We seeken faste after felicité,
But we gon wrong ful ofte trewely.
Thus may we seyen alle, [and] namely I,   410
That wende have had a gret opinioun,
That yif I mighte skape fro prisoun,
Than had I be in joye and perfyt hele,
Ther now I am exiled fro my wele.
Syn that I may not se yow, Emelye,   415
I nam but deed; ther nys no remedye.'

Upon that other syde Palomon,
Whan he wiste that Arcite was agoon,
Such sorwe maketh, that the grete tour
Resowneth of his yollyng and clamour.   420
The pure feteres of his schynes grete
Weren of his bitter salte teres wete.
'Allas!' quod he, 'Arcita, cosyn myn,
Of al oure strif, God woot, the fruyt is thin.
Thow walkest now in Thebes at thi large,   425
And of my woo thou yevest litel charge.
Thou maist, syn thou hast wysdom and manhede,
Assemble al the folk of oure kynrede,
And make a werre so scharpe in this cité,
That by som aventure, or by som treté,   430
Thou mayst hire wynne to lady and to wyf,
For whom that I most[e] needes leese my lyf.
For as by wey of possibilité,
Syn thou art at thi large of prisoun free,
And art a lord, gret is thin avantage,   435
More than is myn, that sterve here in a kage.
For I moot weepe and weyle, whil I lyve,
With al the woo that prisoun may me yyve,
And eek with peyne that love me yeveth also,
That doubleth al my torment and my wo.'   440
Therwith the fuyr of jelousye upsterte
Withinne his brest, and hent him by the herte
So wodly, that lik was he to byholde
The box-tree, or the asschen deed and colde.
Tho seyde he; 'O goddes cruel, that governe   445
This world with byndyng [of youre] word eterne,
And writen in the table of athamaunte
Youre parlement and youre eterne graunte,
What is mankynde more to yow holde

Than is a scheep, that rouketh in the folde?   450
For slayn is man right as another beste,
And dwelleth eek in prisoun and arreste,
And hath seknesse, and greet adversité,
And ofte tymes gilteles, pardé.
What governaunce is in youre prescience,   455
That gilteles tormenteth innocence?
And yet encreceth this al my penaunce,
That man is bounden to his observaunce
For Goddes sake to letten of his wille,
Ther as a beste may al his lust fulfille.   460
And whan a beste is deed, he ne hath no peyne;
But man after his deth moot wepe and pleyne,
Though in this world he have care and woo:
Withouten doute it may[e] stonde so.
The answer of this I lete to divinis,   465
But wel I woot, that in this world gret pyne is.
Allas! I se a serpent or a theef,
That many a trewe man hath doon mescheef,
Gon at his large, and wher him lust may turne.
But I moste be in prisoun thurgh Saturne,   470
And eek thorugh Juno, jalous and eke wood,
That hath destruyed wel neyh al the blood
Of Thebes, with his waste walles wyde.
And Venus sleeth me on that other syde
For jelousye, and fere of him Arcyte.'   475
     Now wol I stynte of Palamon a lite,
And lete[n] him stille in his prisoun dwelle,
And of Arcita forth than wol I telle.
The somer passeth, and the nightes longe
Encrescen double wise the peynes stronge   480
Bothe of the lover and the prisoner.
I noot which hath the wofullere cheer.

For schortly for to sey, this Palomon
Perpetuelly is dampned in prisoun,
In cheynes and in feteres to be deed;   485
And Arcite is exiled upon his heed
For everemo as out of that contré,
Ne nevere mo schal he his lady see.
Now lovyeres axe I this question,
Who hath the worse, Arcite or Palomon?   490
That on may se his lady day by day,
But in prisoun he moot dwelle alway.
That other wher him lust may ryde or go,
But seen his lady schal he never mo.
Now deemeth as you luste, ye that can,   495
For I wol telle forth as I bigan.
   Whan that Arcite to Thebes come was,
Ful ofte a day he swelde and seyde alas!
For seen his lady schal he never mo.
And schortly to concluden al his wo,   500
So moche sorwe had[de] never creature,
That is or schal whil that the world wol dure.
His sleep, his mete, his drynk is him byraft,
That lene he wex, and drye as eny schaft.
His eyen holwe, [and] grisly to biholde;   505
His hewe falwe, and pale as asschen colde.
And solitary he was, and ever alone,
And dwellyng al the night, making his moone.
And if he herde song or instrument,
Then wolde he wepe, he mighte nought be stent;   510
So feble were his spirites, and so lowe.
And chaunged so, that no man couthe knowe
His speche nother his vois, though men it herde.
And in his gir, for al the worlde he ferde
Nought oonly lyke the lovers maladye   515

Of Hercos, but rather lik[e] manye,
Engendrud of humour malencolyk,
Byforen in his selle fantastyk.
And schortly [turned] was al up-so-doun
Bothe abyt and eek disposicioun   520
Of him, this woful lovere daun Arcite.
What schulde I alway of his wo endite?
Whan. he endured hadde a yeer or tuoo
In this cruel torment, [this] peyne and woo,
At Thebes, in his contré, as I seyde,   525
Upon a night in sleep as he him leyde,
Him thought[e] that how the wenged god Mercurie
Byforn him stood, and bad him to be murye.
His slepy *y*erd in hond he bar upright[e];
An hat he wered upon his heres bright[e].   530
Arrayed was this god (as he took· keepe)
As he was whan that Argous took his sleep;
And seyde [him thus] : 'To Athenes schalt thou wende
Ther is the schapen of thy wo an ende.'
And with that word Arcite wook and sterte.   535
'Now trewely how sore that me smerte.'
Quod he, 'to Athenes ri*gh*t now wol I fare;
Ne for the drede of deth schal I not spare
To see my lady, that I love and serve;
In hire presence I recche nat to sterve,'   540
And with that word he caught a gret myrour,
And saugh that chaunged was al his colour,
And saugh his visage was in another kynde.
And right anoon it ran him into mynde,
That seththen his face was so disfigured   545
Of maladie the which he hath endured,
He mighte wel, if that he bar him lowe,
Lyve in Athenes evere more unknowe,

And see his lady wel neih day by day.
And right anon he chaunged his aray, 550
And clothed him as a pore laborer.
And al alone, save oonly a squyer,
That knew his pryvyté and al his cas,
Which was disgysed povrely as he was,
To Athenes is he go the nexte way. 555
And to the court he went upon a day,
And at the *y*ate he profred his servyse,
To drugge and drawe, what-so men wolde devyse.
And schortly of this matier for to seyn,
He fel in office with a chambirleyn, 560
The which that dwellyng was with Emelye.
For he was wys, and couthe sone aspye
Of every servaunt, which that served here.
Wel couthe he hewe woode, and water bere,
For he was *y*ong and mighty for the nones, .565
And therto he was strong and bygge of bones
To doon that eny wight can him devyse.
A *y*eer or two he was in this servise,
Page of the chambre of Emelye the bright[e];
And Philostrate he seide that he hight[e]. 570
But half so wel byloved a man as he
Ne was ther never in court of his degree.
He was so gentil of his condicioun,
That thoruhout al the court was his renoun.
They seyde that it were a charité 575
That Theseus wolde enhaunsen his degree,
And putten him in worschipful servyse,
Ther as he might his vertu excersise.
And thus withinne a while his name spronge
Bothe of his dedes, and of goode tonge, 580
That Theseus hath taken him so neer

That of his chambre he made him squyer,
And *y*af him gold to mayntene his degree;
And eek men brought him out of his countré
Fro *y*eer to *y*er ful pryvyly his rente;   585
But honestly and sleighly he it spente,
That no man wondred how that he it badde.
And thre *y*eer in this wise his lyf he ladde,
And bar him so in pees and eek in werre,
Ther nas no man that Theseus hath so derre.   590
And in this blisse lete I now Arcite,
And speke I wole of Palomon a lyte.

  In derknes and orrible and strong prisoun
This seven *y*eer hath seten Palomoun,
Forpyned, what for woo and for destresse,   595
Who feeleth double sorwe and hevynesse
But Palomon? that love destreyneth so,
That wood out of his witt he goth for wo;
And eek therto he is a prisoner
Perpetuelly, nat oonly for a *y*eer.   600
Who couthe ryme in Englissch propurly
His martirdam? for-sothe it am nat I;
Therfore I passe as lightly as I may.

  Hit fel that in the seventhe *y*eer in May
The thridde night, (as olde bookes seyn,   605
That al this storie tellen more pleyn)
Were it by aventure or destené,
(As, whan a thing is schapen, it schal be,)
That soone aftur the mydnyght, Palomoun
By helpyng of a freend brak his prisoun,   610
And fleeth the cité fast as he may goo,
For he bad[de] *y*ive drinke his gayler soo
Of a clarré, maad of [a] certeyn wyn,
With nercotykes and opye of Thebes fyn,

That al that night though that men wolde him schake,
The gayler sleep, he mighte nou*gh*t awake. 616
And thus he fleeth as fast as ever he may.
The night was schort, and faste by the day,
That needes cost he moste himselven hyde,
And til a grove ther faste besyde 620
With dredful foot than stalketh Palomoun.
For schortly this was his opynyoun,
That in that grove he wolde him hyde al day,
And in the night then wolde he take his way
To Thebes-ward, his frendes for to preye 625
On Theseus to helpe him to werreye.
And shortelich, or he wolde lese his lyf,
Or wynnen Emelye unto his wyf.
This is theffect of his entente playn.
Now wol I torne unto Arcite agayn, 630
That litel wiste how nyh that was his care,
Til that fortune hath brought him in the snare.
  The busy larke, messager of day,
Salueth in hire song the morwe gray;
And fyry Phebus ryseth up so bright, 635
That [al] the orient laugheth of the light,
And with his stremes dryeth in the greves
The silver dropes, hongyng on the leeves.
And Arcite, that is in the court ryal
With Theseus, his squyer principal, 640
Is risen, and loketh on the mery day.
And for to doon his observance to May,
Remembryng of the poynt of his desire,
He on his courser, stertyng as the fire,
Is riden into feeldes him to pleye, 645
Out of the court, were it a myle or tweye.
And to the grove, of which that I yow tolde,

By aventure his wey he gan to holde,
To make him a garland of the greves,
Were it of woodewynde or hawthorn leves, 650
And lowde he song ayens the sonne scheene:
'May, with al thyn floures and thy greene,
Welcome be thou, wel faire freissche May!
I hope that I som grene gete may.'
And fro his courser, with a luste herte, 655
Into the grove ful lustily he sterte,
And in a pathe he romed up and doun,
Ther by aventure this Palamoun
Was in a busche, that no man might him see.
Ful sore afered of his deth was he, 660
Nothing ne knew he that it was Arcite:
God wot he wolde have trowed it ful lite.
For soth is seyd, [a]goon ful many yeres,
That feld hath eyen, and the woode hath eeres.
It is ful fair a man to bere him evene, 665
For al day men meteth atte unset stevene.
Ful litel woot Arcite of his felawe,
That was so neih to herken of his sawe,
For in the busche he stynteth now ful stille.
Whan that Arcite bad[de] romed al his fille, 670
And songen al the roundel lustily,
Into a studie fel he sodeynly,
As doth thes lovers in here queynte geeres,
Now in the croppe, now doun in the breres,
Now up, now doun, as boket in a welle. 675
Right as the Friday, sothly for to telle,
Now it schyneth, now it reyneth faste,
Right so gan gery Venus overcaste
The hertes of hire folk, right as hir day
Is girful, right so chaungeth hire aray. 680

Selde is the Fryday al the wyke i-like.
Whan that Arcite badde songe, he gan to sike,
And sette him doun withouten eny more:
'Alas!' quod he, 'that day that I was bore!
How longe Juno, thurgh thy cruelté   685
Wiltow werreyen Thebes the citee?
Allas! i-brought is to confusioun
The blood royal of Cadme and Amphioun;
Of Cadynus, the which was the furst[e] man
That Thebes bulde, or first the toun bygan,   690
And of that cité first was crowned kyng,
Of his lynage am I, and his ofspring
By verray lyne, and of his stok ryal:
And now I am so caytyf and so thral,
That he that is my mortal enemy,   695
I serve him as his squyer povrely.
And yet doth Juno me wel more schame,
For I dar nought byknowe myn owne name,
But ther as I was wont to hote Arcite,
Now boote I Philostrate, nought worth a myte. 700
Allas! thou felle Mars, allas! Juno,
Thus hath youre ire owre lynage fordo,
Save oonly me, and wrecchid Palomoun,
That Theseus martyreth in prisoun.
And over al this, to slee me utterly,   705
Love hath his fyry dart so brennyngly
I-stykid thorugh my trewe careful herte,
That schapen was my deth erst than my scherte.
Ye slen me with youre eyhen, Emelye;
Ye ben the cause wherfore that I dye.   710
Of al the remenant of al myn other care
Ne sette I nought the mountaunce of a tare,
So that I couthe do ought to youre pleasaunce.'

E

And with that word he fel doun in a traunce
A long tyme; and aftirward upsterte   715
This Palamon, that thought thurgh his herte
He felt a cold swerd sodeynliche glyde;
For ire he quook, he nolde no lenger abyde.
And whan that he hath herd Arcites tale,
As he were wood, with face deed and pale,   720
He sterte him up out of the bussches thikke,
And seyd: 'Arcyte, false traitour wikke,
Now art thou hent, that lovest my lady so,
For whom that I have al this peyne and wo,
And art my blood, and to my counseil sworn,   725
As I ful ofte have told the heere byforn,
And hast byjaped here the duke Theseus,
And falsly chaunged hast thy name thus;
I wol be deed, or elles thou schalt dye.
Thou schalt not love my lady Emelye,   730
But I wil love hire oonly and no mo;
For I am Palomon thy mortal fo.
And though that I no wepen have in this place,
But out of prisoun am y-stert by grace,
I drede not that other thou schalt dye,   735
Or thou ne schalt not love[n] Emelye.
Ches which thou wilt, for thou schalt not asterte.'
This Arcite, with ful despitous herte,
Whan he him knew, and had his tale herde,
As fers as a lyoun pulleth out a swerde,   740
And seide thus: 'By God that sitteth above,
Nere it that thou art sike and wood for love,
And eek that thou no wepne has[t] in this place,
[Thou scholdest never out of this grove pace,]
That thou ne schuldest deyen of myn hond.   745
For I defye the seurté and the bond

Which that thou seyst I have maad to the.
For, verray fool, thenk[e] that love is fre ;
And I wol love hire mawgre al thy might.
But, for thou art a gentil perfi*gh*t knight,   750
And wenest to dereyne hire by batayle,
Have heere my trouthe, to morwe I nyl not fayle,
Withouten wityng of eny other wight,
That heer I wol be founden as a knight,
And bryngen harneys right inough for the ;   755
And ches the best, and lef the worst for me.
And mete and drynke this night wil I bryng[e]
Inough for the, and cloth for thy beddyng[e].
And if so be that thou my lady wynne,
And sle me in this wood that I am inne,   760
Thou maist wel have thy lady as for me.'
This Palomon answereth, 'I graunt it the.'
And thus they ben departed til a-morwe,
Whan ech of hem bad[de] leyd his feith to borwe.

   O Cupide, out of al charité !   765
O regne, that wolt no felaw have with the
Ful soth is seyd, that love ne lordschipe
Wol not, his thonkes, have no fela[w]schipe.
Wel fynden that Arcite and Palamoun.
Arcite is riden anon [un]to the toun,   770
And on the morwe, or it were day light,
Ful prively two harneys hath he dight,
Bothe sufficaunt and mete to darreyne
The batayl in the feeld betwix hem tweyne.
And on his hors, alone as he was born,   775
He caryed al this harneys him byforn ;
And in the grove, at tyme and place i-sette,
This Arcite and this Palamon ben mette.
Tho chaungen gan here colour in here face.

E 2

Right as the honter in the regne of Trace   780
That stondeth in the gappe with a spere,
Whan honted is the lyoun or the bere,
And hereth him comyng in the greves,
And breketh bothe the bowes and the leves,
And thenketh, ' Here cometh my mortel enemy,   785
Withoute faile, he mot be deed or I;
For eyther I mot slen him at the gappe,
Or he moot slee me, if it me myshappe:'
So ferden they, in chaungyng of here hew,
As fer as eyther of hem other knew.   790
Ther nas no 'good[e] day,' ne no saluyng;
But streyt withouten wordes rehersyng,
Every of hem helpeth to armen other,
As frendly as he were his owen brother;
And thanne with here scharpe speres stronge   795
They foyneden ech at other [wonder] longe.
Tho it semed[e] that this Palomon
In his fightyng were [as] a wood lyoun,
And as a cruel tygre was Arcite:
As wilde boores gonne they [to] smyte,   800
That frothen white as fome, for ire wood.
Up to the ancle they faught in here blood.
And in this wise I lete hem fightyng welle;
And forthere I wol of Theseus telle.

    The destné, mynistre general,   805
That executeth in the world overal
The purveans, that God hath seye byforn:
So strong it is, that they the world bad[de] sworn
The contrary of a thing by ye or nay,
Yet som tyme it schal falle upon a day   810
That falleth nought eft in a thousend yeere.
For certeynly oure appetites heere,

Be it of [werre, or] pees, other hate, or love,
Al is it reuled by the sight above.
This mene I [now] by mighty Theseus, 815
That for to honte[n] is so desirous,
And namely the grete hert in May,
That in his bed ther daweth him no day,
That he nys clad, and redy for to ryde
With hont and horn, and houndes him byside. 820
For in his hontyng hath he such delyt,
That [it] is [al] his joye and appetyt
To been himself the grete hertes bane,
For after Mars he serveth now Dyane.

Cleer was the day, as I have told or this, 825
And Theseus, with alle joye and blys,
With his Ypolita, the fayre queene,
And Emelye, clothed al in greene,
On hontyng be thay riden ryally.
And to the grove, that stood ther faste by, 830
In which ther was an hert as men him tolde,
Duk Theseus the streyte wey hath holde.
And to the launde he rydeth him ful right,
Ther was the hert y-wont to have his flight,
And over a brook, and so forth in his weye. 835
This duk wol have of him a cours or tweye
With houndes, which as him lust to comaunde.
And whan this duk was come into the launde,
Under the sonne he loketh, right anon
He was war of Arcite and Palomon, 840
That foughten breeme, as it were boores tuo;
The brighte swerdes wente to and fro
So hidously, that with the leste strook
It seemeth as it wolde felle an ook;
But what they were, nothing yit he woot. 845

This duk with spores his courser he smoot,
And at a stert he was betwixt hem tuoo,
And pullid out a swerd and cride, 'Hoo!
Nomore, up peyne of leesyng of your heed.
By mighty Mars, anon he schal be deed   850
That smyteth eny strook, that I may seen!
But telleth me what mestir men ye been,
That ben so hardy for to fighten heere
Withoute jugge or other officere,
As it were in a lyste really?'   855
This Palamon answerde hastily,
And seyde: 'Sire, what nedeth wordes mo?
We han the deth deserved bothe tuo.
Tuo woful wrecches been we, and kaytyves,
That ben encombred of oure owne lyves;   860
And as thou art a rightful lord and juge,
Ne yeve us neyther mercy ne refuge.
And sle me first, for seynte charité;
But sle my felaw eek as wel as me.
Or sle him first; for, though thou knowe him lyte,
This is thy mortal fo, this is Arcite,   866
That fro thy lond is banyscht on his heed,
For which he hath i-served to be deed.
For this is he that come to thi gate
And seyde, that he highte Philostrate.   870
Thus hath he japed the many a yer,
And thou hast maad of him thy cheef squyer.
And this is he that loveth Emelye.
For sith the day is come that I schal dye,
I make pleynly my confessioun,   875
That I am the woful[le] Palamoun,
That hath thi prisoun broke wikkedly.
I am thy mortal foo, and it am I

That loveth so hoote Emely the bright[e],
That I wol dye present in hire sight[e].   880
Therfore I aske deeth and my juwyse;
But slee my felaw in the same wyse,
For bothe we have served to be slayn.'
    This worthy duk answerde anon agayn,
And seide: 'This is a schort conclusioun: 885
Your owne mouth, by your owne confessioun,
Hath dampned you bothe, and I wil it recorde.
It needeth nought to pyne yow with the corde.
Ye schul be deed by mighty Mars the reede l'
The queen anon for verray wommanhede   890
Gan for to wepe, and so dede Emelye,
And alle the ladies in [the] companye.
Great pité was it, as it thought hem alle,
That evere such a chaunce schulde falle;
For gentil men thei were and of gret estate,   895
And nothing but for love was this debate.
And saw here bloody woundes wyde and sore;
And alle they cryde, lesse and the more,
'Have mercy, Lord, upon us wommen alle!'
And on here bare knees anoon they falle,   900
And wolde have kissed his feet right as he stood,
Til atte laste aslaked was his mood;
For pité renneth sone in gentil herte.
And though he [first] for ire quok and sterte,
He hath it al considered in a clause,   905
The trespas of hem bothe, and here cause:
And although his ire here gylt accused[e],
Yet he, in his resoun, hem bothe excused[e];
And thus he thought[e] that every maner man
Wol help himself in love if that he can,   910
And eek delyver himself out of prisoun.

And eek in his hert had[de] compassioun
Of wommen, for they wepen ever in oon;
And in his gentil hert he thought anoon,
And sothly he to himself[e] seyde: 'Fy   915
Upon a lord that wol have no mercy,
But be a lyoun bothe in word and dede,
To hem that ben in repentaunce and drede,
As wel as to a proud dispitious man,
That wol maynteyne that he first bigan.   920
That lord hath litel of discrecioun,
That in such caas can no divisioun;
But wayeth pride and humblenesse after oon,
And schortly, whan his ire is over-gon,
He gan to loke on hem with eyen light[e],   925
And spak these same wordes al in hight[e].
'The god of love, a! benedicite,
How mighty and how gret a lord is he!
Agayns his might ther gayneth non obstacle,
He may be cleped a god of his miracle;   930
For he can maken at his owen gyse
Of every herte, as him lust devyse.
Lo her is Arcite and Palomon,
That quytely were out of my prisoun,
And might have lyved in Thebes ryally,   935
And witen I am here mortal enemy,
And that here deth lith in my might also,
And yet hath love, maugré here eyghen tuo,
I-brought hem hider bothe for to dye.
Now loketh, is nat that an heih folye?   940
Who may [not] be a fole, if that he love?
Byhold for Goddes [sake] that sitteth above,
Se how they blede! be they nought wel arrayed!
Thus hath here lord, the god of love, hem payed

Here wages and here fees for here servise. 945
And yet they wenen to ben wise,
That serven love, for ought that may bifalle.
But this is yette the beste game of alle,
That sche, for whom they have this jelousye,
Can hem therfore as moche thank as me. 950
Sche woot no more of al this hoote fare,
By God, than wot a cuckow or an hare.
But al moot ben assayed hoot or colde;
A man moot ben a fool other yong or olde;
I woot it by myself ful yore agon: 955
For in my tyme a servant was I on.
And sythen that I knew of loves peyne,
And wot how sore it can a man destreyne,
As he that hath often ben caught in his lace,
I you foryeve holly this trespace, 960
At the request of the queen that kneleth heere,
And eek of Emely, my suster deere.
And ye schullen bothe anon unto me swere,
That never ye schullen my corowne dere,
Ne make werre on me night[e] ne day[e], 965
But be my freendes [in] alle that ye may[e].
I you foryeve this trespas every dele.'
And they him swore his axyng faire and wele,
And him of lordschip and of mercy prayde,
And he hem graunted[e] mercy, and thus he sayde:
' To speke of real lynage and riches[se] 971
Though that sche were a queen or a prynces[se],
Ilk of yow bothe is worthy douteles
To wedde when tyme is, but natheles
I speke as for my suster Emelye, 975
For whom ye have this stryf and jelousye,
Ye woot youreself sche may not wedde two

At oones, though ye faughten ever mo:
That oon of yow, or be him loth or leef,
He may go pypen in an ivy leef;   980
This is to say, sche may nought have bothe,
Al be ye never so jelous, ne so lothe.
For-thy I put you bothe in this degré,
That ilk of you schal have his destyné,
As him is schape, and herken in what wyse;   985
Lo here your ende of that I schal devyse.
My wil is this, for playn conclusioun,
Withouten eny repplicacioun,
If that you liketh, tak it for the best[e],
That every of you schal go wher him lest[e]   990
Frely withouten raunsoun or daungeer;
And this day fyfty wykes, fer ne neer,
Everich of you schal bryng an hundred knightes,
Armed for lystes up at alle rightes
Al redy to derayne hir by batayle.   995
And thus byhote I you withouten fayle
Upon my trouthe, and as I am a knight,
That whethir of yow bothe that hath might,
This is to seyn, that whethir he or thou
May with his hundred, as I spak of now,   1000
Sle his contrary, or out of lystes dryve,
Him schal I yeve[n] Emelye to wyve,
To whom that fortune yeveth so fair a grace.
The lyste schal I make in this place,
And God so wisly on my sowle rewe,   1005
As I schal even juge ben and trewe.
Ye schul non othir ende with me make,
That oon of yow schal be deed or [i-]take.
And if you thinketh this is wel i-sayed,
Say youre avys, and holdeth yow apayed.   1010

This is youre ende and youre conclusioun.'
Who loketh lightly now but Palomoun?
Who spryngeth up for joye but Arcite?
Who couthe telle, or who couthe endite,
The joye that is mad in this place   1015
Whan Theseus hath don so fair a grace?
But down on knees wente every wight,
And thanked him with al here bertes might,
And namely the Thebanes ofte sithe.
And thus with good[e] hope and herte blithe   1020
They taken here leve, and hom-ward they ryde
To Thebes-[ward], with olde walles wyde.
    I trow[e] men wolde it deme necligence,
If I foryete to telle the dispence
Of Theseus, that goth so busily   1025
To maken up the lystes rially.
And such a noble theatre as it was,
I dar wel say that in this world ther nas.
The circuite ther a myle was aboute,
Walled of stoon, and dyched al withoute.   1030
Round was the schap, in maner of compaas,
Ful of degré, the height of sixty paas,
That whan a man was set in o degré
He letted[e] nought his felaw for to se.
    Est-ward ther stood a gate of marbul whit[e],   1035
West-ward such another in opposit[e].
And schortly to conclude, such a place
Was non in erthe in so litel space.
In al the lond ther nas no craftys man,
That geometry or arsmetrike can,   1040
Ne portreyour, ne kerver of ymages,
That Theseus ne yaf hem mete and wages
The theatre for to maken and devyse.

And for to don his right and sacrifise,
He est-ward hath upon the gate above,   1045
In worschip of Venus, goddes[se] of love,
Don make an auter and an oratory;
And westward in the mynde and in memory
Of Mars, he hath i-maked such another,
That coste largely of gold a fother.   1050
And northward, in a toret on the walle,
Of alabaster whit and reed coralle
An oratory riche for to see,
In worschip of Dyane, goddes[se] of chastité,
Hath Theseus i-wrought in noble wise.   1055
But ȝit had I forgeten to devyse
The nobil kervyng, and the purtretures,
The schap, the contynaunce of the figures,
That weren in the oratories thre.
    Furst in the temple of Venus thou may[st] se   1060
Wrought in the wal, ful pitous to byholde,
The broken slepes, and the sykes colde;
The sacred teeres, and the waymentyng;
The fuyry strokes of the desiryng
That loves servauntz in this lyf enduren;   1065
The othes that by her covenantz assuren.
Plesance and hope, desyr, fool-hardynesse,
Beauté and ȝouthe, baudery and richesse,
Charmes and sorcery, lesynges and flatery,
Dispense, busynes, and jelousy,   1070
That werud of ȝolo guldes a gerland,
And a cukkow sittyng on hire hand;
Festes, instrumentz, carols, and daunces,
Lust and array, and al the circumstaunces
Of love, which I rekned and reken schal,   1075
Ech by other were peynted on the wal.

And mo than I can make of mencioun.
For sothly al the mount of Setheroun,
Ther Venus hath hir principal dwellyng,
Was schewed on the wal here portrayng   1080
With alle the gardyn, and al the lustynes.
Nought was foryete; the porter Ydelnes,
Ne Narcisus the fayr of yore agon,
Ne yet the foly of kyng Salomon,
Ne eek the [grete] strengthe of him Hercules,   1085
Thenchauntementz of Medea and Cerces,
Ne of Turnus the hard[e] fuyry corage,
The riche Cresus caytif in servage.
Thus may we see, that wisdom and riches[se],
Beauté ne sleight, strengthe ne hardynes[se],   1090
Ne may with Venus holde champartye,
For as sche lust the world than may sche gye.
Lo, al this folk i-caught were in hire trace,
Til they for wo ful often sayde allas.
Sufficeth this ensample oon or tuo,   1095
And though I couthe reken a thousend mo.
The statu of Venus, glorious for to see,
Was naked fletyng in the large see,
And fro the navel doun al covered was
With wawes grene, and bright as eny glas.   1100
A citole in hire right hand badde sche,
And on hir heed, ful semely on to see,
A rose garland ful swete and wel smellyng,
And aboven hire heed dowves flikeryng.
Biforn hir stood hir sone Cupido,   1105
Upon his schuldres were wynges two;
And blynd he was, as it is often seene;
A bowe he bar and arwes fair and kene.
  Why schuld I nought as wel telle you alle

The portraiture, that was upon the walle   1110
Within the temple of mighty Mars the reede?
Al peynted was the wal in lengthe and breede
Like to the estres of the grisly place,
That hight the gret[e] tempul of Mars in Trace,
In that colde and frósty regioun,   1115
Ther as Mars hath his sovereyn mancioun.
First on the wal was peynted a foreste,
In which ther dwelled[e] neyther man ne beste,
With knotty knarry bareyn trees olde
Of stubbes scharpe and hidous to byholde;   1120
In which ther ran a swymbul in a swough,
As it were a storme schuld[e] berst every bough:
And downward on an hil under a bent,
Ther stood the tempul of Marcz armypotent,
Wrought al of burned steel, of which thentre   1125
Was long and streyt, and gastly for to see.
And therout cam a rage of suche a prise,
That it maad al the gates for to rise.
The northen light in at the dore schon,
For wyndow on the walle was ther noon,   1130
Thorugh the which men might[e] no light discerne.
The dores were alle ademauntz eterne,
I-clenched overthward and endelong
With iren tough; and, for to make it strong,
Every piler the tempul to susteene   1135
Was tonne greet, of iren bright and schene.
Ther saugh I furst the derk ymaginyng
Of felony, and al the compassyng;
The cruel ire, as reed as eny gleede;
The pikepurs, and eek the pale drede;   1140
The smyler with the knyf under his cloke;
The schipne brennyng with the blake smoke;

The tresoun of the murtheryng in the bed;
The open werres, with woundes al bi-bled;
Contek with bloody knyf, and scharp manace.   1145
Al ful of chirkyng was that sory place.
The sleer of himself yet saugh I there,
His herte-blood hath bathed al his here;
The nayl y-dryve[n] in the scbode a-nyght;
The colde deth, with mouth gapyng upright.   1150
Amyddes of the tempul set meschaunce,
With sory comfort and evel contynaunce.
[Yet] saugh I woodnes laughyng in his rage;
[Armed compleint, outehees, and fiers outrage.
The caraigne in the busche, with throte i-korve: 1155
A thousand slayn, and not of qualme i-storve;
The tiraunt, with the pray bi force i-raft;
The toun distroied, there was no thing i-laft.
Yet saugh I brent the schippis hoppesteres;
The hunt[e] strangled with the wilde beeres:]   1160
The sowe freten the child right in the cradel;
The cook i-skalded, for al his longe ladel.
Nought beth forgeten the infortune of Mart;
The carter over-ryden with his cart,
Under the whel ful lowe he lay adoun.   1165
Ther were also of Martz divisioun,
The barbour, and the bowcher, and the smyth,
That forgeth scharpe swerdes on his stith.
And al above depeynted in a tour
Saw I conquest sittyng in gret honour,   1170
With the scharpe swerd over his heed
Hangynge by a sotil twyne threed.
Depeynted was ther the slaught of Julius,
Of grete Nero, and of Anthonius;
Al be that ilke tyme they were unborn,   1175

*Y*et was here deth depeynted ther byforn,
By manasyng of Martz, right by figure
So was it schewed right in the purtreture
As is depeynted in [the] sterres above,
Who schal be slayn or elles deed for love.   1180
Sufficeth oon ensample in stories olde,
[I may not rekene hem alle, though I wolde.]
  The statue of Mars upon a carte stood,
Armed, and loked[e] grym as he were wood;
And over his heed ther schyneth two figures   1185
Of sterres, that been cleped in scriptures,
That oon Puella, that othur Rubius.
This god of armes was arayed thus.
A wolf ther stood byforn him at his feet
With eyen reed, and of a man he eet;   1190
With sotyl pencel depeynted was this storie,
In redoutyng of Mars and of his glorie.
  Now to the temple of Dyane the chaste
As schortly as I can I wol me haste,
To telle you al the descripcioun.   1195
Depeynted ben the walles up and doun,
Of huntyng and of schamefast chastité.
Ther saugh I how woful Calystopé,
Whan that Dyane was agreved with here,
Was turned from a womman to a bere,   1200
And after was sche maad the loode-sterre;
Thus was it peynted I can say no ferre;
Hire son is eek a sterre, as men may see.
Ther saw*gh* I Dane turned intil a tree,
I mene nou*ght* the goddes[se] Dyane,   1205
But Peneus dou*gh*ter, the whiche hight Dane.
Ther saugh I Atheon an hert i-maked,
For vengance that he saugh Dyane al naked;

I saugh how that his houndes han him caught
And freten him, for that they knew him naught. 1210
*Y*it i-peynted was a litel fothermore.
How Atthalaunce huntyd[e] the wilde bore,
And Melyagre, and many another mo,
For which Dyane wrought hem care and woo.
Ther saugh I eek many another story, 1215
The which me list not drawe in to memory.
This goddes[se] on an hert ful hybe seet,
With smale houndes al aboute hire feet,
And undernethe hir feet sche had[de] the moone,
Wexyng it was, and schulde wane soone. 1220
In gaude greene hire statue clothed was,
With bowe in hande, and arwes in a cas.
Hir eyghen caste sche ful lowe adoun,
Ther Pluto hath his derke regioun.
A womman travailyng was hire biforn, 1225
But for hire child so longe was unborn
Ful pitously Lucyna gan she calle,
And seyde, 'Help, for thou mayst best of alle.'
Wel couthe he peynte lyfly that it wrought[e],
With many a floren he the hewes bought[e]. 1230
  Now been thise listes maad, and Theseus
That at his grete cost arayed[e] thus
The temples and the theatres every del,
Whan it was don, it liked him right wel.
But stynt I wil of Theseus a lite, 1235
And speke of Palomon and of Arcite.
  The day approcheth of her attournyng[e],
That every schuld an hundred knightes bryng[e],
The batail to derreyne, as I you tolde;
And til Athenes, her[e] covenant to holde, 1240
Hath every of hem brought an hundred knightes

F

Wel armed for the werre at alle rightes.
And sikerly ther trowed[e] many a man
That never, siththen that this world bigan,
For to speke of knighthod of her hond,　　　1245
As fer as God hath maked see or lond,
Nas, of so fewe, so good a company.
For every wight that loveth chyvalry,
And wold, his thankes, have a passant name,
Hath preyed that he might[e] be of that game; 1250
A[nd] wel was him, that therto chosen was.
For if ther felle to morwe such a caas,
I knowe wel, that every lusty knight
That loveth paramours, and hath his might,
Were it in Engelond, or elleswhere,　　　　1255
They wold, here thankes, wilne to be there.
To fighte for a lady; benedicite!
It were a lusty sighte for to see.
And right so ferden they with Palomon.
With him ther wente knyghtes many oon;　1260
Some wol ben armed in an haburgoun,
In a bright brest-plat and a gypoun;
And som wold have a peyre plates large;
And som wold have a Pruce scheld, or a targe;
Som wol been armed on here legges weel,　1265
And have an ax, and eek a mace of steel.
Ther nys no newe gyse, that it nas old.
Armed were they, as I have [you] told,
Everich after his owen opinioun.
　　Ther maistow se comyng with Palomoun　1270
Ligurge himself, the grete kyng of Trace;
Blak was his berd, and manly was his face.
The cercles of his eyen in his heed
They gloweden bytwixe yolw and reed,

And lik a griffoun loked he aboute, 1275
With kempe heres on his browes stowte;
His lymes greet, his brawnes hard and stronge,
His schuldres brood, his armes rounde and longe.
And as the gyse was in his contré,
Ful heye upon a chare of gold stood he, 1280
With foure white boles in a trays.
In stede of cote-armour in his harnays,
With nayles yolwe, and bright as eny gold,
He had a bere skyn, cole-blak for old.
His lange heer y-kempt byhynd his bak, 1285
As eny raven fether it schon for blak.
A wrethe of gold arm-gret, and huge of wight[e],
Upon his heed, set ful of stoones bright[e],
Of fyne rubeus. and of fyn dyamauntz.
Aboute his chare wente white alauntz, 1290
Twenty and mo, as grete as eny stere,
To hunt at the lyoun or at the bere,
And folwed him, with mosel fast i-bounde,
Colers of golde, and torettz fyled rounde.
An hundred lordes had he in his route 1295
Armed ful wel, with hertes stern and stoute.

  With Arcita, in stories as men fynde,
The gret Emetreus, the kyng of Ynde,
Uppon a steede bay, trapped in steel,
Covered with cloth of gold dyapred wel, 1300
Cam rydyng lyk the god of armes, Mars.
His coote armour was of a cloth of Tars,
Cowched of perlys whyte, round and grete.
His sadil was of brend gold newe bete;
A mantelet upon his schuldre hangyng 1305
Bret-ful of rubies reed, as fir sparclyng.
His crispe her lik rynges was i-ronne,

And that was yalwe, and gliteryng as þe sonne.
His nose was heigh, his eyen bright cytryne,
His lippes rounde, his colour was sangwyn,   1310
A fewe freknes in his face y-spreynd,
Betwixe yolwe and somdel blak y-meynd,
And as a lyoun he his lokyng caste.
Of fyve and twenty yeer his age I caste.
His berd was wel bygonne for to sprynge;   1315
His voys was as a trumpe thunderynge.
Upon his heed he wered of laurer grene
A garlond freisch and lusty for to sene.
Upon his hond he bar for his delyt
An egle tame, as eny lylie whyt.   1320
An hundred lordes had he with him ther,
Al armed sauf here hedes in here ger,
Ful richely in alle maner thinges.
For trusteth wel, that dukes, erles, kynges,
Were gadred in this noble companye,   1325
For love, and for encres of chivalrye.
Aboute the kyng ther ran on every part
Ful many a tame lyoun and lepart.
And in this wise this lordes alle and some
Been on the Sonday to the cité come   1330
Aboute prime, and in the toun alight.
This Theseus, this duk, this worthy knight,
Whan he had[de] brought hem into this cité,
And ynned hem, everich at his degré
He festeth hem, and doth so gret labour   1335
To esen hem, and do hem al honour,
That yit men wene that no mannes wyt
Of non estat that cowde amenden it.
The mynstralcye, the servyce at the feste,
•The grete yiftes to the most and leste,   1340

The riche aray of Theseus paleys,
Ne who sat first ne last upon the deys,
What ladies fayrest ben or best daunsyng[e],
Or which of hem can daunce best or syng[e],
Ne who most felyngly speketh of love;   1345
What haukes sitten on the perche above,
What houndes lyen on the floor adoun :
Of al this make I now no mencioun;
But of theffect; that thinketh me the beste;
Now comth the poynt, and herkneth if you. leste.

   The Sonday night, or day bigan to springe,   1351
When Palomon the larke herde synge,
Although it were nought day by houres tuo,
*Y*it sang the larke, and Palomon also
With holy herte, and with an heih corage   1355
He roos, to wenden on his pilgrymage
Unto the blisful Cithera benigne,
I mene Venus, honorable and digne.
And in hire hour he walketh forth a pass —
Unto the lystes, ther hir temple was,   1360
And doun he kneleth, and, with humble cheer[e]
And her[te] sore, he seide as ye schul heer[e].

   ' Fairest of faire, o lady myn Venus,
Doughter of Jove, and spouse to Vulcanus,
Thou glader of the mount of Citheroun,   1365
For thilke love thou haddest to Adeoun
Have pité on my bitter teéres smerte,
And tak myn humble prayer to thin herte.
Allas ! I ne have no langage for to telle
Theffectes ne the tormentz of myn helle;   1370
Myn herte may myn barmes nat bewreye;
I am so confus, that I may not seye.
But mercy, lady bright[e], that knowest wel

My thought, and felest what harm that I fel,
Consider al this, and rew upon my sore,　　　　1375
As wisly as I schal for evermore
Enforce my might thi trewe servant to be,
And holde werre alday with chastité;
That make I myn avow, so ye me helpe.
I kepe nat of armes for to yelpe,　　　　1380
Ne nat I aske to-morn to have victorie,
Ne renoun in this caas, ne veyne glorie
Of pris of armes, blowyng up and doun,
But I wolde have ful possessioun
Of Emelye, and dye in thi servise.　　　　1385
Fynd thou the maner how, and in what wyse
I recche nat, but it may better be,
To have victorie of him, or he of me,
So that I have my lady in myn armes.
For though so be that Mars be god of armes,　　　1390
And ye be Venus, the goddes[se] of love,
Youre vertu is so gret in heven above,
Thy temple wol I worschipe evermo,
And on thin auter, wher I ryde or go,
I wol do sacrifice, and fyres beete.　　　　1395
And if ye wol nat so, my lady sweete,
Than pray I the, to morwe with a spere
That Arcita me thurgh the herte bere.
Thanne rekke I nat, whan I have lost my lyf,
Though that Arcite have hir to his wyf.　　　1400
This is theffect and ende of my prayeere;
Vif me my love, thou blisful lady deere.'
Whan thorisoun was doon of Palomon,
His sacrifice he dede, and that anoon
Ful pitously, with alle circumstances,　　　1405
Al telle I nat as now his observances.

But at the last the statu of Venus schook,
And made a signe, wherby that he took
That his prayer accepted was that day.
For though the signe schewed a delay,   1410
_Y_et wist he wel that graunted was his boone;
And with glad herte he went him hom ful soone.
    The thrid[de] hour inequal that Palomon
Bigan to Venus temple for to goon,
Up roos the sonne, and up roos Emelye,   1415
And to the temple of Dian gan sche hye.
Hir maydens, that sche with hir thider ladde,
Ful redily with hem the fyr they badde,
Thencens, the clothes, and the [re]menant al
That to the sacrifice longen schal;   1420
The hornes ful of meth, as is the gyse;
Ther lakketh noght to do here sacrifise.
Smokyng the temple, ful of clothes faire,
This Emelye with herte debonaire
Hir body wessch with w[a]tir of a welle;   1425
But how sche dide ne dar I nat telle,
But it be eny thing in general;
And _y_et it were a game to here it al;
To him that meneth wel it were no charge:
But it is good a man be at his large.   1430
Hir brighte her was kempt, untressed al;
A corone of a grene ok cerial
Upon hir heed was set ful fair and meete.
Tuo fyres on the auter gan sche beete,
And did hir thinges, as men may biholde   1435
In Stace of Thebes and the bokes olde.
Whan kynled was the fyre, with pitous cheere
Unto Dyan sche spak, as ye may heere.
    ‘ O chaste goddes[se] of the woodes greene,

To whom bothe heven and erthe and see is seene
Queen of the regne of .Pluto derk and lowe,   1441
Goddes[se] of maydenes, that myn hert has knowe
Ful many a yeer, ye woot what I desire,
As keep me fro the vengans of thilk yre,
That Atheon aboughte trewely: 1445
Chaste goddesse, wel wost thou that I
Desire to ben a mayden al my lyf,
Ne never wol I be no love ne wyf.
I am, thou wost, yit of thi company,
A mayden, and love huntyng and venery,   1450
And for to walken in the woodes wylde,
And nought to ben a wyf, and be with chylde.
Nought wol I knowe the company of man.
Now. helpe me, lady, sythnes ye may and kan,
For the [thre] formes that thou hast in the.   1455
And Palomon, that hath such love to me,
And eek Arcite, that loveth me so sore,
This grace I praye the withouten more,
And sende love and pees betwix hem two;
And fro me torne awey here hertes so,   1460
That al here boote love, and here desire,
Al here besy torment, and al here fyre
Be queynt, or turned in another place.
And if so be thou wol[t] do me no grace,
Or if my destyné be schapid so,   1465
That I schal needes have on of hem two,
So send me him that most desireth me.
Bihold, goddes[se] of clene chastité,
The bitter teeres that on my cheekes falle.
Syn thou art mayde, and keper of us alle,   1470
My maydenhode thou kepe and wel conserve,
And whil I lyve a mayde I wil the serve.'

The fyres bren[ne] upon the auter cleer[e],
Whil Emelye was [thus] in hire preyer[e];
But sodeinly sche saugh a sighte queynt[e],　　1475
For right anon on of the fyres queynt[e],
And quyked agayn, and after that anon
That other fyr was queynt, and al agon;
And as it queynt, it made a whistelyng,
As doth a wete brond in his brennyng.　　1480
And at the brondes. end out ran anoon
As it were bloody dropes many oon;
For which so sore agast was Emelye,
That sche wel neih mad was, and gan to crie,
For sche ne wiste what it signifyed[e];　　1485
But oonely for feere thus sche cryed[e],
And wepte, that it was pité to heere.
And therewithal Dyane gan appeere,
With bow in hond, right as a hunteresse,
And seyd; 'A! doughter, stynt thyn hevynesse.　　1490
Among the goddes hye it is affermed,
And by eterne word write and confermed,
Thou schalt be wedded unto oon of tho,
That have for the so moche care and wo;
But unto which of hem may I nat telle.　　1495
Farwel, for I may her no lenger dwelle.
The fyres which that on myn auter bren[ne]
Schuln the declare[n], or that thou go hen[ne],
Thyn adventure of love, and in this caas.'
And with that word, the arwes in the caas　　1500
Of the goddesse clatren faste and rynge,
And forth sche went, and made a vanysschynge,
For which this Emelye astoneyd was,
And seide, 'What amounteth this, allas!
I put me under thy proteccioun,　　1505

Dyane, and in thi disposicioun.'
And hoom sche goth anon the nexte way[e].
This is theffect, ther nys no mor to say[e].
   The nexte houre of Mars folwynge this,
Arcite to the temple walkyd is,   1510
To fyry Mars to doon his sacrifise,
With al the rightes of his payen wise.
With pitous herte and heih devocioun,
Right thus to Mars he sayd·his orisoun:
'O stronge god, that in the reynes cold[e]   1515
Of Trace honoured and lord art y-hold[e],
And hast in every regne and every land
Of armes al the bridel in thy hand,
And hem fortunest as the lust devyse,
Accept of me my pitous sacrifise.   1520
If so be that my youthe may deserve,
And that my might be worthi [for] to serve
Thy godhed, that I may be on of thine,
Then pray I the to rewe[n] on my pyne.
      *   *   *   *   *
For thilke sorwe that was in thin herte,   1525
Have reuthe as wel upon my peynes smerte.
I am yong and unkonnyng, as thou wost,
And, as I trowe, with love offendid most,
That ever was eny lyves creature;
For sche, that doth me al this wo endure,   1530
Ne rekketh never whether I synke or flete.
And wel I woot, or sche me mercy beete,
I moot with strengthe wyn hir in the place;
And wel I wot, withouten help or grace
Of the, ne may my strengthe nought avayle.   1535
Then help me, lord, to-morn in my batayle,
For thilke fyr that whilom brende the,

As wel as this fir now [that] brenneth me;
And do to-morn that I have the victorie.
Myn be the travail, al thin be the glorie.   1540
Thy soverein tempul wol I most honouren
Of any place, and alway most labouren
In thy plesaunce and [in] thy craftes strong[e].
And in thy tempul I wol my baner hong[e],
And alle the armes of my companye,   1545
And ever more, unto that day I dye,
Eterne fyr I wol bifore the fynde.
And eek to this avow I wol me bynde:
My berd, myn heer that hangeth longe adoun,
That never yit ne felt offensioun   1550
Of rasour ne of schere, I wol the yive,
And be thy trewe servaunt whiles I lyve.
Lord, have rowthe uppon my sorwes sore,
Yif me the victorie, I aske no more.'

The preyer stynt of Arcita the stronge,   1555
The rynges on the tempul dore that honge,
And eek the dores, clatereden ful fast[e],
Of which Arcita somwhat was agast[e].
The fires brenden on the auter bright[e],
That it gan al the tempul for to light[e];   1560
A swote smel anon the ground upyaf,
And Arcita anon his hand up-haf,
And more encens into the fyr yet cast[e],
With othir rightes, and than atte last[e]
The statu of Mars bigan his hauberk ryng[e],   1565
And with that soun he herd a murmuryng[e]
Ful lowe and dym, and sayde thus, ' Victorie.'
For which he yaf to Mars honour and glorie.
And thus with joye, and hope wel to fare,
Arcite anoon unto his inne is fare,   1570

As fayn as foul is of the brighte sonne.
And right anon such stryf [ther] is bygonne
For that grauntyng, in the heven above,
Bitwix[e] Venus the goddes[se] of love,
And Marcz the sterne god armypotent[e],   1575
That Jupiter was busy it to stent[e];
Til that the pale Saturnes the colde,
That knew so many of aventures olde,
Fond in his [olde] experiens an art,
That he ful sone hath plesyd every part.   1580
As soth is sayd, eelde hath gret avantage,
In eelde is bothe wisdom and usage;
Men may the eelde at-ren[ne], but nat at-rede.
Saturne anon, to stynte stryf and drede,
Al be it that it be agayns his kynde,   1585
Of al this stryf he can remedy fynde.
'My deere dou*g*hter Venus,' quod Satourne,
'My cours, that hath so wyde for to tourne,
Hath more power than woot eny man.
Myn is the drenchyng in the see so wan;   1590
Myn is the prisoun in the derke cote;
Myn is the stranglyng and hangyng by the throte;
The murmur, and the cherles rebellyng;
The groynyng, and the pryvé enpoysonyng.
I do vengance and pleyn correctioun,   1595
Whiles I dwelle in the signe of the lyoun.
Myn is the ruen of the hihe halles,
The fallyng of the toures and the walles
Upon the mynour or the carpenter.
I slowh Sampsoun in schakyng the piler.   1600
And myne ben the maladies colde,
The derke tresoun, and the castes olde;
Myn lokyng is the fadir of pestilens.

Now wep nomore, I schal do my diligence,
That Palomon, that is myn owen knight,   1605
Schal have his lady, as thou him bihight.
Thow Marcz schal kepe his kni*gh*t, yet nevertheles
Bitwixe you ther moot som tyme be pees;
Al be ye nou*gh*t of oo complexioun,
That ilke day causeth such divisioun.   1610
I am thi ayel, redy at thy wille;
Wep thou nomore, I wol thi lust fulfille.'
Now wol I stynt of the goddes above,
Of Mars, and of Venus, goddes[se] of love,
And telle you, as pleinly as I can,   1615
The grete effecte for [which] that I bigan.

Gret was the fest in Athenus that day,
And eek that lusty sesoun of that May
Made every wi*gh*t to ben in such plesaunce,
That al the Monday jousten they and daunce,   1620
And spende[n] hit in Venus heigh servise.
But by the cause that they schuln arise
Erly a-morwe for to see that fight,
Unto here rest[e] wente they at nyght.
And on the morwe whan the day gan spryng[e], 1625
Of hors and hernoys noyse and clateryng[e]
Ther was in the oostes al aboute;
And to the paleys rood ther many a route
Of lordes, upon steede and on palfreys.
Ther mayst thou see devysyng of berneys   1630
So uncowth and so riche wrought and wel
Of goldsmithry, of browdyng, and of steel;
The scheldes bright[e], testers, and trappures;
Gold-beten helmes, hauberks, and cote-armures;
Lordes in paramentz on her[e] courses,   1635
Knightes of retenu, and eek squyers

Rayhyng the speres, and helmes bokelyng,
Girdyng of scheeldes, with layneres lasyng;
Ther as need is, they were nothing ydel;
Ther fomen steedes, on the golden bridel   1640
Gnawyng, and faste [the] armurers also
With fyle and hamer prikyng to and fro;
Yemen on foote, and knaves many oon
With schorte staves, as thikke as they may goon;
Pypes, trompes, nakers, and clariounes,   . 1645
That in the batail blewe bloody sownes;
The paleys ful of pepul up and doun,
Heer thre, ther ten, haldyng her[e] questioun,
Dyvynyng of this Thebans knightes two.
Som seyden thus, som seyd it schal be so;   1650
Som heelde with him with the blake berd,
Som with the ballyd, som with [the] thikke hered;
Som sayd he loked[e] grym and wolde fight[e];
He hath a sparth of twenti pound of wight[e].
Thus was the halle ful of devynyng[e],   1655
Lang after that the sonne gan to spring[e].
The gret[e] Theseus that of his sleep is awaked
With menstralcy and noyse that was maked,
Held yit the chambre of his paleys riche,
Til that the Thebanes knyghtes bothe i-liche   1660
Honoured weren, and into paleys fet.
Duk Theseus was at a wyndow set,
Arayed right as he were god in trone.
The pepul presed[e] thider-ward ful sone
Him for to seen, and doon him reverence,   1665
And eek herken his hest and his sentence.
An herowd on a skaffold made a hoo,
Til al the noyse of the pepul was i-doo;
And whan he sawh the pepul of noyse al stille,

Thus schewed he the mighty dukes wille.   1670
 'The lord hath of his heih discrecioun
Considered, that it were destruccioun
To gentil blood, to fighten in this wise
Of mortal batail now in this emprise;
Wherfore to schapen that they schuld[e] not dye, 1675
He wol his firste purpos modifye.
No man therfore, up peyne of los of lyf,
No maner schot, ne pollax, ne schort knyf
Into the lystes sende, or thider bryng[e];
Ne schort swerd for to stoke, the [poynt] bytyng[e] 1680
No man ne drawe, ne bere by his side.
Ne noman schal [un]to his felawe ryde
But oon cours, with a scharpe [ygrounde] spere;
Foyne if him lust on foote, himself to were.
And he that is at meschief, schal be take, 1685
And nat [y]slayn, but be brought to the stake,
That schal be ordeyned on eyther syde;
But thider he schal by force, and ther abyde.
And if so falle, a cheventen be take
On eyther side, or elles sle his make,   1690
No lenger schal the turneynge laste.
God spede you; goth forth and ley on faste.
With long swerd and with mace fight your fille.
Goth now your way; this is the lordes wille.'
 The voice of the peopul touchith heven, 1695
So lowde cried[e] thei with mery steven:
'God save such a lord that is so good,
He wilneth no destruccioun of blood!'
Up goth the trompes and the melodye.
And to the lystes ryde the companye   1700
By ordynaunce, thurgh the cité large,
Hangyng with cloth of gold, and not with sarge.

Ful lik a lord this nobul duk can ryde.
These tuo Theban[e]s on eyther side;
And after rood the queen, and Emelye,   1705
And after hem of ladyes another companye,
And after hem of comunes after here. degre.
And thus they passeden thurgh that cité,
And to the lystes come thei by tyme.
It nas not of the day yet fully pryme,   1710
Whan sette was Theseus riche and hye,
Ypolita the queen and Emelye,
And other ladyes in here degrees aboute.
Unto the seetes preseth al the route;
And west-ward, thorugh the yates of Mart,   1715
Arcite, and eek the hundred of his part,
With baners [rede] ys entred right anoon;
And [in] that selve moment Palomon
Is, under Venus, est-ward in that place,
With baner whyt, and hardy cheer and face.   1720
    In al the world, to seeke[n] up and doun,
So even withoute variacioun
Ther nere suche companyes tweye.
For ther nas noon so wys that cowthe seye,
That any had of other avauntage   1725
Of worthines, ne staat, ne of visage,
So evene were they chosen for to gesse.
And in two renges faire they hem dresse.
And whan he[re] names i-rad were everychon,
That in here nombre gile were ther noon,   1730
Tho were the gates schitt, and cried lowde:
'Doth now your devoir, yonge knightes proude!'
The heraldz laften here prikyng up and doun;
Now ryngede the tromp and clarioun;
Ther is nomore to say, but est and west   1735

In goth the speres [ful sadly] in arest;
Ther seen men who can juste, and who can ryde;
In goth the scharpe spore into the side.
Ther schyveren schaftes upon schuldres thyk[ke];
He feeleth thurh the herte-spon the prik[ke].   1740
Up sprengen speres of twenty foot on hight[e];
Out goon the swerdes as the silver bright[e].
The helmes thei to-hewen and to-schrede;
Out brast the blood, with stoute stremes reede,
With mighty maces the bones thay to-breste.   1745
He thurgh the thikkest of the throng gan threste.
Ther stomblen steedes strong, and doun can falle.
He rolleth under foot as doth a balle.
He foyneth on his foot with a tronchoun,
And him hurteleth with his hors adoun.   1750
He thurgh the body hurt is, and siththen take
Maugré his heed, and brought unto the stake,
As forward was, right ther he most abyde.
Another lad is on that other syde.
And som tyme doth Theseus hem to rest[e],   1755
Hem to refreissche, and drinke[n] if hem lest[e].
Ful ofte a-day have this Thebans twoo
Togider y-met, and wrought his felaw woo;
Unhorsed hath ech other of hem tweye.
Ther nas no tygyr in the vale of Galgopleye,   1760
Whan that hir whelp is stole, whan it is lite,
So cruel on the hunt, as is Arcite
For jelous hert upon this Palomon:
Ne in Belmary ther is no fel lyoun,
That hunted is, or [is] for hunger wood,   1765
Ne of his prey desireth so the blood,
As Palomon to sle his foo Arcite.
This jelous strokes on here helmes byte;

G

Out renneth blood on bothe here sides reede.
Som tyme an ende ther is on every dede;   1770
For er the sonne unto the reste went[e],
The strong[e] kyng Emetreus gan hent[e]
This Palomon, as he faught with Arcite,
And his swerd in his fleissch[e] did[e] byte;
And by the force of twenti he is take   1775
Unyolden, and i-drawe unto the stake.
And in the rescous of this Palomon
The stronge kyng Ligurgius is born adoun;
And kyng Emetreus for al his strengthe
Is born out of his sadel his swerdes lengthe,   1780
So hit him Palomon er he were take;
But al for nought, he was brought to 'the stake.
His hardy herte might him helpe nought;
He most abyde whan that he was caught,
By force, and eek by composicioun.   1785
Who sorweth now but [woful] Palomoun,
That moot nomore gon agayn to fight[e]?
And whan that Theseus had[de] seen that sight[e],
He cryed, 'Hoo! nomore, for it is doon!
Ne noon schal lenger unto his felaw goon.   1790
I wol be trewe juge, and nought partye.
Arcyte of Thebes schal have Emelye,
That hath by his fortune hire i-wonne.'
Anoon ther is [a] noyse [of peple] bygonne
For joye of this, so lowde and heye withalle,   1795
It semed[e] that the listes wolde falle.
What can now fayre Venus doon above?
What seith sche now? what doth this queen of love?
But wepeth so, for wantyng of hir wille,
Til that hire teeres in the lystes fille;   1800
Sche sayde: 'I am aschamed douteles.'

Satournus seyde: 'Dou*gh*ter, hold thy pees.
Mars hath his wille, his knight hath [al] his boone,
And by myn heed thou schalt be esed soone.'
The trompes with the lowde mynstralcy,   1805
The herawdes, that ful lowde *y*olle and cry,
Been in here joye for daun Arcyte.
But herkneth me, and stynteth but a lite,
Which a miracle [ther] bifel anoon.
This fers Arcyte hath don his helm adoun,   1810
And on his courser for to schewe his face,
He priked endlange in the large place,
Lokyng upward upon his Emelye;
And sche agayn him cast a frendly y*gh*e,
(For wommen, as for to speke in comune,   1815
Thay folwe alle the favour of fortune)
And was alle his cheer, and in his hert[e].
Out of the ground a fyr infernal stert[e],
From Pluto send, at the request of Saturne,
For which his hors for feere gan to turne,   1820
And leep asyde, and foundred as he leep;
And or that Arcyte may take keep,
He pight him on the pomel of his heed,
That in that place he lay as he were deed,
His brest to-broken with his sadil bowe.   1825
As blak he lay as eny col or crowe,
So was the blood y-ronne in his face.
Anon he was y-born out of the place
With herte sore, to Theseus paleys.
Tho was he corven out of his harneys,   1830
And in a bed y-brought ful fair and blyve,
For *y*it he was in memory and on lyve,
And alway cryeng after Emelye.
Duk Theseus, and al his companye,

G 2

Is comen hom to Athenes his cité,   1835
With alle blys and gret solempnité.
Al be it that this aventure was falle,
He nolde nought discomfort[en] hem alle.
Men seyde eek, that Arcita schuld[e] nought dye,
He schal be helyd of his maladye.   1840
And of another thing they were as fayn,
That of hem alle ther was noon y-slayn,
Al were they sore hurt, and namely oon,
That with a spere was thirled his brest boon.
To other woundes, and to broken armes,   1845
Some badde salve, and some badde charmes,
Fermacyes of herbes, and eek save
They dronken, for they wolde here lyves have.
For which this noble duk, as he wel can,
Comforteth and honoureth every man,   1850
And made revel al the lange night,
Unto the straunge lordes, as was right.
Ne ther was holden no discomfytyng,
But as a justes or as a turneying;
For sothly ther was no discomfiture,   1855
For fallynge is but an adventure.
Ne to be lad with fors unto the stake
Unyolden, and with twenty knightes take,
A person allone, withouten moo,
And haried forth by arme, foot, and too,   1860
And eek his steede dryven forth with staves,
With footemen, bothe yemen and [eke] knaves,
It was aretted him no vylonye,
Ne no maner man held it no cowardye.
    For which Theseus lowd anon leet crie,   1865
To stynten al rancour and al envye,
The gree as wel on o syde as on other,

And every side lik, as otheres bròther;
And *y*af hem *y*iftes after here degré,
And fully heeld a feste dayes thre;   1870
And conveyed[e] the knightes worthily
Out of his toun a journee largely.
And hom went every man the righte way.
Ther was no more, but 'Farwel, have good day!'
Of this batayl I wol no more endite,   1875
But speke of Palomon and of Arcyte.

    Swelleth the brest of Arcyte, and the sore
Encresceth at his herte more and more.
The clothred blood, for eny leche-craft,
Corrumpith, and [is] in his bouk i-laft,   1880
That nother veyne blood, ne ventusyng,
Ne drynk of herbes may ben his helpyng.
The vertu expulsif, or animal,
For thilke vertu cleped natural,
Ne may the venym voyde, ne expelle.   1885
The pypes of his lounges gan to swelle,
And every lacerte in his brest adoun
Is schent with venym and corrupcioun.

    *   *   *   *   *

Al is to-broken thilke regioun,
Nature hath now no dominacioun.   1890
And certeynly wher nature wil not wirche,
Farwel phisik; go bere the man to chirche.
This al and som, that Arcyte moste dye.
For which he sendeth after Emelye
And Palomon, that was his cosyn deere.   1895
Thanne seyd he thus, as ye schul after heere.

    'Naught may the woful spirit in myn herte
Declare a poynt of [al] my sorwes smerte
To you, my lady, that I love most;

But I byquethe the service of my gost   1900
To you aboven every creature,
Syn that my lyf [ne] may no lenger dure.
Allas, the woo! allas, the peynes stronge,
That I for you have suffred, and so longe!
Allas, the deth! alas, myn Emelye!   1905
Allas, departyng of our companye!
Allas, myn hertes queen! allas, my wyf!
Myn bertes lady, ender of my lyf!
What is this world? what asken men to have?
Now with his love, now in his colde grave   1910
Allone withouten eny companye.
Farwel, my swete! farwel, myn Emelye!
And softe take me in your armes tweye,
For love of God, and herkneth what I seye.
I have heer with my cosyn Palomon   1915
Had stryf and rancour many a day i-gon,
For love of yow, and eek for jelousie.
And Jupiter so wis my sowle gye,
To speken of a servaunt proprely,
With alle circumstaunces trewely,   1920
That is to seyn, trouthe, honour, and knighthede,
Wysdom, humblesse, astaat, and hy kynrede,
Fredam, and al that longeth to that art,
So Jupiter have of my soule part,
As in this world right now ne know I non   1925
So worthy to be loved as Palomon,
That serveth you, and wol do al his lyf.
And if that ye schul ever be a wyf,
Foryet not Palomon, that gentil man.'
And with that word his speche faile gan;   1930
For fro his herte up to his brest was come
The cold of deth, that him had overcome.

And yet moreover in his armes twoo
The vital strength is lost, and al agoo.
Only the intellect, withouten more,   1935
That dwelled in his herte sik and sore,
Gan fayle, whan the herte felte deth,
Duskyng his ey*gh*en two, and fayled[e] breth.
But on his lady *y*it he cast his ye;
His laste word was, 'Mercy, Emelye!'   1940
His spiryt chaunged was, and wente ther,
As I cam never, I can nat tellen wher.
Therfore I stynte, I nam no dyvynistre;
Of soules fynde I not in this registre,
Ne me list nat thopynyouns to telle   1945
Of hem, though that thei wyten wher they dwelle.
Arcyte is cold, ther Mars his soule gye;
Now wol I speke forth of Emelye.

    Shright Emely, and howled[e] Palomon,
And Theseus his sustir took anon   1950
Swownyng, and bar hir fro the corps away.
What helpeth it to tarye forth the day,
To telle how sche weep bothe eve and morwe?
For in swich caas wommen can have such sorwe,
Whan that here housbonds ben from hem ago, 1955
That for the more part they sorwen so,
Or elles fallen in such maladye,
That atte laste certeynly they dye.
Infynyt been the sorwes and the teeres
Of olde folk, and folk of tendre yeeres.   1960
So gret a wepyng was ther noon certayn,
Whan Ector was i-brought, al freissh i-slayn,
As that ther was for deth of this Theban;
For sorwe of him ther weepeth bothe child and man
At Troye, allas! the pité that was there,   1965

Cracchyng of cheekes, rendyng eek of here.
'Why woldist thou be deed,' this wommen crye,
'And haddest gold ynow*gh*, and Emelye?'
No man [ne] mighte glade Theseus,
Savyng his olde fader Egeus,   1970
That knew this worldes transmutacioun,
As he badde seen it torne up and doun,
Joye after woo, and woo aftir gladnesse:
And schewed him ensample and likenesse.

'Right as ther deyde never man,' quod he,   1975
'That he ne lyved in erthe in som degree,
*Y*it ther ne lyvede never man,' he seyde,
'In al this world, that som tyme he ne deyde.
This world nys but a thurghfare ful of woo,
And we ben pilgryms, passyng to and froo;   1980
Deth is an ende of every worldly sore.'
And over al this *y*it seide he mochil more
To this effect, ful wysly to enhorte
The peple, that [they] schulde him recomforte.

Duk Theseus, with al his busy cure,   1985
Cast busyly wher that the sepulture
Of good Arcyte may best y-maked be,
And eek most honurable in his degré.
And atte last he took conclusioun,
That ther as first Arcite and Palomon   1990
Hadden for love the batail hem bytwene,
That in the selve grove, soote and greene,
Ther as he hadde his amorous desires,
His compleynt, and for love his hoote fyres,
He wolde make a fyr, in which thoffice   1995
Of funeral he might al accomplice;
And leet comaunde anon to hakke and hewe
The okes olde, and lay hem on a rewe

In culpouns wel arrayed for to brenne.
His officers with swifte foot they renne,   2000
And ryde anon at his comaundement.
And after this, Theseus hath i-sent
After a beer, and it al overspradde
With cloth of golde, the richest that he hadde.
And of the same sute he clad Arcyte;   2005
Upon his bondes were his gloves white;
Eke on his heed a croune of laurer grene;
And in his hond a swerd ful bright and kene.
He leyde him bare the visage on the beere,
Therwith he weep that pité was to heere.   2010
And for the people schulde see him alle,
Whan it was day he brought hem to the halle,
That roreth of the cry and of the soun.
Tho cam this woful Theban Palomoun,
With flotery berd, and ruggy asshy heeres,   2015
In clothis blak, y-dropped al with teeres,
And, passyng other, of wepyng Emelye,
The rewfullest of al the companye.
In as moche as the service schulde be
The more nobul and riche in his degré,   2020
Duk Theseus leet forth thre steedes bryng[e],
That trapped were in steel al gliteryng[e],
And covered with armes of dan Arcyte.
Upon the steedes, that weren grete and white,
Ther seeten folk, of which oon bar his scheeld, 2025
Another his spere up in bis hondes heeld;
The thridde bar with him his bowe Turkeys,
Of brend gold was the caas and eek the herneys;
And riden forth a paas with sorwful chere
Toward the grove, as ye schul after heere.   2030
The nobles of the Grekes that ther were

Upon here schuldres carieden the beere,
With slak[e] paas, and eyhen reed and wete,
Thurghout the cité, by the maister streete,
That sprad was al with blak, and wonder hye   2035
Right of the same is al the stret i-wrye.
Upon the right hond went olde Egeus,
And on that other syde duk Theseus,
With vessels in here hand of gold wel fyn,
As ful of hony, mylk, and blood, and wyn;   2040
Eke Palomon, with a gret companye;
And after that com woful Emelye,
With fyr in hond, as was that time the gyse,
To do thoffice of funeral servise.

Hey*gh* labour, and ful gret apparailyng   2045
Was at the service and at the fyr makyng,
That with his grene top the heven raughte,
And twenty fadme of brede tharme straughte;
This is to seyn, the boowes were so brode.
Of stree first was ther leyd ful many a loode.   2050
But how the fyr was makyd up on highte,
And eek the names how the trees highte,
As ook, fyr, birch, asp, aldir, holm, popler,
Wilw, elm, plane, assch, box, chesteyn, lynde, laurer,
Mapul, thorn, beech, hasil, ew, wyppyltre,   2055
How they weren feld, schal nou*gh*t be told for me;
Ne how the goddes ronnen up and doun,
Disheryt of here habitacioun,
In which they whilom woned in rest and pees,
Nymphes, Faunes, and Amadryes;   2060
Ne how the beestes and the briddes alle
Fledden for feere, whan the woode was falle;
Ne how the ground agast was of the light,
That was nought wont to see no sonne bright;

Ne how the fyr was couchid first with stree, 2065
And thanne with drye stykkes cloven in three,
And thanne with grene woode and spicerie,
And thanne with cloth of gold and with perrye,
And gerlandes hangyng with ful many a flour,
The myrre, thensens with also swet odour; 2070
Ne how Arcyte lay among al this,
Ne what richesse aboute his body is;
Ne how that Emely, as was the gyse,
Put in the fyr of funeral servise;
Ne how she swowned[e] whan sche made the fyre, 2075
Ne what sche spak, ne what was hire desire;
Ne what jewels men in the fyr tho cast[e],
Whan that the fyr was gret and brente fast[e];
Ne how sum caste here scheeld, and summe her[e] spere,
And of here vestimentz, which that they were, 2080
And cuppes ful of wyn, and mylk, and blood,
Unto the fyr, that brent as it were wood;
Ne how the Grekes with an huge route
Thre tymes ryden al the fyr aboute
Upon the lefte hond, with an heib schoutyng, 2085
And thries with here speres clateryng;
And thries how the ladyes gan to crye;
Ne how that lad was hom-ward Emelye;
Ne how Arcyte is brent to aschen colde;
[Ne how that liche-wake was y-holde] 2090
Al thilke night, ne how the Grekes pleye
The wake-pleyes, kepe I nat to seye;
Who wrastleth best naked, with oyle enoynt,
Ne who that bar him best in no dis[j]oynt.
I wole not telle eek how that they ben goon 2095
Hom til Athenes whan the pley is doon.
But schortly to the poynt now wol I wende,

And maken of my longe tale an ende.
By proces and by lengthe of certeyn yeres
Al styntyd is the mornyng and the teeres   2100
Of alle Grekys, by oon general assent.
Than semed[e] me ther was a parlement
At Athenes, on a certeyn poynt and cas;
Among the whiche poyntes spoken was
To han with certeyn contrees alliaunce,   2105
And have fully of Thebans obeissance.
For which this noble Theseus anon
Let senden after gentil Palomon,
Unwist of him what was the cause and why;
But in his blake clothes sorwfully   2110
He cam at his comaundement in hye.
Tho sente Theseus for Emelye.
Whan they were sette, and hussht was al the place,
And Theseus abyden hadde a space
Or eny word cam fro his wyse brest,   2115
His eyen set he ther as was his lest,
And with a sad visage he syked[e] stille,
And after that right thus he seide his wille.
'The firste moevere of the cause above,
Whan he first made the fayre cheyne of love,   2120
Gret was theffect, and heigh was his entente;
Wel wist he why, and what therof he mente;
For with that faire cheyne of love he bond
The fyr, the watir, eyr, and eek the lond
In certeyn boundes, that they may not flee;   2125
That same prynce and moevere eek,' quod he,
'Hath stabled, in this wrecched world adoun,
Certeyn[e] dayes and duracioun
To alle that er engendrid in this place,
Over the [whiche] day they may nat pace,   2130

Al mowe they *y*it wel here dayes abregge;
Ther needeth non auctorité tallegge;
For it is preved by experience,
But that me lust declare my sentence.
Than may men wel by this ordre discerne,　2135
That thilke moevere stabul is and eterne.
Wel may men knowe, but it be a fool,
That every partye deryveth from his hool.
For nature hath nat take his bygynnyng
Of no partye ne cantel of a thing,　2140
But of a thing that parfyt is and stable,
Descendyng so, til it be corumpable.
And therfore of his wyse purveaunce
He hath so wel biset his ordenaunce,
That spices of thinges and progressiouns　2145
Schullen endure by successiouns,
And nat eterne be, withoute lye:
This maistow understand and se at ye.
　‘ Lo the ook, that hath so long norisschyng[e]
Fro tyme that it gynneth first to spring[e],　2150
And hath so long a lyf, as we may see,
*Y*et atte laste wasted is the tree.
　‘ Considereth eek, how that the harde stoon
Under oure foot, on which we trede and goon,
*Y*it wasteth it, as it lith by the weye.　2155
The brode ryver som tyme wexeth dreye.
The grete townes see we wane and wende.
Than may I see that al thing hath an ende.
　‘ Of man and womman se we wel also,
That wendeth in oon of this termes two,　2160
That is to seyn, in *y*outhe or elles in age,
He moot ben deed, the kyng as schal a page;
Sum in his bed, som in the deepe see,

Som in the large feel[de], as men may se.
Ther helpeth naught, al go[e]th thilke weye.   2165
Thanne may I see wel that al thing schal deye.
What maketh this but Jubiter the kyng?
The which is prynce and cause of alle thing,
Convertyng al unto his propre wille,
From which he is dereyned, soth to telle.   2170
And here agayn no creature of lyve
Of no degré avayleth for to stryve.
  ' Than is it wisdom, as [it] thenketh me,
To maken vertu of necessité,
And take it wel, that we may nat eschewe,   2175
And namely that that to us alle is dewe.
And who-so gruccheth aught, he doth folye,
And rebel is to him that al may gye.
And certeynly a man hath most honour
To deyen in his excellence and flour,   2180
Whan he is siker of his goode name,
Than hath he doon his freend, ne him, no schame,
And glader ought his freend ben of his deth,
Whan with honour is yolden up the breth,
Thanne whan his name appalled is for age;   2185
For al forgeten is his vasselage.
Thanne is it best, as for a worthi fame,
To dye whan a man is best of name.
The contrary of al this is wilfulnesse.
Why grucchen we? why have we hevynesse,   2190
That good Arcyte, of chyvalry the flour,
Departed is, with worschip and honour
Out of this foule prisoun of this lyf?
Why gruccheth heer his cosyn and his wyf
Of his welfare, that loven him so wel?   2195
Can he hem thank? nay, God woot, never a del,

That bothe his soule and eek hemself offende,
And yet they may here lustes nat amende.
  ' What may I conclude of this longe serye,
But aftir wo I rede us to be merye,   2200
And thanke Jubiter of al his grace?
And or that we departe fro this place,
I rede that we make, of sorwes two,
O parfyt joye lastyng ever mo:
And loketh now wher most sorwe is her-inne   2205
Ther wol we first amenden and bygynne.
  ' Sustyr,' quod he, ' this is my ful assent,
With al thavys heer of my parlement,
That gentil Palomon, your owne knight,
That serveth yow with herte, wil, and might,   2210
And ever hath doon, syn fyrst tyme ye him knewe,
That ye schul of your grace upon him rewe,
And take him for your housbond and for lord:
Lene me youre hand, for this is oure acord.
Let see now of your wommanly pité.   2215
He is a kynges brothir sone, pardee;
And though he were a pore bachiller,
Syn he hath served you so many a yeer,
And had for you so gret adversité,
Hit moste be considered, trusteth me.   2220
For gentil mercy aughte passe right.'
Than seyde he thus to Palomon ful right;
' I trowe ther needeth litel sermonyng
To make you assente to this thing.
Com neer, and tak your lady by the hond.'   2225
Bitwix hem was i-maad anon the bond,
That highte matrimoyn or mariage,
By alle the counseil of the baronage.
And thus with blys and eek with melodye

Hath Palomon i-wedded Emelye.   2230
And God, that al this wyde world hath wrought,
Send him his love, that hath it deere i-bought.
For now is Palomon in al his wele,
Lyvynge in blisse, richesse, and in hele,
And Emely him loveth so tendirly,   2235
And he hir serveth al so gentilly,
That never [was ther] wordes hem bitweene
Of gelousy, ne of non othir teene.
Thus endeth Palomon and Emelye;
And God save al this fayre companye! Amen!   2240

THE NONNE PREST HIS TALE.

A PORE wydow, somdel stope in age,
Was whilom duellyng in a pore cotage,
Bisyde a grove, stondyng in a dale.
This wydow, of which I telle yow my tale,
Syn thilke day that sche was last a wif,   5
In paciens ladde a ful symple lyf.
For litel was hir catel and hir rent[e];
For housbondry of such as God hir sent[e],
Sche fond hirself, and eek hir doughtres tuo.
Thre large sowes bad[de] sche, and no mo,   10
Thre kyn, and eek a scheep that highte Malle.
Ful sooty was hir bour, and eek hir halle,
In which she eet ful many a sclender meel.
Of poynaunt saws hir needid[e] never a qeel.
Noon deynteth morsel passid[e] thorugh hir throte;
Hir dyete was accordant to hir cote.   16
Repleccioun [ne] made hir never sik;
Attempre dyete was al hir phisik,
And exercise, and bertes suffisaunce.
The goute lette hir nothing for to daunce,   20

H

Ne poplexie schente not hir heed;
No wyn ne drank sche, nother whit nor reed;
Hir bord was servyd most with whit and blak,
Milk and broun bred, in which sche fond no lak,
Saynd bacoun, and som tyme an ey or tweye,   25
For sche was as it were a maner deye.
A yerd sche had, enclosed al aboute
With stikkes, and a drye dich withoute,
In which she had a cok, hight Chaunteclere,
In al the lond of crowyng was noon his peere.   30
His vois was merier than the mery orgon,
On masse dayes that in the chirche goon;
Wel sikerer was his crowyng in his logge,
Than is a clok, or an abbay orologge.
By nature knew he ech ascencioun   35
Of equinoxial in thilke toun;
For whan degrees fyftene were ascendid,
Thanne crew he, it might[e] not ben amendid.
His comb was redder than the fyn[e] coral,
And batayld, as it were a castel wal.   40
His bile was blak, and as the geet it schon;
Lik asur were his leggis, and his ton;
His nayles whitter than the lily flour,
And lik the burnischt gold was his colour.
This gentil cok had in his governaunce   45
Seven hennes, for to do al his plesaunce,
Whiche were his sustres and his paramoures,
And wonder lik to him, as of coloures.
Of whiche the fairest hiewed on hir throte,
Was cleped fayre damysel Pertilote.   50
Curteys sche was, discret, and debonaire,
And companable, and bar hirself ful faire,
Syn thilke day that sche was seven night old,

That trewely sche hath the hert in hold
Of Chaunteclere loken in every lith;   55
He loved hir so, that wel him was therwith.
But such a joye was it to here him synge,
Whan that the brighte sonne gan to springe,
In swete accord, 'my lief is faren on londe.'
Fro thilke tyme, as I have understonde,   60
Bestis and briddes cowde speke and synge.
And so byfel, that in a dawenynge,
As Chaunteclere among his wyves alle
Sat on his perche, that was in the halle,
And next him sat his faire Pertelote,   65
This Chauntecler gan gronen in his throte,
As man that in his dreem is drecched sore.
And whan that Pertelot thus herd him rore,
Sche was agast, and sayde, 'herte deere,
What eylith yow to grone in this manere?   70
Ye ben a verray sleper, fy for schame!'
And he answerd and sayde thus, 'Madame,
I pray yow, that ye take it nought agreef:
By God, me mette I was in such meschief
Right now, that yit myn hert is sore afright.   75
Now God,' quod he, 'my sweven rede aright,
And keep my body out of foul prisoun!
Me mette, how that I romed up and doun
Withinne oure yerd, wher as I saugh a beest,
Was lik an hound, and wold have maad arrest   80
Upon my body, and wold han had me deed.
His colour was bitwixe yolow and reed;
And tipped was his tail, and bothe his eeres
With blak, unlik the remenaunt of his heres.
His snowt was smal, with glowyng [e]yen tweye;   85
Yet of his look for fer almost I deye;

This caused[e] me my gronyng douteles.'
'Away!' quod sche, 'fy on yow, herteles!
Allas!' quod sche, 'for, by that God above!
Now have ye lost myn hert and al my love;   90
I can nought love a coward, by my feith.
. For certis, what so eny womman seith,
We alle desiren, if it mighte be,
To have housbondes, hardy, riche, and fre,
And secré, and no nygard, ne no fool,   95
Ne him that is agast of every tool,
Ne noon avaunter, by that God above!
How dorst ye sayn for schame unto your love,
That any thing might[e] make yow afferd?
Have ye no mannes hert, and han a berd?   100
Allas! and can ye ben agast of swevenys?
Nought, God wot, but vanité, in sweven is.
Swevens engendrid ben of replecciouns,
And often of fume, and of complexiouns,
Whan humours ben to abundaunt in a wight.   105
Certes this dreem, which ye han met to-night,
Cometh of the grete superfluité
Of youre reede *colera*, pardé,
Which causeth folk to dremen in here dremes
Of arwes, and of fuyr with reede beemes,   110
Of rede bestis, that thai wil hem byte,
Of contek, and of whelpis greet and lite;
Right as the humour of malencolie
Causéth, in sleep, ful many a man to crye,
For fere of beres, or of boles blake,   115
Or elles blake develes wol him take.
Of other humours couthe I telle also,
That wirken many a man in slep ful woo;
But I wol passe as lightly as I can.

Lo Catoun, which that was so wis a man,   120
Sayde he nou*g*ht thus, ne do no force of dremes?
Now, sire,' quod sche, 'whan we fle fro thise beemes,
For Goddis love, as tak som laxatyf;
Up peril of my soule, and of my lyf,
I counsel yow the best, I wol not lye,   125
[That bothe of coloure, and of malencolye
Ye purge yow; and for ye scholne nouht tarye,]
Though in this toun is noon apotecarie,
I schal myself tuo herbes techyn yow,
That schal be for your hele, and for youre prow;   130
And in oure *y*erd tho herbes schal I fynde,
The whiche han of her propreté by kynde
To purgen yow bynethe, and eek above.
Forget not this, for Goddis oughne love!
Ye ben ful colerik of complexioun.   135
Ware the sonne in his ascencioun
Ne fynd yow not replet in humours hote;
And if it do, I dar wel lay a grote,
That ye schul have a fever terciane,
Or an agu, that may be youre bane.   140
A day or tuo ye schul have digestives
Of wormes, or ye take your laxatives,
Of lauriol, century, and fumytere,
Or elles of elder bery, that growith there,
Of catapus, or of gaytre beriis,   145
Of erbe yve that groweth in our *y*erd, that mery is;
Pike hem up right as thay growe, and et hem in.
Be mery, housbond, for your fader kyn!
Dredith non dremes; I can say no more.'
'Madame,' quod he, '*graunt mercy* of your lore.   150
But natheles, as touching daun Catoun,
That hath of wisdom such a gret renoun,

Though that he bad no dremes for to drede,
By God, men may in olde bookes rede
Of many a man, more of auctorité   155
That ever Catoun was. so mot I the, †
That al the revers sayn of his sentence,
And han wel founden by experience,
That dremes ben significaciouns,
As wel of joye, as of tribulaciouns,   160
That folk enduren in this lif present.
Ther nedeth make of this noon argument;
The verray preve schewith it in dede.
Oon of the grettest auctours that men rede
Saith thus, that whilom tway felawes wente 165
On pylgrimage in a ful good entente;
And happed[e] so, thay come into a toun,
Wher as ther was such congregacioun
Of poeple, and eek so streyt of herbergage,
That thay fond nought as moche as oon cotage, 170
In which that thay might[e] bothe i-logged be.
Wherfor thay mosten of necessité,
As for that night, depart her compaignye;
And ech of hem goth to his hostelrye,
And took his loggyng as it wolde falle.   175
That oon of hem was loggid in a stalle,
Fer in a yerd, with oxen of the plough;
That other man was logged wel y-nough,
As was his adventure, or his fortune,
That us governith alle [as] in comune.   180
And so bifel, that, long er it were day,
This oon met in his bed, ther as he lay,
How that his felaw gan upon him calle,
And sayd, 'allas! for in an oxe stalle
This night I schal be murdrid ther I lye.   185

Now help me, deere brother, or I dye;
In alle [haste] cum to me,' he sayde.
This man out of his slep for fere abrayde;
But whan that he was waked out of his sleep,
He torned him, and took of this no keep;　　190
Him thought his dreem nas but a vanité.
Thus twies in his sleepe dremed he.
And at the thridde tyme *yet* his felawe
Com, as him thought, and sayd, 'I am now slawe;
Bihold my bloody woundes, deep and wyde!　　195
Arise up erly in the morwe tyde,
And at the west gate of the toun.' quod he,
'A cart of donge there schalt thou see,
In which my body is hyd [ful] prively;
Do thilke cart arresten boldely.　　200
My gold caused[e] my mourdre, soth to sayn.'
And told him every poynt how he was slayn,
With a ful pitous face, pale of hewe.
And truste wel, his dreem he fond ful trewe;
For on the morwe, as sone as it was day,　　205
To his felawes in he took the way;
And whan that he cam to this oxe stalle,
After his felaw he bigan to calle.
The hostiller answered him anoon,
And sayde, 'Sire, your felaw is agoon,　　210
Als soone as day he went out of the toun.'
This man gan falle in grete suspeccioun,
Remembring on his dremes that he mette,
And forth he goth, no lenger wold he lette,
Unto the west gate of the toun, and fond　　215
A dong cart went as it were to donge lond,
That was arrayed in the same wise
As ye han herd the deede man devise;.

And with an hardy hert he gan to crie
Vengeaunce and justice of this felonye.   220
'My felaw mordrid is this same night,
And in this carte he lith gapeinge upright.
I crye out on the ministres,' quod he,
'That schulde kepe and reule this cité;
Harrow! allas! her lith my felaw slayn!'   225
What schold I more unto this tale sayn?
The peple upstert, and caste the cart to grounde,
And in the middes of the dong thay founde
The dede man, that mordred was al newe.
O blisful God, thou art ful just and trewe!   230
Lo, how thow bywreyest mordre alday!
Mordre wil out, certes it is no nay.
Morder is so wlatsom and abhominable
To God, that is so just and resonable,
That he ne wile nought suffre it hiled be;   235
Though it abyde a yeer, or tuo, or thre,
Morder wil out, this is my conclusioun.
And right anoon, the mynistres of that toun
Han hent the carter, and so sore him pyned,
And eek the hostiller so sore engyned,   240
That thay biknew her wikkednes anoon,
And were anhonged by the nekke boon.
  'Here may men se that dremys ben to drede.
And certes in the same book I rede,
Right in the nexte chapitre after this,   245
(I gabbe nought, so have I joye and blis,)
Tuo men that wolde have passed over see
For certeyn causes into fer contré,
If that the wynd ne badde ben contrarie,
That made hem in a cité for to tarie,   250
That stood ful mery upon an haven syde.

But on a day, agayn the even tyde,
The wynd gan chaunge, and blew right as hem lest[e].
Jolyf and glad they wenten unto rest[e],
And casten hem ful erly for to sayle;   255
But to that oon man fel a gret mervayle.
That oon of hem in slepyng as he lay,
Him met, a wonder drem, agayn the day;
Him thought a man stood by his beddes syde,
And him comaunded[e], that he schuld abyde,   260
And sayd him thus, 'If thou to morwe wende,
Thow schalt be dreynt; my tale is at an ende.'
He wook, and told his felaw what he mette,
And prayde him his viage to lette;
As for that day, he prayd him to abyde.   265
His felaw that lay by his beddis syde,
Gan for to lawgh, and scorned him ful fast[e].
'No dreem,' quod he, 'may so myn herte gaste,
That I wil lette for to do my thinges.
I sette not a straw by thy dremynges,   270
For swevens been but vanitees and japes.
Men dreme al day of owles and of apes,
And [eke] of many a mase therwithal;
Men dreme of thinges that never be schal.
But sith I see that thou wilt her abyde,   275
And thus forslouthe wilfully thy tyde,
God wot it reweth me, and have good day.'
And thus he took his leve, and went his way.
But er he badde half his cours i-sayled,
Noot I nought why, ne what meschaunce it ayled,   280
But casuelly the schippes bothom rent[e],
And schip and man undir the watir went[e]
In sight of other schippes ther byside,
That with him sailed at the same tyde.

'And therfore, faire Pertelot so deere,   285
By such ensamples olde maistow leere
That no man scholde be so recheles
Of dremes, for I say the douteles,
That many a dreem ful sore is for to drede.
Lo, in the lif of seint Kenelm, I rede,   290
That was Kenulphus sone, the noble king
Of Mercinrike, how Kenilm mette a thing.
A litil [or] he was mordred, upon a day
His mordre in his avysioun he say.
His norice him expouned every del   295
His sweven, and bad him for to kepe him wel
For traisoun; but he nas but seven yer old,
And therfore litel tale hath he told
Of eny drem, so holy was his hert[e].
By God, I badde lever than my schert[e],   300
That ye bad[de] rad his legend, as have I.
Dame Pertelot, I say yow trewely,
Macrobius, that writ the avisioun
In Auffrik of the worthy Cipioun,
Affermeth dremes, and saith that thay been   305
Warnyng of thinges that men after seen.
And forthermore, I pray yow loketh wel
In the olde Testament, of Daniel,
If he huld dremes eny vanyté.
Rede eek of Joseph, and ther schal ye see   310
Whethir dremes ben som tyme (I say nought alle)
Warnyng of thinges that schul after falle.
Lok of Egipt the king, daun Pharao,
His baker and his botiler also,   •
Whethir thay felte noon effect in dremis.   315
Who so wol seke [the] actes of sondry remys,
May rede of dremes many a wonder thing.

Lo Cresus, which that was of Lydes king,
Mette [he not] that he sat upon a tre,
Which signified he schuld [an]hanged be?   320
Lo hir Andromachia, Ectors wif,
That day that Ector schulde lese his lif,
Sche dremed on the same night byforn,
How that the lif of Ector schulde be lorn,
If thilke day he wente to batayle;   325
Sche warned him, but it might[e] nou*gh*t availe;
He wente forth to fighte natheles,
And he was slayn anoon of Achilles.
But thilke tale is al to long to telle,
And eek it is neigh day, I may not duelle.   330
Schortly I say, as for conclusioun,
That I schal have of this avisioun
Adversité; and I say forthermore,
That I ne telle of laxatifs no store,
For thay ben venemous, I wot right wel;   335
I hem defye, I love hem never a del.
  'Now let us speke of mirthe, and lete al this;
Madame Pertilot, so have I blis,
Of o thing God hath sent me large grace;
For whan I see the beauté of your face,   340
Ye ben so scarlet hiew about your ey*gh*en,
It makith al my drede for to dey*gh*en,
For, als siker as *In principio,*
Mulier est hominis confusio.
(Madame, the sentence of this Latyn is,   345
Womman is mannes joye and mannes blis.)
        *   *   *   *   *
I am so ful of joye and solas
That I defye bothe sweven and drem.'
And with that word he fleigh doun fro the beem,

For it was day, and eek his hennes alle;　　　350
And with a chuk he gan hem for to calle,
For he had found a corn, lay in the yerd.
Real he was, he was nomore aferd;

     *   *   *   *   *   *

He lokith as it were a grim lioun;
And on his toon he rometh up and doun,　　　355
Him deyneth not to set his foot to grounde.
He chukkith, whan he hath a corn i-founde,
And to him rennen than his wifes alle.
   Thus real, as a prince is in his halle,
Leve I this chaunteclere in his pasture;　　　360
And after wol I telle his aventure.
Whan that the moneth in which the world bigan,
That highte March, whan God first maked[e] man,
Was complet, and [y-]passed were also,
Syn March bygan, tway monthes and dayes tuo,　365
Byfel that Chaunteclere in al his pride,
His seven wyves walkyng by his syde,
Cast up his eyghen to the brighte sonne,
That in the signe of Taurus had i-ronne
Twenty degrees and oon, and somwhat more;　　370
He knew by kynde, and by noon other lore,
That it was prime, and crew with blisful steven.
'The sonne,' he sayde, 'is clomben up on heven
Twenty degrees and oon, and more i-wis.
Madame Pertelot, my worldes blis,　　　375
Herknith these blisful briddes how they synge,
And seth these freissche floures how they springe;
Ful is myn hert of revel and solaas.'
But sodeinly him fel a sorwful caas;
For ever the latter end of joye is wo.　　　380
God wot that worldly joye is soone ago;

And if [a] rethor couthe faire endite,
He in a chronique saufly might it write,
As for a soverayn notabilité.

Now every wys man let him herkne me; 385
This story is also trewe, I undertake,
As is the book of Launcelot the Lake,
That womman huld in ful gret reverence.
Now wol I torne agayn to my sentence.
A cole-fox, ful sleigh of iniquité, 390
That in the grove bad[de] woned yeres thre,
By heigh ymaginacioun forncast,
The same nighte thurgh the hegge brast
Into the yerd, ther Chaunteclere the faire
Was wont, and eek his wyves, to repaire; 395
And in a bed of wortes stille he lay,
Til it was passed undern. of the day,
Waytyng his tyme on Chaunteclere to falle;
As gladly doon these homicides alle,
That in awayte lyn to morther men. 400
O false mordrer lurkyng in thy den!
O newe Scariot, newe Genilon!
Fals[e] dissimulour; O Greke Sinon,
That broughtest Troye al outrely to sorwe!
O Chauntecler, accursed be the morwe, 405
That thou into the yerd flough fro the bemys!
Thow were ful wel iwarned by thy dremys,
That thilke day was perilous to the.
But what that God forwot most[e] needes be
After the opynyoun of certeyn clerkis. 410
Witnesse on him, that eny [perfit] clerk is,
That in scole is gret altercacioun
In this matier, and gret desputesoun,
And hath ben of an hundred thousend men.

But *y*it I can not bult it to the bren,   415
As can the holy doctor Augustyn,
Or Boece, or the bischop Bradwardyn,
Whether that Goddis worthy forwetyng
Streigneth me need[e]ly for to do a thing,
(Needely clepe I simple necessité);   420
Or elles if fre choys be graunted me
To do that same thing, or to do it noug*h*t,
Though God forwot it, er that it was wrought;
Or if his wityng streyneth never a deel,
But by necessité condicionel.   425
I wol not have to do of such matiere;
My tale is of a cok, as ye schal hiere,
That took his counseil of his wyf with sorwe,
To walken in the *y*erd upon the morwe,
That he bad[de] met the dreme, that I tolde.   430
Wymmens counseiles ben ful ofte colde;
Wommannes counseil broug*h*t us first to woo,
And made Adam fro paradys to go,
Ther as he was ful mery, and wel at ease.
But for I not, to whom it might[e] displease,   435
If I counseil of womman wolde blame,
Pas over, for I sayd it in my game.
Red auctours, wher thay trete of such matiere,
And what thay sayn of wommen ye may heere.
These been the cokkes wordes, and not myne;   440
I can noon harme of [no] wommen divine.
    Faire in the sond, to bathe hir merily,
Lith Pertelot, and alle hir sustres by,
Agayn the sonne; and Chaunteclere so free
Sang merier than the meremayd in the see;   445
For Phisiologus seith sicurly,
How that thay syngen wel and merily.

And so byfel that as he cast his ye
Among the wortes on a boterflye,
He was war of this fox that lay ful lowe.　　450
No thing ne list him thanne for to crowe,
But cryde anon, 'cok, cok,' and up he stert[e],
As man that was affrayed in his hert[e].
For naturelly a beest desireth flee
Fro his contrarie, if he may it see,　　455
Though he never had er sayn it with his ye.
　This Chaunteclere, whan he gan him aspye,
He wold han fled, but that the fox anon
Said, 'Gentil sire, allas! why wol ye goon?
Be ye affrayd of me that am youre frend?　　460
Certes, I were worse than eny feend,
If I to yow wold harm or vilonye.
I am not come your counsail to espye.
[Bot trewely the cause of my comynge
Was onely for to herken how ye singe.]　　465
For trewely ye have als mery a steven,
As eny aungel hath, that is in heven;
Therwith ye han of musik more felynge,
Than had[de] Boece, or eny that can synge.
My lord your fader (God his soule blesse)　　470
And [eke] youre moder of her gentilesse
Han in myn hous[e] been, to my gret ease;
And certes, sire, ful fayn wold I yow please.
But for men speke of syngyng, I wol say,
So mot I brouke wel myn [e]yen tway,　　475
Save ye, I herde never man so synge,
As dede youre fadir in the morwenynge.
Certes it was of hert al that he song.
And for to make his vois the more strong,
He wold[e] so peynen him, that with bothe his yen　480

He moste wynke, so lowde he wolde crien,
And stonden on his typtoon therwithal,
And strecche forth his necke long and smal.
And eek he was of such discressioun,
That ther nas no man in no regioun   485
That him in song or wisdom mighte passe.
I have wel rad in daun Burnel thasse
Among his verses, how ther was a cok,
That, for a prestes sone yaf him a knok
Upon his leg, whil he was young and nyce,   490
He made him for to lese his benefice.
But certeyn ther is no comparisoun
Bitwix the wisdom and discressioun
Of youre fader, and of his subtilté.
Now syngeth, sire, for seinte Charité,   495
Let se, can ye your fader countrefete ?'
This Chaunteclere his wynges gan to bete,
As man that couthe his tresoun nought espye,
So was he ravyssht with his flaterie.

Allas! ye lordlynges, many a fals flatour   500
Is in your hous, and many a losengour,
That pleasen yow wel more, by my faith,
Than he that sothfastnesse unto yow saith.
Redith Ecclesiast of flaterie;
Beth war, ye lordes, of her treccherie.   505

This Chaunteclere stood heighe upon his toos,
Strecching his necke, and [held] his [e]yhen cloos,
And gan to crowe lowde for the noones;
And daun Russel the fox stert up at oones,
And by the garget hente Chaunteclere,   510
And on his bak toward the woode him bere.
For yit was there no man that [badde] him sewed.
O desteny, that maist not ben eschiewed!

Allas, that Chaunteclere fleigh fro the bemis!
Allas, his wif ne roughte nou*gh*t of dremis!   515
And on a Friday fel al this mischaunce.
O Venus, that art godd[esse] of pleasaunce,
Syn that thy servant was this Chaunteclere,
And in thy service did al his powere,
More for delit, than the world to multiplie,   520
Why woldest thou suffre him on thy day to dye?
O Gaufred, dere mayster soverayn,
That, whan the worthy king Richard was slayn
With schot, compleynedist his deth so sore,
Why ne had I nou*gh*t thy sentence and thy lore,   525
The Friday for to chiden, as dede ye?
(For on a Fryday sothly slayn was he.)
Than wold I schewe how that I couthe pleyne,
For Chauntecleres drede, and for his peyne.

Certis such cry ne lamentacioun   530
Was never of ladies maad, whan Ilioun
Was wonne, and Pirrus with his streite swerd,
Whan he hente kyng Priam by the berd,
And slough him (as saith us *Eneydos*),
As maden alle the hennes in the clos,   535
Whan thay had[de] sayn of Chauntecler the sight[e].
But soveraignly dame Pertelote schright[e],
Ful lowder than did Hasdrubaldes wyf;
Whan that hir housebond had[de] lost his lyf,
And that the Romayns had i-brent Cartage,   540
Sche was so ful of torment and of rage,
That wilfully unto the fuyr sche stert[e],
And brend hirselven with a stedfast hert[e].
O woful hennes, right so cride ye,
As whan that Nero brente the cité   545
Of Rome, criden the senatoures wyves,

For that her housbondes losten alle here lyves;
Withouten gult this Nero hath hem slayn.
Now wol I torne to my matier agayn.
The sely wydow, and hir doughtres tuo,   550
Herden these hennys crie and maken wo,
And out at dores starte thay anoon,
And sayden the fox toward the woode is goon,
And bar upon his bak the cok away;
They criden, 'Out! harrow and wayleway!   555
Ha, ha, the fox!' and after him thay ran[ne],
And eek with staves many another man[ne];
Ran Colle our dogge, and Talbot, and Garlond,
And Malkyn, with a distaf in hir hond;
Ran cow and calf, and eek the verray hogges   560
So were they fered for berkyng of [the] dogges
And schowtyng of the men and wymmen eke,
Thay ronne that thay thought her herte breke.
Thay yelleden as feendes doon in helle;
The dokes criden as men wold hem quelle;   565
The gees for fere flowen over the trees;
Out of the hyves came the swarm of bees;
So hidous was the noyse, a *benedicite!*
Certes he Jakke Straw, and his meyné,
Ne maden schoutes never half so schrille,   570
Whan that thay wolden eny Flemyng kille,
As thilke day was maad upon the fox.
Of bras thay brought[en] hornes and of box,
Of horn and boon, in which thay blew and powped[e],
And therwithal thay schryked and thay howped[e]; 575
It semed as that heven schulde falle.
    Now, goode men, I pray [you] herkneth alle;
Lo, how fortune torneth sodéinly
The hope and pride eek of her enemy!

This cok that lay upon this foxes bak,   580
In al his drede, unto the fox he spak,
And saide, 'Sire, if that I were as ye,
*Y*et schuld I sayn (as wis God helpe me),
Turneth ayein, ye proude cherles alle!
A verray pestilens upon yow falle!   585
Now I am come unto this woodes syde,
Maugre youre hede, the cok schal heer abyde;
I wol him ete in faith, and that anoon.'
The fox answerd, 'In faith, it schal be doon.'
And whil he spak that word, al sodeinly   590
This cok brak from his mouth delyverly,
And heigh upon a tree he fleigh anoon.
And whan the fox seigh that he was i-goon,
'Allas!' quod he, 'O Chaunteclere, allas!
I have to yow,' quod he, 'y-don trespas,   595
In-as-moche as I makid yow aferd,
Whan I yow hent, and brou*gh*t out of the *y*erd;
But, sire, I dede it in no wicked entent[e];
Com doun, and I schal telle yow what I ment[e].
I schal say soth to yow, God help me so.'   600
'Nay than,' quod he, 'I schrew us bothe tuo,
And first I schrew myself, bothe blood and boones,
If thou bigile me any ofter than oones.
Thou schalt no more, thurgh thy flaterye,
Do me to synge and wynke with myn ye.   605
For he that wynkith, whan he scholde see,
Al wilfully, God let him never the!'
'Nay,' quod the fox, 'but God *y*ive him meschaunce,
That is so undiscret of governaunce,
That jangleth, whan he scholde holde his pees.'   610
    Lo, such it is for to be recheles,
And necgligent, and trust on flaterie.

But ye that holde this tale a folye,
As of a fox, or of a cok and hen,
Takith the moralité therof, goode men.   615
For seint Poul saith, that al that writen is,
To oure doctrine it is i-write i-wys.
Takith the fruyt, and let the chaf be stille.
  Now, goode God, if that it be thy wille,
As saith my lord, so make us alle good men;   620
And bring us alle to his blisse. *Amen.*

NOTES.

THE PROLOGUE.

l. 1. *swoote*, pl. of *swot*. *swete* in l. 5 is the definite form of *swet*.

l. 4. *vertue*, power, corresponding to the O.E. *miht* (might).

l. 5. *breeth*[*e*], breath. The dative takes a final *e*.

l. 6. *holte*, dat. of *holt*, a wood or grove.

l. 7. *yonge sonne*. The sun is here said to be young because it has only just entered upon his annual course through the signs of the zodiac.

l. 8. *Ram*. Tyrwhitt says, ' rather the *Bull*,' because in April the sun has entered the sign of Taurus.

l. 13. *palmer*, originally one who made a pilgrimage to the Holy Land and brought home a *palm*-branch as a token. Chaucer, says Tyrwhitt, seems to consider all pilgrims to foreign parts as palmers. The essential difference between the two class of persons here mentioned, the palmer and the pilgrim, was, that the latter had " one dwelling place, a palmer had none; the pilgrim travelled to some certain place, the palmer to all, and not to any one in particular; the pilgrim must go at his own charge, the palmer must profess wilful poverty; the pilgrim might give over his profession, the palmer must be constant." (Saunders.)

l. 14. *ferne halwes*, distant saints. *ferne* = O.E. *ferrene, ferren*, afar, from *fer*, far. *halwes*, saints; cp. Scotch *Hallow-e'en*, the eve of All Hallows, or All Saints.

l. 16. *wende*, to go; pret. *wente*. Eng. *went*. The old preterite of *go* being *eode*, *ȝede*, or *ȝode*.

l. 17. *the holy blisful martir*, Thomas à Becket.

l. 18. *holpen*, pp. of *helpen*. The older preterites of this verb are *heolp, help, halp*.

l. 20. *Tabbard*. Of this word Speght gives the following account in his Glossary to Chaucer :—" Tabard—a jaquet or slevelesse coate, worne in times past by noblemen in the warres, but now only by heraults (heralds), and is called theyre ' coate of armes in servise.' It is the signe of an inne in Southwarke by London, within the which was the lodging of the Abbot of Hyde by Winchester. This is the hostelry where *Chaucer* and the other

Pilgrims mett together, and, with Henry Baily their hoste, accorded about the manner of their journey to Canterbury. And whereas through time it hath bin much decayed, it is now by Master *J. Preston*, with the Abbot's house thereto adgoyned, newly repaired, and with convenient rooms much encreased, for the receipt of many guests." The *Taberdars* of Queen's College, Oxford, were scholars, supposed originally to have worn the *tabard*, since called, by mistake, the Talbot.

l. 23. *hostelrie*, a lodging, inn, house, residence. *Hostler* properly signifies the keeper of an inn, and not, as now, the servant of an inn who looks after the horses. (The O.E. *hors-hus* signifies an inn—another term was *gest-hus*; and *hors-herde* = an inn-keeper.)

l. 24. *wel* is here used like our word *full*.

l. 25. *by aventure i-falle*, by adventure (chance) fallen.

l. 26. *felawschipe*, fellowship, from O.E. *felaw*, companion, fellow.

l. 29. *esud atte beste*, accommodated or entertained in the best manner. *Easement* is still used as a law term, signifying accommodation.

atte = *at þan* = *at tan* or *atten*. In the older stages of the language we find *atte* used only before masc. and neuter nouns beginning with a consonant; the feminine form is *atter*, which is not used by Chaucer.

l. 30. *to reste* = at rest.

l. 34. *ther as to I you devyse*, to that place that I tell you of (scil. Canterbury). *ther* in O.E. frequently signifies *where*; *devyse*, to speak of, describe.

whiles, whilst. Eng. *while*, time. O.E. *hwile*, awhile; *while whilen*. The form in *-es* is a double adverbial form, and may be compared with O.E. *hennes*, *thennes*, hence, thence; *ones*, *twies*, *thries*, once, twice, thrice, of which older forms are found in *-ene* and *-e*.

l. 37. It seemeth to me it is reasonable.

me thinketh = *me thinks*, where *me* is the dative before the impersonal vb. *thinke* to appear, seem; cp. *me liketh*, *me list*, it pleases me. So the phrase *if you please* = if it *please you*, you being the *dative* and not the nominative case. *semed[e] me* = it seemed to me, occurs in l. 39.

l. 41. *inne*. In O.E. *in* is the preposition, and *inne* the adverb.

l. 43. *Knight*. It was a common thing in this age for knights to seek employment in foreign countries which were at war. Tyrwhitt cites from Leland the epitaph of a knight of this period, Matthew de Gourney, who had been at the battle of Benamaryn, at the siege of Algezir, and at the battles of Crecy, Poitiers, &c.

worthy, worthy, is here used in its literal signification of distinguished, honourable. See ll. 47, 50.

l. 45. *chyvalrye*, knighthood; also the manners, exercises, and exploits of a knight.

l. 49. *ferre*, the comp. of *fer*, far. Cp. *derre*, dearer.

l. 50. *hethenesse*, heathen lands, as distinguished from *Cristendom*, Christian countries.

l. 51. *Alisandre*, in Egypt, was won, and immediately after abandoned, in 1365, by Pierre de Lusignan, King of Cyprus.

l. 52. *he had the bord bygonne*. Some commentators think *bord* = *board*, table, so that the phrase signifies 'he had been placed at the head of the dais, or *table* of state.' Mr. Marsh suggests that *bord* or *bourd* is the Low Germ. *boort* or *buhurt*, joust, tournament.

ll. 53, 54. *Pruce.* When our English knights wanted employment, it was usual for them to go and serve in Pruce or Prussia, with the knights of the Teutonic order, who were in a state of constant warfare with their heathen neighbours in Lettow (Lithuania), *Ruce* (Russia), and elsewhere. (Tyrwhitt.)

ll. 56–58. *Gernade,* Granada. The city of Algezir was taken from the Moorish King of *Granada* in 1344.

Belmarie and *Tremassene* (Tramessen, l. 62) were Moorish kingdoms in Africa.

Layas (Lieys), in Armenia, was taken from the Turks by Pierre de Lusignan about 1367.

Satalie was taken by the same prince soon after 1352. (Attalia.)

Palatye (Palathia, see l. 65), in Anatolia, was one of the lordships held by Christian knights after the Turkish conquests.

l. 59. *the Grete See.* The name Great Sea is applied by Sir J. Maundeville to that part of the Mediterranean which washes the coast of Palestine, to distinguish it from the two so-called inland seas, the sea of Tiberias and the Dead Sea. Cp. its proper name in Scripture, Numb. xxxiv. 6, 7; Josh. i. 4.

l. 60. *arive,* arrival or disembarkation of troops. Tyrwhitt, following MS. Lansd. 851, and other MSS., reads *armee.*

be = ben, been. Cp. *ydo = ydon,* done, &c.

l. 62. *foughten,* pp. fought. This verb belongs to the strong, and not to the weak verbs, like *sought, brought,* &c. The older forms of *fought* are *faght* and *foght.*

l. 63. *slayn; hadde* must be supplied from l. 61.

l. 67. *sovereyn prys,* exceeding great renown.

l. 70. *vilonye,* any conduct unbecoming a gentleman.

" The *villain* is, *first,* the serf or peasant, *villanus,* because attached to the *villa* or farm. He is, *secondly,* the peasant, who, it is taken for granted, will be churlish, selfish, dishonest, and generally of evil moral conditions, these having come to be assumed as always belonging to him, and to be permanently associated with his name, by those who were at the springs of language. At the *third* step nothing of the meaning which the etymology suggests—nothing of *villa*—survives any longer; the peasant is quite dismissed, and the evil moral conditions of him who is called by this name, alone remains." (Trench, in English Past and Present.)

l. 71. *no maner wight,* no kind of person whatever.

perfight, perfect. It is sometimes spelt *perfit, parfit.*

l. 74. *ne ... nought.* In O.E. two negatives do not make an affirmative.

gay seems here to signify decked out in various colours.

l. 75. *gepoun = gipoun,* a diminutive of *gipe,* a short cassock.

l. 76. *haburgeoun* is properly a diminutive of *hauberk,* although often used as synonymous with it. It was a defence of an inferior description to the hauberk; but when the introduction of plate-armour, in the reign of Edward III, had supplied more convenient and effectual defence for the legs and thighs, the long skirt of the hauberk became superfluous; from that period the *habergeon* alone seems to have been worn. (Way.)

ll. 77, 78. For he had just returned from his voyage, and went to perform his pilgrimage (which he had vowed for a safe return) in his knightly 'array.'

l. 79. *squyer* = esquire, one who attended on a knight, and bore his lance and shield.

l. 80. *lovyer*, lover. The *y* in this word is not euphonic like the *y* in *lawyer*; lovyer is formed from the verb *lovie*, A.S. *lofian*, to love.

l. 82. *yeer*. In the older stages of the language, year, goat, swine, &c., being neuter nouns, underwent no change in the nom. case of the plural number; but after numerals the *genitive* case was usually required.

I *gesse*, I should think. In O.E. *gesse* signifies to judge, believe, suppose.

l. 85. *chivachie*. Fr. *chevauchée*. It most properly means an expedition with a small party of *cavalry*; but is often used generally for any military expedition. Holingshed calls it a *rode* (i. e. *raid*).

l. 87. *born him wel*, conducted himself well, behaved bravely.

l. 88. *lady grace*, ladies' grace. In the earlier stages of our language the genitive of feminine nouns terminated in -*e*, so that *lady* is for *ladye*. Cp. the modern phrase 'Lady-day.'

l. 98. *sleep*, also written *slep*, *slepte*. Cp. *wep*, *wepte*; *lep*, *lepte*, &c.

l. 100. *carf*, the past tense of *kerven*, to carve (pp. *corven*).

l. 101. *Yeman*, yeoman, is an abbreviation of *yeonge man* (A.S. *geong*, young). As a title of service, it denoted a servant of the next degree above a *garçon* or groom. The title of *yeoman* was given in a secondary sense to people of middling rank not in service; and in more modern times it came to signify a small landholder. (Tyrwhitt.)

l. 102. *him lust*, it pleased him. *lust* is for *luste*, past tense, pleased; *lust* = pleaseth. See note on l. 37.

l. 104. *a shef of pocock arwes*, a sheaf of arrows with peacocks feathers.

l. 109. *not-heed*. Tyrwhitt explains this as *a head like a nut*; from the hair probably being cut short. In later days the name of Roundhead came in for the same reason. The phrase '*nut-headed knave*' occurs in Shakespeare's Henry VIII.

l. 111. *bracer*, a piece of armour for the arm. Fr. *bras*, the arm, whence *bracelet*.

l. 114. *harneysed*. The word *harness* signifies equipage, furniture, tackling for sea or land.

l. 115. *Cristofre*. A figure of St. Christopher, used as a brooch. The figure of St. Christopher was looked upon with particular reverence among the middle and lower classes; and was supposed to possess the power of shielding the person who looked on it from hidden danger. (Wright.)

l. 120. *ooth[e]*, oath. 'Lansd. MS. reads *othe*, which is a genitive *plural*, and means *of oaths*.

Seynt Loy. Tyrwhitt says that *Loy* is for *Eloy*, a corruption of St. *Eligius*. It may be merely another form of St. *Louis*.

l. 121. *clept*. Lansdowne MS. reads *cleped*, which improves the metre. The passage may originally have been as follows:—

And sche yclept was Madame Englantyne.

l. 123. *entuned*, intoned.

nose. This is the reading of Harleian MS. 7334, and Lansd. 851. Speght reads *voice*.

semyly for *semely.* The *e* is here to be distinctly sounded. *hertily* is sometimes written for *hertely.* See l. 136.

l. 125. *scole,* school; here used for style.

l. 126. *Frensch.* The French taught in England was the debased form of the Old Anglo-Norman, somewhat similar to that used at a later period in the courts of law; and it was at this at which Chaucer and some of his contemporaries sneered. The writer of the Vision of Piers Ploughman speaks of French of Norfolk, l. 2949. (Wright.) Chaucer thought but meanly of the English-French spoken in his time. It was proper, however, that the Prioress should speak some sort of French; not only as a woman of fashion, a character she is represented to affect (ll. 139, 140), but as a religious person. (Tyrwhitt.)

l. 127. *At mete.* These simple conditions of good breeding are to be found in most of the mediæval tracts on *Courtesy* and *Nurture,* written for the purpose of teaching manners at table.

l. 132. *leste = liste,* pleasure. The following reading would be more metrical than the one found in the text :—

In curtesie yset was al hire leste.

l. 134. *ferthing* signifies literally a fourth part, and hence a small portion. Lansd. MS. reads *fat thing.*

l. 139. *peyned hire,* took pains, endeavoured.

ll. 139, 140. *to counterfete cheere of court,* to imitate courtly behaviour.

l. 141. *to ben holden,* &c., to be esteemed worthy of reverence.

l. 147. *wastel breed.* Horses and dogs were not usually fed on *wastel breed* or cake bread (bread made of the best flour), but on coarse lentil bread baked for that purpose. "The domestic baker prepared several kinds and qualities of bread, suitable to the various departments of a household: the *manchet* loaf of wheaten flour was for the master's table, the fine *chete* for the side-tables, and the brown bread for the board's end. The finer quality was made of flour passed through a sieve or boulting-cloth, and sometimes called boulted bread; the chete was of unboulted flour, and the household was made of a mixture of flour and rye-meal, called mystelon or maslin; the latter was the quality usually made in the houses of the middle class; the poor ate bread made of rye, lentils, and oatmeal. Fancy bread, such as paynepuff and march-pane, was prepared for company; the latter was in old times a favourite delicacy, made of flour, sugar, and almonds; originally it was used especially at Easter, and called mass-pane, or mass-bread, and sometimes payne-mayne." (Our English Home, pp. 79, 80.) In l. 336 we read that the Frankeleyn loved a 'sop in wyn.' In the Anturs of Arther at the Tarnewathelan, we read that

> " Three sops of demayn (i. e. paindemayne)
> Were brought to Sir Gawayn
> For to comfort his brain."

And in Harl. MS. 279, fol. 10, we have the necessary instruction for the making of these sops. " Take mylke and boyle it, and thanne (then) tak (take) yolkys (yolks) of eyroun (eggs), ytryid (separated) fro (from) the whyte, and hete it, but let it nowt boyle, and stere (stir) it wel tyl it be somwhat thikke; thanne caste therto salt and sugre, and kytte (cut) fayre paynemaynnys in round soppys, and caste the soppys theron, and serve it forth for a potage." (Way, in Promptorium Parvulorum, p. 378.)

l. 149. *men smot.* If *men* were the ordinary plural of *man*, *smot* ought to be *smite* (pl. past), but *men*, Old Eng. *me*, is like the Ger. *man*, French *on*.

yerde, stick, rod. Cp. *yard*-measure, and *yard* as a nautical term. A *gird* of land (about 7 acres of ploughland, and pasture for 2 oxen, 1 cow, and 6 sheep).

l. 151. *wymple.* The *wimple* or *gorger* is stated first to have appeared in Edward the First's reign. It was a covering for the neck, and was used by nuns and elderly ladies.

l. 152. *eyen grey.* This seems to have been the favourite colour of ladies' eyes in Chaucer's time.

l. 156. *hardily* is here used for *sikerly*, certainly.

l. 157. *fetys* literally signifies 'made after the fashion of another,' and hence well-made, *feat*, neat, handsome. See Glossary, s. v. *Fetys*.

waar = war, aware; I was *waar* = I perceived.

l. 159. *bedes.* The word *bede* signifies, 1. a prayer; 2. a string of grains upon which the prayers were counted, or the grains themselves. See Glossary, s. v. *Bede*.

gaudid al with grene, having the *gawdies* green. Some were of silver gilt. The *gawdies* or *gaudees* were the larger beads in a roll for prayer. "*Gaudye* of beedes, *signeau de paternoster*." (Palsgrave.)

> "A paire of bedes blacke as sable
> She toke and hynge my necke about;
> Upon the *gaudees* all without
> Was wryte of gold, *pur reposer*."
>
> (Gower, Confessio Amantis, f. 190.)

l. 160. *broch = brooch*, signified,—1, a pin; 2, a breast-pin; 3, a buckle or clasp; 4, a jewel or ornament. It was an ornament common to both sexes. The 'crowned A' is supposed to represent *Amor* or *Charity*, the greatest of all the Christian graces.

l. 163. *Anothur Nonne.* It was not usual for Prioresses to have female chaplains, and we are therefore unacquainted with the duties belonging to the office, which was probably instituted in imitation of the monastic chaplain.

l. 165. *a fair*, i. e. a fair one.

for the maistrie is equivalent to the French phrase *pour la maistrie*, which in old medical books is applied to such medicines as we usually call sovereign, excellent above all others. (Tyrwhitt.) In the Promptorium Parvulorum we find "*maystrye*, or *soverenté*, and heyare (higher) hond yn stryfe or werre (war). Dextre, pl. victoria, triumphus." Another copy reads, "*maistri* or worchip (honour) or the heyer hond," &c.

l. 166. *venerye*, hunting. The monks of the middle ages were extremely attached to hunting and field sports; and this was a frequent subject of complaint with the more austere ecclesiastics, and of satire with the laity. (Wright.)

l. 168. *deynté*, dainty, is frequently used by Chaucer in the sense of precious, valuable, rare.

l. 169. *rood*, or *rod*, the past tense of *riden*, to ride.

l. 170. *gyngle*, jingle. Fashionable riders were in the habit of hanging small bells on the bridles and harness of their horses. Wycliffe, in his Triloge, inveighs against the clergy of his time for their "fair hors, and joly and gay sadeles and bridles ringing by the way." (Lewes' Wickliffe, p. 121.) At a much later period Spenser makes mention of these 'bells' in his description of a lady's steed :—

> " Her wanton palfrey all was overspread
>   With tinsel trappings, woven like a wave,
>   Whose bridle rung with golden bells and bosses brave."

l. 172. *ther as* = where that.

l. 173. *The reule* (rule) *of seynt Maure* (St. Maur) *and seint Beneyt* (St. Benet or Benedict) were the oldest forms of monastic discipline in the Romish Church.

l. 175. This same monk caused them to be passed by; *hem* refers to the rules of St. Maur and St. Benet, which were too *streyt* (strict) for this 'lord' or superior of the house, who seems to have preferred a milder form of discipline. Lansdowne MS. reads *olde thinges* instead of *forby him;* and Mr. Wright admits the former reading into his text, because the latter, he says, "appears to give no clear sense." *Forby* is still used in Scotland for *by* or *past*, and occurs frequently in the North English literature of the fourteenth century in the sense of by, past, near.

l. 176. *space*. Lansd. MS. reads *pace* (steps). Tyrwhitt reads *trace*, path.

l. 177. *a pulled hen*. As Tyrwhitt says, "I do not see much force in the epithet *pulled*." It is sometimes explained as a *plucked hen ; pullid* is evidently for *pilled*, bald, or scalled (scurfy). "*Pyllyd*, or scallyd, depilatus glabellus." (Prompt. Parv.) Cp. *peeled* in Isaiah xviii. 2, 7 (l. 6); Ezek. xxix. 18 ; Shakespeare, Hen. VI., i. 1, 3.

l. 179. *cloysterles*. Lansd. MS. reads *recheles*, negligent. This passage is a literal translation of one from the Decretal of Gratian : "*Sicut piscis sine aqua caret vita, ita sine monasterio monachus.*" Joinville says, " The Scriptures do say that a monk cannot live out of his cloister without falling into deadly sins, any more than a fish can live out of water without dying."

l. 182. *hild* for *held* (esteemed), past tense of *holden* to hold.

l. 184. *what* has here its earlier sense of *wherefore*.
wood, mad, foolish.

l. 186. *swynke*, to toil, whence *swinker*, used by Milton for a labourer, workman.

l. 187. *byt*, the 3rd pers. sing. of *bidden*, to command.

ll. 187, 188. *Austyn*. St. Augustine made his cathedral clergy, as far as their duties permitted it, live as strictly as the monkish orders.

l. 189. *a pricasour*, a hard rider.

l. 192. *for no cost*, &c., for no expense would he abstain from these sports.

l. 193. *purfiled*. The O.E. *purfil* signifies the embroidered or furred hem of a garment, so that *purfile* is to work upon the edge. *purfiled* has also a more extended meaning, and is applied to garments overlaid with gems or other ornaments. "*Pourfiler d'or*, to *purfile*, tinsill, or overcast with gold thread, &c. *Pourfileure*, *purfling*, a purfling lace or work, bodkin work, tinselling " (Cotgrave.)

l. 194. *grys*, a sort of costly fur, formerly very much esteemed; what species of fur it was is not clear. Some suppose it to be the fur of the *grey* squirrel.

l. 198. *ballid*, bald. See Specimens of Early English, p. 75, l. 408.

l. 200. *in good poynt* = Fr. embonpoint.

l. 201. *steep*, O.E. *steap*, does not here mean *sunken* but *bright*, burning, fiery. Mr. Cockayne has illustrated the use of this word in his Seinte Marherete; " his twa ehnen [semden] *steappre* þene sterren," his two eyes seemed brighter than stars. (p. 9.)

l. 202. *stemed as a forneys of a leede*, shone like the fire under a cauldron.

l. 203. *bootes souple*. This is part of the description of a smart abbot, by an anonymous writer of the thirteenth century: " Ocreas habebat in cruribus quasi innatæ essent, sine plicâ porrectas." Bod. MS. James, n. 6, p. 121. (Tyrwhitt.)

l. 205. *for-pyned*, tormented, and here wasted away; from *pine*, torment, pain; *pined* also signifies wasted, as in the modern verb *pine*. The *for-* is intensive (as in Eng. *forswear*), and not negative (as in Eng. *forgo, fordo*).

l. 208. *frere*, friar. The four orders of mendicant friars mentioned in l. 210 were:—1. The Dominicans, or friars-preachers, who took up their abode in Oxford in 1221, known as the Black Friars. 2. The Franciscans, founded by St. Francis of Assisi in 1207, and known by the name of Grey Friars. They made their first appearance in England in 1224. 3. The Carmelites, or White Friars. 4. The Augustin (or Austin) Friars.

wantoun, sometimes written *wantowen*, literally signifies untrained, and hence wild, brisk, lively. *wan* is a common O.E. prefix, equivalent to our *un-* or *dis-*, as *wanhope*, despair; *wanbeleve*, unbelief; *wantruste*, distrust: *towen* or *town* occurs in O.E. writers for well-behaved, good. See Glossary.

merye, pleasant; cp. O.E. *merrywether*, pleasant weather.

l. 209. *lymytour* was a begging friar to whom was assigned a certain district or *limit*, within which he was permitted to solicit alms. Hence in later times the verb *limit* signifies to beg.

l. 210. *can* here signifies *knows*. See Glossary.

l. 211. *daliaunce and fair langage*, gossip and flattery. *daliaunce* in O.E. signifies tittle-tattle, gossip. The verb *dally* signified not only to loiter or idle, but to play, sport, from *daly* a die, plaything; Prov. Eng. *dally-bones*, sheep's trotters. See Glossary.

l. 214. *post*, pillar or support. See Gal. ii. 9.

l. 220. *licentiat*. He had a licence from the Pope to give absolution for all sins without being obliged to refer to his bishop. The *curate*, or parish priest, could not grant absolution in all cases, some of which were reserved for the bishop's decision.

l. 224. *pitance* here signifies a mess of victuals. It originally signified an extraordinary allowance of victuals given to monastics, in addition to their usual commons, and was afterwards applied to the whole allowance of food for a single person, or to a small portion of anything.

l. 226. *i-schreve* = *i-schriven*, confessed, *shriven*.

l. 233. *typet*, hood, cuculla, or cowl, which seems to have been used as a pocket.

l. 235. *certayn* [*li*]. This reading is sanctioned by Lansdowne MS. 851.

l. 236. *rote*, is by some explained as a kind of cymbal, by others it is said to be the same as the hurdy-gurdy. "Dulcimers or double harps called a *roote*, barbitos." (Huloet, 1552.)

l. 237. *yeddynges*, songs embodying some popular tales or romances.

l. 241. *tapstere*, a female tapster. In olden times the retailers of beer, and for the most part the brewers also, appear to have been females. The *-stere* or *-ster* as a feminine affix occurs in O.E. *brewstere*, *webbestere*; Eng. *spinster*. In *buckster*, *maltster*, *songster*, this affix has acquired the meaning of an agent; and in *youngster*, *gamester*, *punster*, &c., it implies contempt.

l. 242. *bet.* Lansd. MS. reads *beter*.

lazer, a leper, from *Lazarus*, in the parable of Dives and Lazarus; hence *lazarette*, an hospital for lepers, a lazar-house.

l. 246. It is not becoming, it may not advance (profit) to deal with (associate with) such poor people.

l. 248. *riche*, i. e. rich people.

l. 250. Courteous he was and humble in offering his services.

l. 258. *purchace* = beggary. What he acquired in this way was greater than his *rent* or income.

> "To wynnen is always myn entente,
> *My purchace is bettir than my rente.*"
> (Romaunt of the Rose, l. 6840.)

l. 260. *love-dayes.* Love-days (dies amoris) were days fixed for settling differences by umpire, without having recourse to law or violence. The ecclesiastics seem generally to have had the principal share in the management of these transactions, which, throughout the Vision of Piers Ploughman, appear to be censured as the means of hindering justice and of enriching the clergy.

> "Ae now is Religion a rydere
> A romere aboute,
> A ledere of *love-dayes*," &c.
> (Piers Ploughman, l. 6219.)

See Wright's Vision of Piers Ploughman, vol: ii. p. 535. Mr. Kitchin suggests that these private days of peace are analogous to the *Treuga Dei*, truce of God, so often proclaimed by bishops between 1000 and 1300. This truce lasted from 3 p.m. on Saturday to 6 a.m. on Monday.

l. 262. *cope*, a priest's vestment; a cloak forming a semicircle when laid flat; the *semy-cope* (l. 264) was a short cloak or cape.

l. 272. *a forked berd.* In the time of Edward III *forked beards* were the fashion among the franklins and bourgeoisie.

l. 278. *were kepud*, should be guarded; so that he should not suffer from *pirates* or privateers. The old subsidy of tonnage and poundage was given to the king for the safeguard and custody of the sea.

l. 279. *Middulburgh and Orewelle.* *Middleburgh* is still a well-known port of the island of Walcheren, in the Netherlands, almost immediately opposite Harwich, beside which are the estuaries of the rivers Stoure and

Orewelle. The spot was formerly known as the port of *Orwell* or *Orewelle.* (Saunders.)

l. 280. He well knew how to make a profit by the exchange of his crowns in the different money-markets of Europe ; *sheeldes* are French crowns (*ecus*), from their having on one side the figure of a shield.

l. 281. *his witte bisette,* employed his knowledge to the best advantage.

ll. 283, 284. So steadily did he order his bargains and agreements in borrowing money.

l. 286. *not* = *ne* + *wot*, know not; so *nost* = *ne* + *wost* (thou) knowest not.

l. 287. *Clerk,* a university student, a scholar preparing for the priesthood. It also signifies a man of learning, a man in holy orders.

Oxenford, Oxford, as if the ford of the oxen (A.S. *Oxnaford*) ; but the root *ox* (*esk, ouse*) is of Celtic origin, and signifies *water*.

l. 289. *Also . . . . as* = as . . . . as.

l. 292. His uppermost short cloak of coarse cloth.

l. 301. Lansd. MS. reads *But al that he might of his frendes hente.*

l. 304. *yaf him.* An allusion to the common practice, at this period, of poor scholars in the Universities, who wandered about the country begging, to raise money to support them in their studies. In a poem in MS. Lansd. 762, the husbandman, complaining of the many burdens he supports in taxes to the court, payments to the church, and charitable contributions of different kinds, enumerates among the latter the alms to scholars :—

> " Than cometh clerkys of Oxford, and make their mone,
> To her scole-hire they most have money."
>
> (See Piers Ploughman, p. 525, ed. Wright, 1856.)

scolay, to attend school. It is used in the same sense by Lydgate.

l. 309. *sowynge in,* tending to. Cp. our phrase, ' it *sounds* bad.'

> " That day (Domesday) sal (shall) na man be excused
> Of nathyng that he wrang (wrong) here used,
> That *sounes in* ille on any manere,
> Of whilk (which) he was never delyvered here."
>
> (Pricke of Conscience, p. 164, l. 6079.)

Ascham evidently plays upon the word in the following passage :—" Some siren shall sing him a song sweete in tune, but *sounding in* the ende to his utter destruction." (The Schoolmaster, p. 72, ed. Mayor, 1863.)

l. 310. *atte parvys,* at the *church-porch,* or portico of St. Paul's, where the lawyers were wont to meet for consultation. Cp. *Parvisum,* church-porch of St. Mary's, Oxford, where the examinations used to be held.

l. 322. *to him suspecte.* Tyrwhitt reads *in suspect* = in suspicion. *to him* does not seem necessary to the sense. The line may have originally been, *His purchasyng might[e] nought ben suspecte,* i. e. suspected.

ll. 325, 326. He was well acquainted with all the legal cases and decisions (or decrees) which had been ruled in the courts of law since the time of William the Conqueror. The MS. reads, *that King [Will.] were falle* (= were fallen, had befallen or occurred).

l. 328. *pynche at,* find fault with. Its original meaning was to act in a niggardly manner (as in the modern verb *pinch*), to deny oneself common necessaries ; from which sprang a secondary meaning, to deny or refuse the courtesy or praise due to another, and hence to blame. Palsgrave uses the phrase, "*I pynche courtaysye* (as one that doth that is nyce of condyscions, i. e. fays le nyce)."

l. 330. *medled coote*, a coat of·a mixed stuff or colour. Tyrwhitt reads *medlee*.

l. 331. *gird*, pp., is the same as *girt*, girded. The past tense would be *girde*.

seynt of silk, &c., a girdle of silk with small ornaments. The *barres* were called *cloux* in French, and were a usual ornament of a girdle (Lat. *clavus*). They were perforated to allow the tongue of the buckle to pass through them. Originally they were attached transversely to the wide tissue of which the girdle was formed, but subsequently were round or square, or fashioned like the heads of lions, and similar devices, the name of *barre* being still retained improperly. (Way, in Promptorium Parvulorum.)

l. 333. Fortescue describes a franklin to be a *pater familias—magnis ditatus possessionibus*. The following extract from the Boke of Nurture gives us a good idea of a franklin's feast:—

" A Franklen may make a feste Improberabill,
brawne with mustard is concordable, } bakoun serued with pesoun,
beef or motoun stewed seruysable,
Boyled Chykoun or capoune agreable, } convenyent for þe sesoun ;
Rosted goose & pygge·fulle profitable,
Capoun / Bakemete, or Custade Costable, } whenne eggis & crayme be gesoun.
Þerfore stuffe of household is behoveable,
Mortrowes or Iusselle ar delectable } for þe second course by resoun.
Thanne veel, lambe, kyd, or cony,
Chykoun or pigeoun rosted tendurly, } bakemetes or dowcettes with alle.
þenne followynge frytowrs, & a leche lovely ;
suche seruyse in sesoun is fulle semely } To serue with bothe chambur and halle.
Thenne appuls & peris with spices delicately
Aftur þe terme of þe yere fulle deynteithly. } with bred and chese to calle.
spised cakes and wafurs worthily,
with bragot & meth, þus men may meryly } plese welle bothe gret & smalle."

l. 336. The MS. reads '*a sop of wyn*,' and the true reading adopted from Lansd. MS., 851 is '*a sop in wyn ;*' see note to l. 147.

l. 342. *St. Julian* was eminent for providing his votaries with good lodgings and accommodation of all sorts. In the title of his legend, Bod. MS. 1596, fol. 4, he is called "St. Julian the gode herberjour" (St. Julian the good harbourer). It ends thus:—

" Therfore yet to this day thei that over lond wende (go),
Thei biddeth (pray) Selnt Julian anon that gode herborw (lodging) he hem sende,
And Seint Julianes Paternoster ofte seggeth (say) also
For his fader scule and his moderes, that he hem bringe therto."

(Tyrwhitt.)

l. 344. *envyned*, stored with wine. Cotgrave has preserved the French word *enviné* in the same sense. (Tyrwhitt.)

l. 345. *bake mete = baked meat ;* the old past participle of *bake* was *baken*.

l. 347. The verb *snewed* is usually explained as a metaphor from snowing; but the O.E. *snewe*, like the Prov. Eng. *snie* or *snive*, signifies to *abound*, *swarm*.

l. 351. *mewe.* The *mewe* was the place where the hawks were kept while moulting; it was afterwards applied to the *coop* wherein fowl were fattened, and lastly to a place of confinement or secresy.

l. 352. *stewe*, fish-pond. "To insure a supply of fish, stew-ponds were attached to the manors, and few monasteries were without them; the moat around the castle was often converted into a fish-pond, and well stored with luce, carp, or tench." (Our English Home, p. 65.)

l. 353. *woo was his cook*, woeful or sad was his cook. We only use *woo* or *woe* as a substantive.

ll. 353, 354. *sauce—poynant* is like the modern phrase *sauce piquant.* "Our forefathers were great lovers of 'piquant sauce.' They made it of expensive condiments and rare spices. In the statute of Edward III to restrain high living, the use of sauce is prohibited unless it could be procured at a very moderate cost." (Our English Home, p. 63.)

l. 355. *table dormant.* "Previous to the fourteenth century a pair of common wooden trestles and a rough plank was deemed a table sufficient for the great hall. . . . Tables, with a board attached to a frame, were introduced about the time of Chaucer, and, from remaining in the hall, were regarded as indications of a ready hospitality." (Our English Home, p. 30.)

l. 357. *sessions.* At the Sessions of the Peace.

l. 359. *anlas* or *anelace.* Speght defines this word as a *falchion*, or wood-knife. It seems, however, to have been a kind of knife or dagger usually worn at the girdle.

gipser was properly a pouch or budget used in hawking, &c., but commonly used by the merchant, or with any secular attire. (Way.)

l. 360. *heng*, the past tense of *hongen* or *hangen*, to hang.

morne mylk = morning milk.

l. 361. *schirreve*, the *reve* of a *shire*, governor of a county; our modern word *sheriff.*

counter. A counter appears to have been one retained to defend a cause or plead for another (Old Fr. *conter*). It may, however, be questionable whether Chaucer used the term in this sense, and it seems possible that *escheator* may be meant; the office, like that of sheriff, was held for a limited time, and was served only by the gentry of name and station in the county. (Way.)

l. 362. *vavaser*, or *vavasour*, a kind of inferior gentry, one who held his lands in fealty. Tyrwhitt says "it should be understood to mean the whole class of middling landholders."

l. 363. *Haburdassher.* Haberdashers were of two kinds: haberdashers of small wares—sellers of needles, tapes, buttons, &c.; and haberdashers of hats.

l. 364. *Webbe*, a male weaver; *websterre* was the female weaver.

l. 365. *lyveré*, livery. Under the term livery was included whatever was dispensed (*delivered*) by the lord to his officials or domestics annually or at certain seasons, whether money, victuals, or garments. The term chiefly denoted external marks of distinction, such as the *roba estivalis* and *hiemalis*, given to the officers and retainers of the court, as appears by the Wardrobe Book, 28 Edw. I, p. 310, and the Household Ordinances. The practice of distributing such tokens of general adherence to the service or interests of the individual who granted them, for the maintenance of any private quarrel, was carried to an injurious extent during the reigns of Edward III and Richard II, and was forbidden by several statutes, which allowed liveries to be borne only by menials, or the members of guilds. (See Stat. of Realm, ii. pp. 3, 74, 93, 156, 167.) The "*liverée des chaperons,*" often mentioned in these documents, was a hood or tippet, which being of a colour strongly contrasted to that of the garment, was a kind of livery much in fashion, and well adapted to serve as a distinctive mark. This, in later times, assumed the form of a round cap, to which was appended the long *liripipium,* which might be rolled around the head, but more commonly was worn hanging over the arm; and vestiges of it may still be traced in the dress of civic liverymen. The Stat. 7 Hen. IV expressly permits the adoption of such distinctive dress by fraternities and "*les gentz de mestere,*" the trades of the cities of the realm, being ordained with good intent; and to this prevalent usage Chaucer alludes when he describes five artificers of various callings, who joined the pilgrimage, clothed all "*in oo lyveré of a solempne and gret fraternité.*" (Way.)

l. 367. *piked.* Lansd. MS. 851 reads *apiked;* but the prefix is not needed, as the *e* in *gere* is sounded as a distinct syllable. *piked* signifies cleaned, trimmed. Bullinger in his fortieth sermon on the Apocalypse, inveighing against the Roman clergy, says, " They be commed, and *piked,* and very finely apparelled."

l. 368. *i-chapud = i-chaped,* having *chapes* (i. e. plates of metal at the point of the sheath or scabbard). Tradesmen and mechanics were prohibited from using knives adorned with silver, gold, or precious stones. So that Chaucer's pilgrims were of a superior estate, as indicated in l. 369.

l. 372. *deys.* Lansd. MS. 851 reads *bihe deys.* The term *deys, dese,* or *dais* (Fr. *deis* or *daix,* Lat. *dasium*), is used to denote the raised platform which was always found at the upper end of a hall, the table or the seat of distinction placed thereon, and finally the hanging drapery, called also *seler,* cloth of estate, and in French *ceil,* suspended over it.

l. 373. *that he can,* that he knows; *as he couthe,* as he knew. See l. 392.

l. 374. *schaply,* adapted, fit. It sometimes signifies comely, of good *shape* or form.

l. 375. For they had sufficient property and income (to entitle them to undertake the office of alderman).

l. 378. *clept* (Lansd. MS. reads *cleped*), called.

l. 379. *And for to go to vigilies al byfore.* It was the manner in times past, upon festival evens, called vigils, for parishioners to meet in their church-houses, or church-yards, and there to have a drinking-fit for the time. Here they used to end many quarrels betwixt neighbour and neighbour. Hither came the wives in comely manner, and they that were of the better sort had their mantles carried with them, as well for show as to keep them from cold at table. (Speght.)

l. 381. *for the nones = for the nonce;* this expression if grammatically written would be *for then once*, O. E. *for þan anes*, for the once, i. e. for the occasion. Such phrases as *at the nale*, *at the noke* = at the ale, at the oak, contain also a remnant of the dative case of the article; *for then* or *for þan* was originally *for þam.* Cp. O.E. atte = *atten* = at þan = *at þam.*

l. 382. Lansd. MS. reads *with the mery bones*, i. e. with the marrow-bones.

l. 383. *poudre marchaunt* may be the same as *pouldre blanche*, a powder compounded of ginger, cinnamon, and nutmegs.

galyngale is the root of sweet cyperus. In the Boke of Nurture (Harl. MS. 4011) we read that

"Mustard is meete for brawn beef, or powdred motoun;
Verdjus to boyled capoun, veel, chiken, or bakoun;

.   .   .   .   .

Roost beeff and goos with garlek, vinegre, or pepur; . .
Gynger sawce to lambe, to kyd, pigge, or fawn; . . .
To feysand (pheasant), partriche, or cony, mustard with the sugure."

l. 384. *Londone ale.* London ale was famous as early as the time of Henry III, and much higher priced than any other ale.

l. 386. *mortreux* or *mortrewes.* There were two kinds of 'mortrews,' '*mortrewes de chare*' and 'mortrewes of fysshe.' The first was a kind of soup in which chickens, fresh pork, crumbs of bread, yolks of eggs, and saffron formed the chief ingredients; the second kind was a soup containing the roe (or milt) and liver of fish, bread, pepper, ale. The ingredients were first stamped or brayed in a *mortar*, whence it probably derived its name. Lord Bacon (Nat. Hist. i. 48) speaks of "a *mortress* made with the brawn of capons stamped and strained."

l. 388. *mormal*, a cancer or gangrene. Jonson, in imitation of this passage, has described a cook with an ' old *mort mal* on his skin.' (Sad Shepherd, act ii. sc. 6.)

l. 392. *rouncy*, a common hackney horse, a nag.

l. 393. ' *a gowne of faldyng*,' a gown (robe) of coarse cloth. The term *faldyng* signifies a kind of frieze or rough-napped cloth, which was probably supplied from the North of Europe, and identical with the woollen wrappers of which Hermoldus speaks, ' *quos nos appellamus Faldones.*'

l. 396. *the boote somer.* Probably this is a reference to the summer of the year 1351, which was long remembered as the hot and dry summer. (Wright.)

ll. 398–400. Very many a draught of wine had he drawn (from the casks) while the chapman (merchant or supercargo to whom the wine belonged) was asleep, for he paid no regard to any conscientious scruples.

l. 401. *heigher hand*, upper hand.

l. 410. Many MSS. have *Gotland* (i.e. *Gothland*), the reading adopted by Tyrwhitt.

l. 411. *cryk* = *cryke*, creek, harbour, port.

l. 416. A great portion of the medical science of the middle ages depended upon astrological and other superstitious observances. (Wright.)

l. 418. *magik naturel.* Chaucer alludes to the same practices in the House of Fame, ll. 169-180 :—

" Ther saugh I pleyen jugelours
. . . .
And clerkes eke, which konne wel
Alle this *magike naturel,*
That craftely doon her ententes
To maken *in certeyn asceṅdentes,*
Ymages, lo ! thrugh which magike,
To make a man ben hool or syke."

l. 426. *his boote,* his remedy.

l. 428. *dragges.* Lansd. MS. reads *drugges;* but *dragges* is correct, for the Promptorium Parvulorum has *dragge,* dragetum ; and Cotgrave defines *dragée* the French form of the word *dragge* as a kind of digestive powder prescribed unto weak stomachs after meat, and hence any jonkets, comfits, or sweetmeats served in the last course for stomach closers. Old English writers employ occasionally *dragy* in the sense of a small comfit, and *dragoir, dragenall,* a vessel for *dragees.*

ll. 431–436. The authors mentioned here wrote the chief medical text-books of the middle ages. Rufus was a Greek physician of Ephesus, of the age of Trajan ; Haly, Serapion, and Avicen were Arabian physicians and astronomers of the eleventh century; Rhasis was a Spanish Arab of the tenth century; and Averroes was a Moorish scholar who flourished in Morocco in the twelfth century. Johannes Damascenus was also an Arabian physician, but of a much earlier date (probably of the ninth century); Constantius Afer, a native of Carthage, and afterwards a monk of Monte Cassino, was one of the founders of the school of Salerno—he lived at the end of the eleventh century; Bernardius Gordonius, professor of medicine at Montpellier, appears to have been Chaucer's contemporary ; John Gatisden was a distinguished physician of Oxford in the earlier half of the fourteenth century ; Gilbertyn is supposed by Warton to be the celebrated Gilbertus Anglicas. The names of Hippocrates and Galen were, in the middle ages, always (or nearly always) written Ypocras and Galienus. (Wright.)

l. 441. In cloth of a blood-red colour and of a blueish-grey.

l. 442. *taffata* (or *taffety*), a sort of thin silk.

sendal (or *cendal*), a kind of rich thin silk used for lining, very highly esteemed. Palsgrave however has ' *cendell,* thynne lynnen, *sendal.*'

l. 443. *esy in dispence,* moderate in his expenditure.

l. 444. *wan in pestilence,* acquired during the pestilence. Wright supposes that this is an allusion to the great pestilence which devastated Europe in the middle of the fourteenth century.

l. 447. *of byside,* &c. from (a place) near Bath.

l. 448. But she was somewhat deaf, and that was her misfortune.

l. 449. *cloth makyng.* The West of England, and especially the neighbourhood of Bath, from which the ' good wif' came, was celebrated, till a comparatively recent period, as the district of cloth-making. Ypres and Ghent were the great clothing marts on the Continent. (Wright.)

l. 452. *to the offryng.* We have here an allusion to the offering on Relic-Sunday, when the congregation went up to the altar in succession to kiss the relics. "But the relics we must kiss and offer unto, especially on Relic-Sunday." (Book of Homilies.)

l. 455. *keverchef*, (*coverchef*, or *kerchere*, *kerché*). The kerchief, or covering for the head, was, until the fourteenth century, almost an indispensable portion of female attire.

"Upon hir hed a *kerché* of Valence."

(Lydgate's Minor Poems, p. 47.)

ful fyne of grounde, of a very fine texture.

l. 459. *moyste* here means only recently purchased. It is properly applied to new or unfermented wine; and also to other liquors. Chaucer uses the phrase *moisty ale* as opposed to *old ale*.

l. 462. *chirche dore.* The priest married the couple at the church-porch, and immediately afterwards proceeded to the altar to celebrate mass, at which the newly-married persons communicated.

l. 468. *in Galice* (Galicia), at St. James of Compostello, a famous resort of pilgrims in the fourteenth and fifteenth centuries. As the legend goes, the body of St. James the Apostle was supposed to have been carried in a ship without a rudder to Galicia, and preserved at Compostello.

Coloyne. At Cologne, where the bones of the Three Kings or Wise Men of the East are said to be preserved.

l. 470. *gattothud = gat-toothed*, having teeth wide apart or separated from one another. Speght reads *cat-tothed*.

l. 474. *foot-mantel.* Tyrwhitt supposes this to be a sort of *riding-petticoat*, such as is now used by market-women.

l. 477. *remedyes.* An allusion to the title and subject of Ovid's book, De Remedio Amoris.

l. 478. *the old daunce*, the old game, or customs. Cotgrave has the French phrase, "*Elle sçait asses de la vieille danse.*"

l. 480. *Persoun of a toun*, the parson or parish priest. Chaucer in his description of the parson, contrasts the piety and industry of the secular clergy with the wickedness and laziness of the religious orders or monks.

l. 483. *gladly.* Lansd. MS. has *trewly.*

l. 488. He did not excommunicate those who failed to pay the tithes that were due to him.

l. 491. *offrynge*, the voluntary contributions of his parishioners.

substaunce, income derived from his benefice.

l. 494. *lafte not*, left not, ceased not.

l. 496. *moche*, great. Lansd. MS. reads *moste*, greatest.

l. 499. *after that.* Lansd. MS. reads *afterwards.*

l. 504. *lewid*, unlearned, ignorant. *Lewid* or *lewd* originally signified the people, laity, as opposed to the clergy; the modern sense of the word is not common in Old English.

l. 507. *to huyre*, to hire. The parson did not leave his parish duties to be performed by a strange curate, that he might have leisure to seek a chantry in St. Paul's.

l. 510. *chaunterie*, chantry, an endowment for the payment of a priest to sing mass agreeably to the appointment of the founder. Lansd. MS. 851 reads '*to singe* for soules.'

l. 517. *daungerous*, not affable, difficult to approach.

l. 519. *fairnesse*, i. e. by leading a fair or good life. The MS. has *clennesse*, that is, a life of purity.

l. 525. *waytud after*, looked for. See l. 571. Cp. Knightes Tale, l. 58.

l. 526. *spiced conscience. Spiced* here seems to signify, says Tyrwhitt, nice, scrupulous. It occurs in the Mad Lover, act iii. (Beaumont and Fletcher). When Cleanthe offers a purse, the priestess says,—

> " Fy! no corruption——.
>   *Cle.* Take it, it is yours;
>   Be not so *spiced;* it is good gold;
>   And goodness is no gall to the conscience."

" Under pretence of *spiced* holinesse." (Tract dated 1594, ap. Todd's Illustrations of Gower, p. 380.)

l. 528. *and.* Lansd. MS. reads *bot* (but).

l. 529. Lansd. MS. reads *was* before *bis.*

l. 534. *though him gamed or smerte*, though it was pleasant or unpleasant to him.

l. 541. *mere.* People of quality would not ride upon a mare.

l. 548. *the ram.* This was the usual prize at wrestling-matches.

l. 549. *a thikke knarre*, a thickly knotted (fellow), i. e. a muscular fellow.

l. 550. *of harre*, off its hinges.

l. 551. *at.* MS. reads *with.*

l. 560. *golyardeys*, one who gains his living by following rich men's tables, and telling tales and making sport for the guests. Tyrwhitt says, " This jovial sect seems to have been so called from *Golias*, the real or assumed name of a man of wit, towards the end of the twelfth century, who wrote the Apocalypsis Goliæ, and other pieces in burlesque Latin rhymes, some of which have been falsely attributed to Walter Map." In several authors of the thirteenth century, quoted by Du Cange, the *goliardi* are classed with the *' joculatores et buffones.'*

l. 563. *a thombe of gold.* If the allusion be, as is most probable, to the old proverb, " Every honest miller has a thumb of gold," this passage may mean that our miller, notwithstanding his thefts, was an *honest* miller, i. e. as honest as his brethren. (Tyrwhitt.) " It appears much more probable that the line, coming, as it does, immediately after the notice of thefts,

> ' And yet he had a thombe of gold, pardé,'

is neither a bit of satire directed at the miller's own pretensions to honesty, nor at the pretensions of his brethren of the white coat generally; but refers simply to his skill, as shewing how little need there was for his thefts. Mr. Yarrell says, ' It is well known that all the science and tact of a miller are directed so to regulate the machinery of his mill that the meal produced should be of the most valuable description that the operation of grinding will permit when performed under the most advantageous circumstances. His profit or his loss, even his fortune or his ruin, depends upon the exact adjustment of all the various parts of the machinery in operation. The miller's ear is constantly directed to the note made by the running stone, in its circular course over the bed-stone; the exact parallelism of their two surfaces, indicated by a particular sound, being a matter of the first consequence, and his hand is constantly placed under the meal-spout, to ascertain by actual contact the character and qualities of the meal produced. The thumb, by a particular movement, spreads the sample over the fingers; the thumb is the gauge of the value of the produce; and hence have arisen the sayings of

" Worth a miller's thumb," and " An honest miller hath a golden thumb," in reference to the amount of the profit that is the reward of his skill.   By this incessant action of the miller's thumb, a peculiarity in its form is produced, which is said to resemble exactly the shape of the head of the fish constantly found in the mill-stream, and has obtained for it the name of the Miller's Thumb, which occurs in the comedy of Wit at Several Weapons, by Beaumont and Fletcher, act v. sc. 1 ; and also in Merrett's Pinax.   Although the improved machinery of the present time has diminished the necessity for the miller's skill in the mechanical department, the thumb is still constantly resorted to as the best test for the quality of flour.'"—British Fishes. (Saunders.)

l. 567. *Maunciple* or *manciple*, an officer who had the care of purchasing provisions for a college, an inn of court, &c.

l. 570. *took by taille*, took on credit.

l. 572. *ay biforn*, ever before (others).   Lansd. MS. reads *al* instead of *ay*.

l. 578. *an house.*   Lansd. MS. reads *that house.*

l. 584. *al a*, a whole.

l. 586. *bere aller cappe*, the caps of them all.   *Here aller* = eorum omnium.   ' *To sette* ' a man's *cappe* is to overreach him, to cheat him, and also to befool him.

l. 589. *neighe.*   Lansd. MS. reads *rounde.*

l. 593. *and.*   Lansd. MS. reads *or.*

l. 617. *pers.*   The MS. reads *blew.*

l. 621. *tukkud*, clothed in the long habit or frock of the friars.

l. 624. *cherubyne's face.*   H. Stephens, Apol. Herod. i. c. 30, quotes the same thought from a French epigram—" Nos grands docteurs *au cherubin visage.*"

l. 625. *sawceflem* or *sawsfleam*, having a red pimpled face.   The Old Eng. corresponding term is *redgownd* or *redgund*, which is often applied to the eruptive humours that usually make their appearance in very young children. It also applied to the running or impure secretion of the eyes.   Tyrwhitt quotes the phrase "*facies alba*—interdum sanguinis fleumate viciata."

l. 645. *questio quid juris.*   This kind of question occurs frequently in Ralph de Hengham.   After having stated a case, he adds, *quid juris*, and then proceeds to give the answer to it.

ll. 649, 652. He would teach his friend to stand in no awe of the archdeacon's curse (excommunication), except he set store upon his money ; for in his purse he should be punished (i. e. by paying a good round sum he could release himself from the archdeacon's curse).

l. 657. *significavit*, i.e. of a writ *de excommunicato capiendo*, which usually began, ' Significavit nobis venerabilis frater,' &c.

l. 658. *in daunger*, in his jurisdiction, within the reach or control of his office.

l. 660. *and was here aller red*, and was the adviser of them all.   The MS. reads *and was al here red.*   The Lansd. MS. reads *and what was*, &c.

l. 662. *ale-stake*, a sign-post in front of an ale-house.

l. 665. *of Rouncival.*   I can hardly think that Chaucer meant to bring his Pardoner from Roncevaux, in Navarre, and yet I cannot find any place of that name in England.   An hospital, Beatæ Mariæ de Rouncyvalle, in Charing, London, is mentioned in the Monast. t. ii. p. 443 ; and there was a

Runceval Hall in Oxford. (Stevens, v. ii. p. 262.) So that it was perhaps the name of some fraternity. (Tyrwhitt.)

l. 667. *Come hider, love, to me.* This, I suppose, was the beginning, or the burthen of some known song. (Tyrwhitt.)

l. 668. *bar . . . a stif burdoun,* sang the bass. Cp. Fr. *bourdon,* the name of a deep organ stop.

l. 675. *but.* MS. reads *and; bot* is the reading of the Lansd. MS.

l. 677. *the newe get,* the new fashion, which is described in ll. 675–678.

l. 680. *vernicle,* a diminutive of *Veronike* (Veronica). A copy in miniature of the picture of Christ, which is supposed to have been miraculously imprinted upon a handkerchief, preserved in the church of St. Peter at Rome. It was usual for persons returning from pilgrimages to bring with them certain tokens of the several places which they had visited; and therefore the Pardoner, who is just arrived from Rome, is represented with *a vernicle sowed on his cappe.* (Tyrwhitt.) See Piers Ploughman, vol. i. p. 109 (ed. Wright, 1856) :—

> " A bolle and a bagge he bar by his syde ;
> An hundred of ampulles on his hat seten,
> Signes of Synay, and shelles of Galice,
> And many a crouche on his cloke and Keyes of Rome,
> And the *vernicle* bifore, for men sholde knowe
> And se bi hise signes, whom he sought hadde."

l. 682. *bret-ful of pardoun,* brim-full of indulgences.

l. 709. *schortly,* briefly. Lansd. MS. reads *sothely,* truly.

l. 710. *thestat, tharray,* = the estate, the array ; the coalescence of the article with the noun is very common in Old Eng. writers.

l. 715. *bare.* Lansd. MS. reads *beren,* and omits *in* after *us.*

l. 720. That ye ascribe it not to my ill-breeding.

l. 728. *al speke he,* if he speak. See *al have I,* l. 738.

ll. 735, 736. This saying of Plato is taken from Bŏethius, De Consolatione, lib. iii.

l. 746. *in an.* Lansd. MS. reads *in a lordes.*

l. 764. May the blessed martyr reward you !

l. 766. *talken.* Lansd. MS. reads *talen,* to tell tales.

l. 779. *to make it wys,* to make it a matter of wisdom or deliberation ; *made it straunge* = made it a matter of difficulty.

l. 792. *of solas.* Lansd. MS. reads *most solas.*

l. 804. *and oure othus swore,* and *we* our oaths swore.

l. 811. *in heygh and lowe.* Lat. *In,* or *de alto et basso,* Fr. *de haut en bas,* were expressions of entire submission on one side, and sovereignty on the other. (Tyrwhitt.)

l. 816. Lansd. MS. omits *that.*

l. 829. *draweth cut,* draw lots. Froissart calls it *tirer à la longue paille,* to draw the long straw.

l. 841. *as was resoun,* as was reasonable or right.

l. 847. *syn I.* Lansd. MS. reads *seththe that I.*

l. 852. Lansd. MS. reads *anon* after *tale;* and for *right,* &c., reads *as ye mai here.*

THE KNIGHTES TALE.

l. 3. *governour.* It should be observed that Chaucer continually accents words (of Romance origin) in the Norman-French manner, on the *last* syllable. Thus we have here *governóur;* again in the next line, *conqueróur;* in l. 7, *chivalríe;* in l. 11, *contré;* in l. 18, *manére,* &c. &c. The most remarkable examples are when the words end in *-oun* or *-ing* (ll. 25, 26, 35, 36).

l. 6. *contre* is here accented on the *first* syllable; in l. 11, on the *last.* This is a good example of the unsettled state of the accents of such words in Chaucer's time, which afforded him an opportunity of licence, which he freely uses.

l. 7. *chivalrie,* knightly exploits. In l. 20, *chivalrye* = knights; Eng. *chivalry.*

l. 8. *regne of Femynye.* The kingdom (Lat. *regnum*) of the Amazons. *Femenye* is from Lat. *fœmina,* a woman.

l. 9. *Cithea,* Scythia.

l. 27. *as-now,* at present, at this time. Cf. the O.E. adverbs *as-swithe, as-sone,* immediately.

l. 31. *I wol not lette eek non of al this rowte,* I desire not to hinder eke (also) none of all this company. *Wol* = desire; cf. ' I *will* have mercy,' &c.

l. 43. *creature* is a word of three syllables.

l. 45. *ne wolde* was no doubt pronounced (as so often written) *nolde,* would not, otherwise the *ne* appears redundant. So *ne hath,* hath not, is pronounced *nath.* Lansd. MS. reads *thei nolde never,* &c.

stenten, stop. '' She *stinted,* and cried aye.'' (Romeo and Juliet.)

l. 50. *that thus*—i. e. ye that thus.

l. 54. *alle* is to be pronounced *al-lè,* but Tyrwhitt reads *than,* then, after *alle.*

l. 55. *a dedly chere,* a deathly countenance.

l. 60. *we beseken,* we beseech, ask for. For such double forms as *beseken* and *besechen;* cf. mod. Eng. *dik* and *ditch, kirk* and *chirch, sack* and *satchel, stick* and *stitch.* In the Early Eng. period the harder forms with *k* were very frequently employed by *Northern* writers, who preferred them to the softer *Southern* forms with *ch.*

l. 68. This line means 'that no estate ensureth to be well.'

l. 70. *Clemence,* clemency.

l. 78. *lesten,* lost. The Harl. MS. reads *leften,* left, but Lansd. MS. reads *losten.*

l. 83. *for despyt,* out of vexation.

l. 84. *To do the deede bodyes vilonye,* to treat the dead bodies shamefully.

l. 90. *withoute more respite,* without longer delay.

l. 91. *they fillen gruf,* they fell flat with the face to the ground. In O.E. we find the phrase *to fall grovelinges,* or *to fall groveling.*

l. 96. *him thoughte,* it seemed to him; cf. *methinks,* it seems to me. In O.E. the verbs *like, list, seem, rue* (pity), are used impersonally, and take the dative of the pronoun. Cf. the modern expression 'if you please' = if it be pleasing to you.

l. 102. *ferforthly*, i. e. *far-forth-like*, to such an extent, as far as.

l. 107. *abood*, delay, awaiting, abiding. Lansd. MS. reads *withoute more* for *withoute eny.*

l. 108. *his baner he displayeth*, i. e. he summoneth his troops to assemble for military service. Lansd. MS. reads *displeide.*

l. 110. *no ner = no nerre*, no nearer. Lansd. MS. reads *nerre.*

l. 119. *feeldes*, field, is an heraldic term for the ground upon which the various charges, as they are called, are emblazoned. The whole of this description is taken from the Thebais, lib. xii.

l. 130. *in pleyn bataille*, in open or fair fight.

l. 134. *housbondes.* Lansd. MS. reads *frendes.*

l. 136. We ought perhaps to read *But it were al to longe to devyse. Longe* being an adverb requires a final -*e.*

l. 146. *as him leste*, as it pleased him.

l. 147. *cas*, heap, collection. Tyrwhitt reads *tas*, heap, from the Fr. *tas*, heap, troop. Lansd. MS. reads *caas.* In l. 162 it is written *chaas*, as if for chaos, medley.

l. 152. *thurgh girt*, pierced through.

l. 153. *liggyng by and by*, lying separately. In later English, *by and by* signifies presently, immediately, as " the end is not *by and by.*"

l. 154. *in oon armes*, in one (kind of) arms or armour, showing that they belonged to the same house. Lansd. MS. reads, *Bothen in armes samen wrouht ful richely.*

l. 157. *nat fully quyk*, not wholly alive.

l. 158. *by here coote-armure*, by their coat armour, by the devices over armour covering the breasts.

by here gere, by their *gear*, i. e. equipments.

l. 160. *they.* Tyrwhitt reads *tho*, those.

l. 165. *tathenes*, to Athens.

l. 166. *he wolde no ranceoun*, he would accept of no ransom.

l. 167. Lansd. MS. reads, *And whan this worthi duc had thus ydone.*

l. 171. *terme of his lyf*, the remainder of his life.

what wolle ye, &c., wherefore will ye hear more words. Lansd. MS. reads *what nedeth.*

l. 173. Lansd. MS. reads, *Dwellen this Palomon and eke Arcite.*

l. 180. *strof hire hewe*, strove her hue, i. e. her complexion contested the superiority.

l. 181. *I not*, I know not; *not = ne wot.*

fairer. The MS. reads *fyner.* Lansd. MS. reads *faireste.*

l. 187. Lansd. MS. reads, *And sithen arise and done May observance.*

l. 189. *May.* Against Maie, every parishe, towne, and village, assembled themselves together, bothe men, women, and children, olde and yonge, even all indifferently, and either going all together or devidying themselves into companies, they goe, some to the woodes and groves, some to the hills and mountaines, some to one place, some to another, when they spend all the night in pastimes; in the morninge they return, bringing with them birche, bowes and branches of trees, to deck their assemblies withalle. (Stubbs, Anatomie of Abuses, p. 94.)

l. 191. *Hire yolwe heer was browdid*, Her yellow hair was braided.

l. 193. *the sonne upriste*, the sun's uprising; the *-e* in *sonne* represents the old genitive inflexion.

l. 194. *wher as hire liste*, wherever it pleased her.

l. 195. *party*, partly; Fr. *en partie.*

l. 196. *sotil gerland*, a subtle garland; subtle has here the exact force of the Lat. *subtilis*, finely woven. Harl. MS. reads *certeyn.*

l. 202. *evene joynyng*, closely joining, or adjoining.

l. 203 *Ther this Emily hadde hire pleyinge*, i. e. where she was amusing herself.

l. 216. *by aventure or cas*, by adventure or hap.

l. 217. *and many a barre.* Tyrwhitt reads *with*, &c. Lansd. MS. reads *of.*

l. 218. *sparre*, a square wooden bolt; the bars which were of iron were as thick as they must have been if wooden. See l. 132.

l. 220. *bleynte*, the past tense of *blenche*, or *blenke* (to blink), to start, draw back suddenly.

l. 221. Lansd. MS. reads *thouhe* (though) instead of *that.*

l. 224. *for to see*, for to be seen, i. e. in appearance. Lansd. MS. reads *on* instead of *for.*

l. 233. *the schort and pleyn*, the brief and manifest statement of the case.

l. 241. *rome.* Lansd. MS. reads *romeynge.*

l. 243. *whethur.* Lansd. MS. reads *where*, a very common form for *whether.*

l. 247. *yow* (used reflexively), yourself.

l. 250. *schape = schapen*, shaped, determined. " *Shapes* our ends." (Shakespeare.)

l. 261. Lansd. MS. reads *rometh in that yonder place.*

l. 262. And except I have her pity and her favour.

l. 263. *atte leste weye*, at the least.

l. 264. *I am not but* (no better than) *dead*, there is no more to say. Chaucer uses *ne—but* much in the same way as the Fr. *ne—que.* Cp. North English, " I'm *nobbut* clemmed " = I am almost dead of hunger.

l. 265. *tho*, those. Lansd. MS. reads *thes.*

l. 268. *in good fey*, in good faith.

l. 269. *me lust ful evele pleye*, it pleaseth me very badly to play.

l. 271. *bit nere = it were not*, it would not be.

l. 275. That never, even though it cost us a miserable death.

l. 276. Till that death shall part us two.

l. 278. *cas*, case. It properly means event, hap. See l. 216.
my leevè brother, my dear brother.

l. 289. *counseil*, advice. Lansd. MS. reads *cosin* (cousin), and for *to* reads *my.* See l. 303.

l. 293. *I dar wel sayn*, I dare maintain.

l. 295. *thou schalt be.* Chaucer occasionally uses *shall* in the sense of *owe*, so that the true form of *I shall* is *I owe* (Lat. *debeo*); it expresses a strong obligation. So here it is not so much the sign of a future tense as a separate verb, and the sense is ' Thou art sure to be false sooner than I am.'

l. 297. *par amour*, with love, in the way of love. To love *par amour* is an old phrase for to love excessively.

erst then thou. Lansd. MS. reads *ar* for *then.* The correct phrase *erthan* = before that, before.

l. 298. Lansd. MS. reads *it* before *not,* which is omitted in the Harleian MS.

l. 300. *affeccioun of holynesse,* a sacred affection, or aspiration after.

l. 304. *I pose,* I put the case, I will suppose.

l. 305. 'Knowest thou not well the old writer's saying?' The *olde clerke* is Boethius, from whose book, De Consolatione, Chaucer has borrowed largely in many places. The passage alluded to is in lib. iii. met. 12 :—

> " Quis legem det amantibus?
> Major lex amor est sibi."

l. 309. *and such decré,* and (all) such ordinances.

l. 310. *in ech degree,* in every rank of life.

l. 314. *and eke it is,* &c., and moreover it is not likely that ever in all thy life thou wilt stand in her favour. The MS. reads *And that is.* The reading here adopted is from the Lansd. MS.

l. 321. *were wrothe.* Lansd. MS. reads *so* before *wrothe.*

l. 328. *every of us,* each of us, every one of us. Lansd. MS. reads *everyche.*

l. 331. *to the effect,* to the result, or end.

l. 342. *in helle.* An allusion to Theseus accompanying Peirithous in his expedition to carry off Proserpina, daughter of Aidoneus, king of the Molossians, when both were taken prisoners, and Peirithous torn in pieces by the dog Cerberus.

l. 354. *o stounde,* one moment, any short interval of time.

l. 360. *his nekke lith to wedde,* his neck is in jeopardy.

l. 364. *To slen himself he wayteth pryvyly,* he watches for an opportunity to slay himself unperceived.

l. 367. *now is me schape,* now am I destined; literally, now is it *shapen* (or appointed) for me.

l. 371. Lansd. MS. omits *for.*

l. 374. *nat,* in the text, seems redundant. Lansd. MS. reads,—

> *Thouhe that I nevere hire grace miht deserve.*

l. 379. Lansd. MS. omits *in.*

l. 399. And another man would fain (get) out of his prison.

l. 401. *mateere,* in the *matter* of thinking to excel God's providence.

l. 402. *We wo / te nevere / what thing / we pray / en heere,* We never know what thing it is that we pray for here below. See Romans viii. 26.

l. 404. This is from Boethius, De Consolatione, lib. iii. But I returne again to the studies of men, of which men the corage always reherseth and seeketh the soveraine good, al be it so that it be with a dyrked memory; but he not by whiche pathe, *right as a dronken man note nought by which pathe he may returne home to his house.* (Chaucer's Translation of Boethius.)

l. 405. Lansd. MS. omits *nat.* The correct reading is as follows :—

> *But he / not which / the righ / te wey / is thider.*

l. 409. According to the text this line must be scanned as follows :—

> *But we / gon wrong / ful of / te trew / ely.*

The Lansd. arrangement is—

> *But we / gon wrong / of tè / ful trew / ely.*

Wrong is an adverb, and should be written *wronge;* and in the Lansd. reading it becomes elided before *ofte.*

l. 421. *pure feteres,* the very fetters. So in the Duchesse, v. 583, *the pure deth.* The Greeks used καθαρός in the same sense. (Tyrwhitt.) For *of* the Lansd. MS. reads *on.*

l. 425. *at thi large,* at large.

l. 428. *oure.* Lansd. MS. reads *youre.*

l. 429. *in.* Lansd. MS. reads *on.*

l. 432. The following reading is more grammatical and harmonious than that in the text :—

> For *whom | I nee | des lee | se mot | my lyf.*

l. 436. *sterve,* may die. Lansd. MS. reads *sterveth.*

l. 459. *to letten of his wille,* to refrain from his wille (or lusts).

l. 461. *ne hath* is to be pronounced (as it is often written) *nath.*

l. 484. *in prisoun.* Lansd. MS. reads *to.*

l. 486. *upon his heed.* Froissart has *sur sa teste* and *sur la teste, sur peine de la teste.*

l. 489. *this question.* An implied allusion to the mediæval courts of love, in which questions of this kind were seriously discussed. (Wright.)

l. 502. *wol.* Lansd. MS. reads *mai.*

l. 508. *dwellyng.* Lansd. MS. reads *weyleynge* (wailing).

making his moone, making his complaint or *moan.*

ll. 514–517. And in his manner for all the world he conducted himself not like to ordinary lovers, but rather like many whose brains were affected by the 'humour melancholy' (or a bilious attack).

l. 518. *in his selle fantastyk.* Tyrwhitt reads *Biforne his hed in his celle fantastike.* The division of the brain into cells, according to the different sensitive faculties, is very ancient, and is found depicted in mediæval manuscripts. The *fantastic cell (fantasia)* was in front of the head. (Wright.)

l. 527. *that* is rightly omitted in the Lansd. MS.

l. 543. *was in.* Lansd. MS. reads *al in.*

l. 547. *bar him lowe,* conducted himself as one of low estate.

l. 566. *strong.* The MS. reads *long.*

l. 579. *[is] spronge. Is* is supplied from the Lansd. MS.; *spronge* is the past participle, not the past tense, which is *sprong.*

l. 590. *so derre.* Lansd. MS. omits *so,* and rightly, for *derre* is the comparative of *der,* dear, beloved.

l. 612. Lansd. MS. reads,—

> He had[de] gif his gailer drinke so.

We ought perhaps to put an *-e* after *gif,* and read as follows :—

> He had / dè giv / e drinke / his gay / ler so.

l. 613. *clarré.* The French term *claré* seems simply to have denoted a clear transparent wine, but in its most usual sense a compound drink of wine with honey and spices, so delicious as to be comparable to the nectar of the gods. In Sloan MS. l. 2584, f. 173, the following directions are found for making *clarré* :—" Take a galoun of honi, and skome (skim) it wel, and loke whanne it is isoden (boiled) that ther be a galoun; thanne take viii galouns of red wyn, than take a pounde of pouder canel (cinnamon), and a half a pounde of pouder gynger, and a quarter of a pounde of pouder pepper, and medle (mix) alle these thynges togeder and (with) the wyn; and do hym in a clene barelle, and stoppe it fast, and rolle it wel ofte sithes, as men don verjous iii dayes." (Way.)

l. 619. *needes cost,* for *needes coste,* by the force of necessity. It seems to be equivalent to O.E. *needes-wyse,* of necessity.

l. 620. *And til / a gro / ve fas / te ther / besyde.*

l. 629. *for of* Lansd. MS. reads *and.*

l. 656. *lustily.* Lansd. MS. reads *hastely.* We ought perhaps to omit *ful,* and read

> *Into / the gro / vè lus / tèly / he sterte.* See l. 620.

l. 658. Lansd. MS. reads *as* after *ther.*

l. 666. *atte unset stevene,* at a meeting not previously fixed upon, an unexpected meeting or appointment.

l. 669. *stynteth* (stops). Lansd. MS. reads *sitteth.*

l. 673. *here queynte geeres,* their strange behaviour.

l. 674. Now in the top (i. e. elevated, in high spirits), now down in the briars (i. e. depressed, in low spirits).

l. 679. A writer in Notes and Queries quotes the following Devonshire proverb: " Fridays in the week are never aleek."

l. 696. *as his.* The MS. reads *and am his.*

l. 708. Compare Legend of Goode Women,—

> *Sens first that day that shapen was my sherte,*
> *Or by the fatal suster had my dome.*

l. 713. *that* seems to be superfluous.

l. 721. *bussches.* Lansd. MS. reads *boskes* (bushes).

l. 735. *I drede not,* I have no fear, I doubt not.

ll. 735, 736. *other . . . or* = either . . . or.

l. 740. *pulleth.* Lansd. MS. reads *pulled.*

l. 748. *For.* Lansd. MS. reads *what* = lo!

l. 764. *to borwe.* This expression has the same force as *to wedde,* in pledge. See l. 360.

l. 768. *his thonkes,* willingly, with his good will. Cp. O.E. *myn unthonkes* = ingratis.

l. 783. *comyng.* Lansd. MS. reads *come rosseheinge.*

l. 785. *thenketh* and *cometh* are to be pronounced as *thenkth* and *comth.*

l. 800. The MS. reads *And as wilde boores gonne they smyte.*

l. 807. *hath seye byforn,* hath seen before, hath foreseen.

l. 808. *they* is for *thegh* or *theigh,* though.

l. 818. *ther daweth him no day,* no day dawns upon him.

l. 820. *hont* is here written for *hunte,* hunter.

l. 830. *ther* seems to be redundant.

> *And to / the gro / vè that / stood fas / tè by.*

l. 848. *Hoo,* an exclamation made by heralds, to stop the fight. It was also used to enjoin silence. See l. 1667.

l. 878. *it am I.* This is the regular construction in early English. In modern English the pronoun *it* is regarded as the direct nominative, and *I* as forming part of the predicate.

l. 881. Therefore I ask my death and my doom. The rhyme has compelled the poet to invert the regular order of the terms.

l. 889. *Mars the reede.* Bocaccio uses the same epithet in the opening of his Teseide: *O rubiconde Marte.* *Reede* refers to the colour of the planet.

l. 901. The MS. has *bare* feet, which renders the line too long.

l. 912. The line reads better without the word *his.* The Lansd. MS. omits *in.* We ought perhaps to read,—

    And eek / in hert / hadde he / compas / sioun.

l. 922. *can no divisioun,* knows no distinction.

l. 923. *after oon = after one mode,* according to the same rule.

l. 925. *eyen lighte,* cheerful looks.

l. 950. *can . . . thank,* acknowledges an obligation, owes thanks.

l. 959. We ought perhaps to read *As he / that ofte / hath ben,* &c.

l. 961. The metre requires the omission of *the* before *request.*

l. 965. Read as follows:—

    Ne ma / kè werre / on me / nightè / ne daye.

Nighte is an adverb (originally a noun in the dative case), and should there-fore take a final *-e.*

l. 967. Read [*And*] *I / foryè / ve you / this tres / pas ev / ery dele.*

l. 970. *graunted*[*e*]. Lansd. MS. reads *graunteth.*

l. 979. *loth or leef,* displeasing or pleasing.

l. 980. *pypen in an ivy leef* is an expression like ' blow the buck's-horn,' to console oneself with any useless or frivolous employment. Cp. the expres-sion ' to go and whistle.' Lydgate uses similar expressions :—

    " But let his brother blowe in an horn,
      Where that him list, or pipe in a reede."

                    (Destruction of Thebes, part ii.)

l. 992. *fer ne neer,* farther nor nearer, more nor less. The following remarks on the *fyfty wykes* are taken from Notes and Queries, v. iii. p. 202 :—" With respect to the time of year at which the tournament takes place, there seems to be an inconsistency." Theseus fixes ' this day fifty wekes' from the fourth of May, as the day on which the final contention must come off, and yet the day previous to the final contention is afterwards alluded to as ' the lusty season of that May' which, it is needless to say, would be inconsistent with an interval of fifty ordinary weeks.

" But fifty weeks, if taken in their literal sense of 350 days, would be a most unmeaning interval for Theseus to fix upon,—it would almost require explanation as much as the difficulty itself; it is therefore much easier to suppose that Chaucer meant to imply the interval of a solar year. Why he should choose to express that interval by fifty, rather than by fifty-two weeks, may be surmised in two ways: first, because the latter phrase would be unpoetical and unmanageable ; and secondly, because he might fancy that the week of the pagan Theseus would be more appropriately represented by a lunar quarter than by a Jewish hebdomad.

" Chaucer sometimes makes the strangest jumble—mixing up together pagan matters and Christian, Roman and Grecian, ancient and modern ; so that, although he names Sunday and Monday as two of the days of the week in Athens, he does so evidently for the purpose of introducing the allocation of the hours, alluded to before, to which the planetary names of the days of the week were absolutely necessary. But in the fifty weeks appointed by Theseus, the very same love of a little display of erudition would lead

Chaucer to choose the hebdomas lunæ, or lunar quarter, which the Athenian youth were wont to mark out by the celebration of a feast to Apollo on every seventh day of the moon. But after the first twenty-eight days of every lunar month, the weekly reckoning must have been discontinued for about a day and a half (when the new moon was what was called 'in coitu,' or invisible), after which a new reckoning of sevens would recommence. Hence there could be but four hebdomades in each lunar month; and as there are about twelve and a half lunar months in a solar year, so must there have been fifty lunar weeks in one solar year."

l. 1015. The MS. reads *The joye that is mad in this place*. The MS. reads *made*, which, being a participle, should be *mad*. We ought perhaps to read,—

The joy / e that / y mad / is in / this place.

l. 1017. Lansd. MS. reads *manere* before *wight*.

l. 1020. *And thus / with goo / de hope / and her / te blithe.*

l. 1021. The original reading appears to have been,

They taken / here leve / and ho / me ward / they ryde.
Lansd. MS. reads *gan* before *they*.

l. 1032. *ful of degré*, full of steps (placed one above another, as in an amphitheatre).

l. 1071. *guldes*, a *gold* or turnsol. "*Goolde* herbe. Solsequium, quia sequitur solem, elitropium, calendula." The corn-marigold in the North is called *goulans*, *guilde*, or *goles*, and in the South, *golds*. Gower says that Leucothea was changed

" Into a floure was named *golde*,
   Which stont governed of the sonne." (Conf. Am.)

l. 1078. *Setheroun* = *Cithæron*, sacred to Venus.

l. 1083. *of yore agon*, of years gone by.

l. 1104. *flikeryng*, fluttering. The MS. reads *fleyng*, flying.

l. 1108. *kene*, sharp. The MS. reads *grene*.

l. 1121. *a swymbul in a swough*, a moaning (or sighing) in a general commotion (caused by the wind). Lansd. MS. reads *rombel* for *swymbul*.

l. 1122. We ought perhaps to read,—

As it were / a storm / e schul / de berst / en ev / ery bough.
Lansd. MS. *as thouhe a storm*, &c.

l. 1127. *a rage of suche a prise*, a rabble of so great a press. Perhaps we ought to read *and*, as in the Lansd. MS.

l. 1129. "I suppose the *northern light* is the aurora borealis, but this phenomenon is so rarely mentioned by mediæval writers, that it may be questioned whether Chaucer meant anything more than the faint and cold illumination received by reflexion through the door of an apartment fronting the north." (Marsh.)

l. 1131. Read *Thorough which / e men / mightè / no light / discerne*.
The has evidently been inserted by the transcriber. It is omitted in the Lansd. MS.

l. 1146. *chirkyng* is properly the cry of birds. The Lansd. MS. has a better reading, *schrikeinge* (shrieking).

l. 1149. This line contains an allusion to the death of Sisera, Judges iv.

l. 1154. Harl. MS. reads *The hunt[e] strangled with wilde boores corage.*

This reading is evidently corrupt, for the *boar* does not strangle (see l. 1160). The reading in the text is from Lansd. MS. 851.

l. 1159. *hoppesteres.* Speght explains this word by pilots (*gubernaculum tenentes*); Tyrwhitt, female dancers. *Hoppesteres* is in an apposition with *schippis* (ships).

l. 1162. *for al,* notwithstanding.

l. 1163. *infortune of Mart.* Tyrwhitt thinks that Chaucer might intend to be satirical in these lines: but the introduction of such apparently undignified incidents arose from the confusion already mentioned of the god of war with the planet to which his name was given, and the influence of which was supposed to produce all the disasters here mentioned. The following extract from the Compost of Ptholemeus gives some of the supposed effects of Mars. " Under Mars is borne theves and robbers that kepe hye wayes, and do hurte to true men, and nyght walkers, and quarell pykers, bosters, mockers, and skoffers, and these men of Mars causeth warre and murther, and batayle, they wyll be gladly *smythes* or workers of yron, lyght fyngred, and lyers, gret swerers of othes in vengeable wyse, and a great summyler and crafty. He is red and angry, with blacke heer, and lytell iyen ; he shall be a great walker, and a maker of swordes and knyves, and a sheder of mannes blode, and a fornycatour, and a speker of rybawdry . . . . and good to be a *barboure* and a blode letter, and to drawe tethe, and is peryllous of his handes." The following extract is from an old astrological book of the sixteenth century :—" Mars denoteth men with red faces and the skinne redde, the face round, the eyes yellow, horrible to behold, furious men, cruell, desperate, proude, sedicious, souldiers, captaines, *smythes*, colliers, bakers, alcumistes, armourers, furnishers, *butchers*, chirurgions, *barbers*, sargiants, and hangmen, according as they shal be well or evill disposed." (Wright.)

ll. 1171, 1172. *With / the schar / pe swerd / over / his heed*
      Hang / ynge by / a so / til twy / ne threed.
Apparently an allusion to the sword of Damocles.

l. 1198. *Calystopè = Calliste,* a daughter of Lycaon, King of Arcadia. See Ovid's Fasti, ii. 153.

l. 1204, 1205. *Dyane* or *Dane = Daphne.* See Ovid's Metamorph. i. 450.

l. 1207. *Atheon = Actæon.* See Ovid's Metamorph. iii. 138.

l. 1211. The *i* is silent in *ipeynted,* or *yit* is to be omitted.

l. 1212. *Atthalaunce = Atalanta.* See Ovid's Metamorph. x. 560.

l. 1216. *not drawe in to memory = not drawen to memory,* not call to mind. The Lansd. MS. omits *in.*

l. 1217. The MS. reads *by he seet,* as if for *by she seet;* but the correct reading is *byè seet. Hye* being an adverb has a final -e.

l. 1228. *thou mayst best,* art best able to help, thou hast most power.

l. 1234. *right.* Lansd. MS. has *wonder.*

l. 1237. *attournynge.* Lansd. MS. has *retournynge.*

l. 1262. Lansd. MS. reads *liht* (light) before *gypoun.*

l. 1267. This line seems to mean that there is nothing new under the sun.

l. 1276. *kempe heres,* shaggy, rough hairs. Tyrwhitt and subsequent editors have taken for granted that *kempe = kemped,* combed ; but *kempe* is rather the reverse of this, and, instead of smoothly combed, means bent.

curled, and hence rough, shaggy. In an early English poem it is said of Nebuchadnezzar that

> " Holghe (hollow) were his *yghen* anunder (under) *campe hores*."
>
> (Early Eng. Alliterative Poems, p. 88, l. 1695.)

Compe hores = shaggy hairs (about the eyebrows), and corresponds exactly in form and meaning to *kempe heres*.

l. 1284. *for old* = *for eld*, for age.

l. 1286. *for blak* is generally explained as *for blackness;* it may mean *very black.*

l. 1294. *colers of,* having collars of. Some MSS. read *colerd with.*

l. 1309. *bright cytryne.* The MS. reads *were cytryne.*

l. 1319. *delyt.* Lansd. MS. reads *deduyte.*

l. 1329. *alle and some,* all (individually) and collectively, one and all.

l. 1359. *and in hire houre.* I cannot better illustrate Chaucer's astrology than by a quotation from the old Kalendrier de Bergiers, edit. 1500, Sign. K. ii. b.:—" Qui veult savoir comme bergiers scevent quel planete regne chascune heure du jour et de la nuit, doit savoir la planete du jour qui veult s'enquerir; et la premiere heure temporelle du soleil levant ce jour est pour celluy planete, la seconde heure est pour la planete ensuivant, et la tierce pour l'autre," &c., in the following order: viz. Saturn, Jupiter, Mars, Sol, Venus, Mercury, Luna. To apply this doctrine to the present case: the first hour of the Sunday, reckoning from sunrise, belonged to the sun, the planet of the day; the second to Venus, the third to Mercury, &c., and continuing this method of allotment, we shall find that the twenty-second hour also belonged to the Sun, and the twenty-third to Venus; so that the hour of Venus really was, as Chaucer says, two hours before the sunrise of the following day.

Accordingly, we are told in l. 1413, that the third hour after Palamon set out for the temple of Venus, the Sun rose, and Emelie began to go to the temple of Diane. It is not said that this was the hour of Diane, or the Moon, but it really was; for, as we have just seen, the twenty-third hour of Sunday belonging to Venus, the twenty-fourth must be given to Mercury, and the first hour of Monday falls in course to the Moon, the presiding planet of that day.

After this Arcite is described as walking to the temple of Mars, l. 1509, *in the nexte houre of Mars*, that is, the *fourth* hour of the day. It is necessary to take these words together, for *the nexte houre*, singly, would signify the *second* hour of the day; but that, according to the rule of rotation mentioned above, belonged to Saturn, as the *third* did to Jupiter. The *fourth* was *the nexte houre of Mars* that occurred after the hour last named. (Tyrwhitt.)

l. 1366. *Adeoun*, Adonis.

l. 1380. I care not of arms (success in arms) to boast.

l. 1392. The Lansd. MS. reads,—

> Youre vertue is so grete in heven above,
> That if thou liste I shal wel have my love.

l. 1394. *wher I ryde or go,* whether I ride or walk.

l. 1395. *fyres beete*, to kindle or light fires. *Beete* also signifies to mend or make up the fire.

l. **1413**. *the thridde hour inequal.* In the astrological system, the day, from sunrise to sunset, and the night, from sunset to sunrise, being each divided into twelve hours, it is plain that the hours of the day and night were never equal except just at the equinoxes. The hours attributed to the planets were of this *unequal* sort. See Kalendrier de Berg. loc. cit., and our author's treatise on the Astrolobe. (Tyrwhitt.)

l. **1426**. From the Lansd. MS. it is probable that the original reading was as follows :—

> *But how / sche dide / hir right / I dar / nat telle.*

l. **1428**. *a game,* a pleasure.

l. **1436**. *in Stace of Thebes,* in the Thebaid of Statius.

l. **1442**. For *has* read *has[t].*

l. **1444**. *the vengans.* Lansd. MS. reads *thi venjance and thi ire.*

l. **1445**. *aboughte,* atoned for. Cp. the phrase ' to *buy* dearly.'

l. **1455**. *thre formes.* Diana is called *Diva Triformis ;*—in heaven, Luna; on earth, Diana and Lucina, and in hell, Proserpina.

l. **1507**. *the nexte waye,* the nearest way.

l. **1510**. *walkyd is,* has walked.

l. **1515**. *reynes.* Lansd. MS. has *regne.*

l. **1529**. *lyves creature,* creature alive, living creature.

l. **1539**. *do,* bring it about, cause it to come to pass.

l. **1553**. Lansd. MS. reads *Now lord,* &c.

l. **1561**. *swote.* The *-e* final represents an older *-ne.*

l. **1571**. As joyful as the bird is of the bright sun.

l. **1572**. Lansd. MS. reads *frissche* for *such.*

l. **1573**. *that;—thilke,* adopted by Tyrwhitt from Lansd. MS., is a better reading.

l. **1583**. Men may outrun old age but not outwit (surpass its counsel).

l. **1585**. *agayns his kynde.* According to the Compost of Ptholemeus Saturn was influential in producing strife : "And the children of the sayd Saturne shall be great jangeleres and chyders . . . . and they will never forgyve tyll they be revenged of theyr quarell."

l. **1589**. *more power.* The Compost of Ptholemeus says of Saturn, "He is myghty of hymself. . . . It is more than xxx yere or he may ronne his course. . . . Whan he doth reygne, there is moche debate."

l. **1601**.   *And my / ne ben / the ma / ladi / es colde.*
Tyrwhitt reads, *Min ben / also / the ma / ladi / es colde.*

l. **1604**.   *Now wep / no more / I shal do / my di / ligence.*
A better reading is obtained by omitting *my* with the Lansd. MS.

l. **1606**. *bihight.* The verb *hast* is to be understood before *bihight,* for if *bihight* were the 2nd pers. sing. pret. it would be written *bihighte.* Lansd. MS. reads *bihte.*

l. **1607**. *nevertheless. Natheles* = nevertheless is a better reading, and is adopted by Tyrwhitt. Lansd. MS. has *Mars schal helpe his knyht natheles.*

l. **1627**. *oostes.* Tyrwhitt reads *hostelries.* Lansd. MS. has *hostries.*

l. **1637**. *rayhyng.* Some MSS. read *naylyng.*

l. **1638**. *girdyng.* Some MSS. read *gideing,* others *gniding.* Tyrwhitt adopts *gniding,* rubbing.

l. **1675**. *schulde.* This gives us a syllable too many ; the original reading may have been *schul* or *schuln* (shall), the 3rd pl. present. Lansd. MS. reads *schal*.

l. 1680. Nor short sword having a *biting* (sharp) point for to stab with. Lansd. MS. has *with pointe*, &c.

l. 1731. Lansd. MS. reads *was* before *lowde*.

l. 1734. Lansd. MS. reads *now ryngen tompes loude*, &c.

l. 1736. In go the spears full firmly into the *rest ;*—a sort of holster attached to the stirrup, in which the butt end of the lance was placed, to keep it steady.

l. 1739. *schuldres.* Lansd. MS. has *scheldes* (shields).

l. 1749. *foot.* Tyrwhitt proposes to read *foo*, foe, enemy.

l. 1758. *wrought . . . woo*, done harm.

l. 1760. *Galgopleye.* This word is variously written *Colaphey, Galgaphey, Galapey.* There was a town called *Galapha* in Mauritania Tingitana, upon the river Malva (Cellar. Geog. Ant. vii. p. 935), which perhaps may have given name to the vale here meant. (Tyrwhitt.)

l. 1774. A better reading is furnished by the Lansd. MS.,—
> *And made his swerd depe in his flesche bite.*

l. 1807. Lansd. MS. reads, *Ben in here wele for joye of daun Arcite.*

l. 1809. *which*, what, how great.

l. 1810. Lansd. MS. reads, *This fers Arcite hath of his helm ydon.*

l. 1815. *as for to speke.* Lansd. MS. reads *as to speken.*

l. 1817. Lansd. MS. reads, *And was al his chere as in his herte.* Tyrwhitt inserts *in* before *chere*, but upon no good authority. *Alle his cheer[e]* may mean ' altogether his, in countenance, as she was really so in his heart.'

l. 1830. Then was he cut out of his armour.

l. 1832. *in memory*, conscious.

l. 1839. *schulde.* Lansd. MS. has *schal.*

l. 1845. As a remedy *for* (to) other wounds, &c.

ll. 1846, 1847. *charmes . . . save.* It may be observed that the salves, charms, and pharmacies of herbs were the principal remedies of the physician in the age of Chaucer. *save* (*salvia*, the herb sage) was considered one of the most universally efficient mediæval remedies (Wright); whence the proverb of the school of Salerno,—
> " Cur moriatur homo,
> Dum salvia crescit in horto ? "

l. 1859. *a person*, one person.

l. 1860. *baried.* The MS. reads *rent.*

l. 1870. *dayes thre.* Wright says the period of three days was the usual duration of a feast among our early forefathers. As far back as the seventh century, when Wilfred consecrated his church at Ripon, he held " magnum convivium trium dierum et noctium reges cum omni populo bætificantes." (Eddius, Vit. S. Wilf. c. 17.)

l. 1893. *this al and som*, one and all *said* this—that Arcite must die. Some editors explain the phrase as *this* (is) *the al and som*, i. e. this is the short and long of it.

l. 1931. *herte.* Lansd. MS. has *fete.*

l. 1932. *overcome.* Tyrwhitt reads *overnome*, overtaken, the pp. of *overnimen.*

l. 1941. *was.* Lansd. MS. has *house.*

l. 1947. *ther Mars,* &c., O that Mars would, &c., may Mars. Lansd. MS. has *lat.* for *ther.*

l. 1954. *such sorwe,* so great sorrow. Lansd. MS. has *han* for *have.*

l. 2017. And surpassing others in weeping came Emely.

l. 2048. *of brede.* Lansd. MS. reads *on brede* = in breadth.

l. 2060. *Amadryes* is a corruption of *Hamadryades.*

l. 2085. *an heih schoutyng.* Lansd. MS. reads *a bowe scheteinge* (shooting).

l. 2094. *in no disjoynt,* with no disadvantage.

l. 2123. *that fayre cheyne of love.* This sentiment is taken from Boethius, lib. ii. met. 8 :—

> " Hanc rerum seriem ligat,
> Terras ac pelagus regens,
> Et cælo imperitans, amor."

What follows is taken from lib. iv. pr. 6.

l. 2148. *se at ye,* see at a glance.

l. 2166. *see.* Lansd. MS. reads *sei,* say.

l. 2205. *her* is omitted in the Lansd. MS.

l. 2221. *aughte passe right,* should surpass mere equity or justice.

THE NONNE PREST HIS TALE.

l. 1. *stope.* Lansd. MS. reads *stoupe,* as if it signified bent, *stooped.* It is, however, the past participle of the verb *steppen,* to step, advance.

l. 2. *pore.* Lansd. MS. reads *narwe,* narrow.

l. 5. *syn.* Lansd. MS. reads *seththen,* since.

l. 8. *for housbondry,* by economy. Lansd. MS. reads *be* instead of *for.*

l. 9. *doughtres.* Lansd. MS. reads *douhtren.*

l. 12. *Ful sooty was hir bour, and eek hir halle.* The widow's house consisted of only two apartments, designated by the terms bower and hall. Whilst the widow and her ' daughters two ' slept in the bower, chanticleer and his seven wives roosted on a perch in the hall, and the swine ensconced themselves on the floor. The smoke of the fire had to find its way through the crevices of the roof. (See Our English Home, pp. 139, 140.)

l. 19. *hertes suffisaunce,* a satisfied or contented mind; literally heart's satisfaction. Cp. our phrase ' to your heart's content.'

l. 22. *wyn . . . whit nor need.* The white wine was sometimes called ' the wine of Ossey;' the red wine of Gascony, sometimes called ' Mountrose,' was deemed a liquor for a lord. (See Our English Home, p. 83.)

l. 25. *saynd bacoun,* singed or broiled bacon.

an ey or tweye, an egg or two.

l. 26. *deye.* The *daia* is mentioned in Domesday among assistants in husbandry; and the term is again found in 2nd Stat. 25 Edw. III (A.D. 1351). In Stat. 37 Edw. III (A.D. 1363), the *deye* is mentioned among others of a certain rank, not having goods or chattels of 40s. value. The *deye* was mostly a female, whose duty was to make butter and cheese, attend to the calves and poultry, and other odds and ends of the farm. The *dairy* (in some parts of England, as in Shropshire, called a *dey*-house) was the department assigned to her.

l. 31. *orgon.* This is put for *orgons* or *organs.* It is plain, from *goon* in the next line, that Chaucer meant to use this word as a plural from the Lat. *organa.*

l. 40. *and batayld.* Lansd. MS. reads *embateled*, indented like a battlement.

l. 41. *as the geet*, like the jet. Beads used for the repetition of prayers were frequently formed of *jet.*

l. 50. *damysel Pertilote.* Cp. our 'Dame Partlet.'

l. 54. *in bold*, in possession.

l. 55. *loken in every lith*, locked in every limb.

l. 59. *my lief is faren on londe*, my beloved is gone away. Probably the refrain of a popular song of the time.

l. 64. *the balle.* The MS. reads *his balle.*

l. 65. *his fair.* MS. reads *this faire.*

l. 69. *herte deere.* This expression corresponds to ' dear heart,' or ' deary heart,' which still survives in some parts of the country.

l. 73. *take it agreef = take it in grief*, i. e. to take it amiss, to be offended.

l. 74. *me mette*, I dreamed ; literally *it dreamed to me.*

l. 76. *my sweven rede aright*, bring my dream to a good issue ; literally ' interpret my dream favourably.'

l. 80. *was lik.* The relative *that* is often omitted by Chaucer before a relative clause.

l. 82. *yolow.* Lansd. MS. reads *white.*

l. 94. *riche.* Lansd. MS. reads *wise.*

l. 104. *fume*, the effects arising from drunkenness.

l. 108. *colera.* Lansd. MS. reads *coloures.*

l. 111. *that thai*, &c. Lansd. MS. reads *that willen hem bite.*

l. 118. That cause many a man in sleep to be very distressed.

l. 120. *Catoun.* Cato de Moribus, l. ii. dist. 32 ; *somnia ne cures.* " I observe by the way, that this distich is quoted by John of Salisbury, Polycrat. l. ii. c. 16, as a precept *viri sapientis.* In another place, l. vii. c. 9, he introduces his quotation of the first verse of dist. 20 (l. iii.) in this manner :— ' *Ait vel Cato vel alius*, nam autor incertus est.'" (Tyrwhitt.)

l. 121. *do no force of* = take no notice of.

l. 144. *elder bery.* Lansd. MS. reads *elobore.*

l. 146. *that groweth*, &c. Lansd. MS. reads *groinge in owre gardine that mery is.*

l. 149. Lansd. MS. reads *yowe* (you) before *no.*

l. 150. *graunt mercy;* this in later authors is corrupted into *grammercy.*

l. 156. *so mot I the*, so may I thrive (or prosper).

l. 162. Lansd. MS. reads, *The nedeth nouht to make of this none argument.*

l. 164. *oon of the grettest auctours.* Cicero, De Divin. l. i. c. 27, relates this and the following story, but in a different order, and with so many other differences, that one might be led to suspect that he was here quoted at second-hand, if it were not usual with Chaucer, in these stories of familiar life, to throw in a number of natural circumstances, not to be found in his original authors. (Tyrwhitt.)

l. 165. *wente.* Lansd. MS. reads *yede.*

l. 166. *good entente.* Lansd. MS. reads *grete nede.*

l. 171. Lansd. MS. omits *that,* to the improvement of the metre.

l. 173. *depart.* Lansd. MS. reads *departen of.* The original reading was probably *departen compaignye* = part company, separate. Tyrwhitt has *departen compaignie.*

l. 182. *in his bed, there as he lay.* Lansd. MS. reads *in his bedde, there he ley.* In the latter reading *bedde* is the dative, and is to be pronounced as a dissyllable. This may have been the original reading, for it often happens that the scribe of the Harl. MS. omits the final *-e* of the dative, and to render the line metrically complete adds an additional word.

l. 184. *oxe stalle. Oxe* is here a dissyllable. It is not quite certain that *oxe stalle* is a compound = *ox-stall;* it seems rather to be for the older English *oxan stalle,* the stall of an ox—*oxe* standing for *oxen* (as in *Oxenford,* note on l. 287, p. 10), of an ox.

l. 190. *took of this no keep,* took no heed of this, paid no attention to it.

l. 198. Lansd. MS. reads *ful* before *of.*

l. 201. *soth to sayn,* to say (tell) the truth.

l: 212. *grete.* This is the reading of the Lansd. MS. 851. Harl. MS. reads *a.*

l. 216. Lansd. MS. reads, *A donge cart as he went to donge the londe.* The correct reading is probably as follows :—*A dong cart as it went to donge lond.*

l. 222. *gapeinge.* This is taken from the Lansd. MS. 851. The Harl. copy reads *heer;* but the phrase *gapyng upright* occurs elsewhere (see Knightes Tale, l. 1150), and signifies lying flat on the back with the mouth open.

l. 225. *harrow,* a cry of distress ; a cry for help.

l. 231. *alday.* Lansd. MS. reads *alweie* = always.

l. 232. *certes,* &c. Lansd. MS. reads *that se we daie bi daie.*

it is no nay, there is no denial (to this assertion) ; it is beyond contradiction.

l. 235. *wile.* Harl. MS. reads *wold[e].*

l. 240. *so sore engyned.* Lansd. MS. reads *so ferre engyned.*

l. 257. Harl. MS. reads *his slepyng;* but *his* is omitted by the Lansd. MS. 851.

l. 264. *And pray / de him / his vi / agè / to lette,* And prayed him to abandon his journey.

l. 265. *to abyde.* This was pronounced (and often written) *tabyde* (to postpone).

l. 269. *my thinges,* my business matters.

l. 272. *al day.* Lansd. MS. reads *alweie.*

l. 274. Lansd. MS. reads, *Men dremen of thinge that never was ne schal.*

l. 290. Kenelm succeeded his father Kenulph on the throne of the Mercians in 821, at the age of seven years, and was murdered by order of his aunt, Quenedreda. He was subsequently made a saint, and his legend will be found in Capgrave, or in the Golden Legend. (Wright.)

l. 297. *for traisoun,* i. e. *fro traisoun,* from treason.

l. 304. *Cipioun.* The Somnium Scipionis of Macrobius was a favourite work during the middle ages.

l. 308. Lansd. MS. omits *in,* to the improvement of the metre.

l. 321. *lo hir Andromacha.* Andromache's dream is not to be found in Homer. It is related in the 24th chapter of Dares Phrygius, the authority for the history of the Trojan war most popular in the middle ages. (Tyrwhitt.)

l. 331. *as for conclusioun,* in conclusion.

l. 334. *telle . . . no store,* set no store by them; reckon them of no value; count them as useless.

l. 335. *riht.* Harl. MS. reads *it.*

l. 336. *never a del,* never a whit, not in the slightest degree.

l. 341. *hiew,* for *hiewed,* coloured. Lansd. MS. reads *red.*

ll. 343–346. By way of quiet retaliation for 'Partlet's sarcasm, he cites a Latin proverbial saying, in l. 344, 'Mulier est hominis confusio,' which he turns into a pretended compliment by the false translation in ll. 345, 346. (Marsh.)

l. 352. *lay,* for *that lay.* Chaucer frequently omits the relative. We ought to read,—

For he / found had / a corn / lay in / the yerd.
Had before a consonant would be written *haddè.*

l. 363. We ought perhaps to read,—

That high / te March / whan God / first ma / de man.

l. 370. *twenty.* Lansd. MS. reads *thretté.* " The reading of the greatest part of the MSS. is *fourty degrees.* But this is evidently wrong, for Chaucer is speaking of the altitude of the sun at or about prime, i. e. six o'clock a.m. When the sun is in 22° Taurus he is 21° high—about three-quarters after six a.m. (Tyrwhitt.)

l. 380. *is wo.* Lansd. MS. 851 reads *sone ago.*

l. 381. Lansd. MS. 851 reads, *And comunly oft time it falleth so.*

l. 390. *cole-fox,* a treacherous fox. Tyrwhitt quotes Heywood for *cole-prophets* and *colepoysoun.* See Glossary for the explanation of the prefix *cole.*

ful sleigh of. Lansd. MS. 851 reads *ful of sleihte and.*

l. 393. *thurgh.* Lansd. MS. 851 reads *oute* after *thurgh;* but the line is metrical enough without this addition.

The sa / me nigh / te thurgh / the heg / ge brast.

l. 400. *lyn.* Lansd. MS. reads *ligge.*

l. 401. *lurkyng.* Lansd. MS. reads *roukeing,* i. e. lying huddled up.

l. 409. Some MSS. read *mot* (= must), which improves the metre.

l. 413. *desputesoun.* Lansd. MS. reads *disputacioun.*

l. 415. *bult it to the bren,* sift the matter; cp. the phrase *to boult the bran.*

l. 419. *for* was probably inserted by the scribe, who did not know that *needely* was a word of three syllables. See l. 420, where it is properly written.

l. 430. We ought perhaps to read,—

That had / de met / the dre / me that / I tolde.

l. 441. Lansd. MS. reads *no woman.*

l. 446. *Phisiologus.* He alludes to a book in Latin metre, entitled

Physiologus de Naturis xii. Animalium, by one Theobaldus, whose age is not known.　The chapter *De Sirenis* begins thus :—

> " Sirenæ sunt monstra maris resonantia magnis,
> Vocibus et modulis cantus formantia multis,
> Ad quas incaute veniunt sæpissime nautæ,
> Quæ faciunt sompnum nimia dulcedine vocum." (Tyrwhitt.)

　　sicurly.　Lansd. MS. reads *witterly* (indeed, truly).

　l. 455. *if.*　Lansd. MS. reads *whan.*

　l. 456. Lansd. MS. 851 reads, *Theihe he nevere hadde seen it erst with his ye.*

　l. 457. *him.*　Lansd. MS. 851 reads *him;* the Harl. MS. has *it.*

　l. 459. *why wol ye goon.*　Lansd MS. 851 reads *what wille ye done.*

　ll. 461, 462. Lansd. MS. reads,—

> *Certes sire that bien ye unhende* (uncivil)
> *If I to yowe wolde harme or velonye.*

　l. 472. *house* is here the dative ; the nominative is *hous.*

　l. 478. *of hert,* from his heart.

　l. 480. *hothe* is probably an addition by the writer of the MS., and should be omitted, the line would then read thus :—

> *He wol / de so / peyne him / that with / his yen.*

　l. 481. *wolde.*　Lansd. MS. reads *dide.*

　l. 487. *daun Burnel thasse* (= the asse).　The story alluded to is in a poem of Nigellus Wireker, entitled Burnellus seu Speculum Stultorum, written in the time of Richard l.　In the Chester Whitsun Playes, *Burnell* is used as a nickname for an ass.　The original was probably *brunell*, from its *brown* colour ; as the *fox* below is called *Russel*, from its *red* colour. (Tyrwhitt.)

　l. 501. *hous.*　Lansd. MS. reads *courte.*

　l. 510. *garget.*　Lansd. MS. reads *gorge.*

　l. 511. Lansd. MS. reads *bakke*, which, grammatically, is more correct than *bak.*

　l. 512. *that* is omitted in the Lansd. MS.

　l. 522. *O Gaufred.*　He alludes to a passage in the Nova Poetria of Geoffrey de Vinsauf, published not long after the death of Richard l.　In this work the author has not only given instructions for composing in the different styles of poetry, but also examples.　His specimen of the plaintive style begins thus :—

> " Neustria, sub clypeo regis defensa Ricardi,
> Indefensa modo, gestu testare dolorem;
> Exundent oculi lacrymas; exterminet ora
> Pallor; connodet digitos tortura; cruentet
> Interiora dolor, et verberet æthera clamor;
> Tota peris ex morte sua.　Mors non fuit ejus,
> Sed tua, non una, sed publica mortis origo.
> *O veneris lacrymosa* dies! O sydus amarum l
> Illa dies tua nox fuit, et Venus illa venenum
> Illa dedit vulnus," &c.

These lines are sufficient to show the object and the propriety of Chaucer's ridicule.　The whole poem is printed in Leyser's Hist. Po. Med. Ævi, pp. 862-978. (Tyrwhitt.)

l. 527. *sotbly*. Lansd. MS. reads *schortly* (suddenly).

l. 542. *unto*. Lansd. MS. reads *into*.

l. 547. *losten*, &c. Lansd. MS. reads *scholde lese here lyves*.

l. 549. *matier*. Lansd. MS. reads *tale*.

l. 550. *the*. Lansd. MS. reads *this*.

l. 553. *sayden* is probably an error for *sayen* (saw). Lansd. MS. reads *sawe*.

  woode. Lansd. MS. reads *grove*, and omits *is*. The meaning of the line is, ' They saw the fox go toward the wood.'

l. 561. Lansd. MS. reads, *Sore aferde for berkeinge of the dogges*.

l. 573. *hornes*. Lansd. MS. reads *beemes* (trumpets).

l. 575. *howpede*. Lansd. MS. reads *schowted*.

l. 581. *fox he*. Lansd. MS. omits *he*. The original reading may have been *the foxe*.

l. 584. *cherles*. Lansd. MS. reads *clerkes*.

l. 586. *woodes syde*. Lansd. MS. has the older form, *wode side*.

l. 598. Lansd. MS. reads *noubt* after *it*.

l. 603. *any*. Lansd. MS. properly omits this word.

   If thou / bi gi / le me / ofter / than oones.

l. 604. *thurgh*. Lansd. MS. has *with*.

l. 614. MS. reads *or of an hen*. Lansd. MS. reads *and a kok and of an hen*, instead of *or of a cok*, &c.

l. 615. *therof* is omitted in the Lansd. MS.

l. 621. Lansd. MS. reads *hihe* (high) before *blisse*.

GLOSSARY.

A.

A, one, single. A.S. *an*, Ger. *ein*, one; Eng. indef. article *an* or *a*. Cp. O.E. *o*, *oo*, one; *ta*, *to*, the one, the first.

A, in, on; cp. *a-night*, *a-morwe*; *a Goddus name*, in God's name; cp. Mod. Eng. *a-foot*, *afraid*, *a-hunting*, *a-building*, &c. A.S. and O.S. *an*, in, on. It is still used in the South of England.

Abbay, abbey.

Abide, Abiden, Abyde (pret. *abod, abood*; p.p. *abiden, abyden*), abide, delay, wait for, await. A.S. *abidan*, *bidan*, to wait, remain; Goth. *beidan*, to expect.

Able, fit, capable, adapted. Lat. *babilis* (Lat. *babeo*, to have), convenient, fit; O. Fr. *babile*, able, expert, fit.

Aboad, delay. See **Abide**.

Aboughte (the pret. of *abegge* or *abye*), atoned for, suffered for. A.S. *abicgan*, to redeem, pay the purchase-money, to pay the penalty (from *bycgan*, to buy). Cp. the modern expression ' to buy it dear.' Shakespeare and Milton have, from similarity of sound, given the sense of *abye* to the verb *abide*, as in the following examples:—

" If it be found so, some will dear *abide* it." (Julius Cæsar.)
" Disparage not the faith thou dost not know,
Lest to thy peril thou *abide* it dear." (Mids. Night's Dream.)
" How dearly I *abide* that boast so vain." (Paradise Lost.)

Aboven, above. A.S. *abufan*, *beufan*, *ufan*; Du. *boven*. Cp. O.E. forms, *buve*, *buven*, *aboon*, above.

Abrayde, Abreyde, started (suddenly), awoke. A.S. *brægdan*, to move, turn, weave; O.N. *bragða*, to draw out a sword, to pull down, to awake, to leap. The O.E. *braide* has all these meanings, and signifies also to cry out suddenly, to scold; whence Eng. *braid*, *upbraid*. The A.S. *brægd*, *bregd*, O.N. *bragð*, signifies a sudden start, blow, deceit; hence the O.E. phrase ' at a braid,' = in a trice. The Icel. *bragð* is also applied to the features, to the gestures, by which an individual is characterized; hence Prov. Eng. *braid*, to resemble, pretend; Eng. *braid*, appearance (Bailey). Shakespeare uses *braid* = of deceitful manner.

Abregge, to shorten, *abridge*. Fr. *a-bréger*; Lat. *abbreviare*. Cp. *allay*, O.E. *allegge*, from Fr. *alléger* (from Lat. *levis*) ; O. E. *agregge*, *agredge*, to aggravate, from Fr. *aggréger* (from Lat. *gravis*).

Acate, purchase. O. Fr. *achepter*, to buy; Fr. *acheter*, It. *accattare*, to acquire, get ; Mid. Lat. *accapitare* (Lat. *ad-captare*). Cp. O. E. *acates*, cates, victuals, provision, delicacies ; *catery*, store-room; Eng. *cater*. Fr. *achat*, purchase.

Accomplice, to accomplish.

Accordant, Acordant, according to, agreeing, suitable.

Accorde, Acord, agreement, decision.

Accorde, Acorde, to agree, suit, decide. Fr. *accorder*, to agree (from Lat. *cor*, the heart).

Achatour, purchaser, caterer. See **Acate**.

Acorded, agreed.

Acqueyntaunce, acquaintance.

Ademauntz, adamant. Gr. *à-δά-μas* (*a* privative, *δαμάω*, to tame, subdue), the hardest metal, probably steel (also the diamond); whence Eng. *adamantine*. "In *adamantine* chains and penal fire." (Milton, Par. Lost, l. 48.)

Adown, down, downwards, below. A.S. *of-dune*, *a-dun* (cp. O. Fr. *à val*, to the valley, downwards), from the hill, downwards; from *dun*, a hill, down.

Adrad, in dread, afraid. For the force of the prefix *a-* see **A = in**, **on**.

Adventure, Aventure, chance, luck, misfortune. O. Fr. *advenir* (Lat. *advenire*), to happen; whence Eng. *peradventure*.

Aferd, Afered, Afferd, in fear, afraid. O. E. *ferd*, *ferdnesse*, fear.

Affeccioun, affection, hope.

Affermed, confirmed.

Affrayed, terrified, scared. Fr. *effrayer*, scare, appal; *effroi*, terror: whence *fray* and *affray*.

Affyle, to file, polish. Fr. *affiler*, It. *affilare*, to sharpen; Fr. *fil*, edge; Lat. *filum*, a thread.

Afright, in fright, afraid. A.S. *forht*, Ger. *furcht*, fear; Goth. *faurhts*, timid.

Again, Agayn, Ageyn, again, against, towards. A.S. *on-gean*, *on-gen*, *a-gen*, opposite, towards, against ; *gean*, opposite, against ; O. Sw. *gen*, opposite ; Ger. *gegen*, against.

Agast, terrified, *aghast*. Cp. O. E. *gastlic*, ghastly, *gastnes*, fear ; A.S. *gæstan*, Goth. *us-geisnian*, *us-gaisnian*, to frighten, terrify; Dan. *gys*, terror.

Ago, Agon, Agoo, Agoon, gone, past ; the past participle of O. E. verb *agon*, to go, pass away. A.S. *agan*, *agangan*. We also meet with *ygo* in the same sense, and some etymologists have erroneously supposed that the prefix *a-* is a corruption of *y-*.

Agreef, in grief. 'To take *agrief*' = to take it amiss, feel aggrieved, be displeased.

Al, all, whole (cp. *al a* = a whole); quite, wholly (cp. *al redy*, *al armed*, &c.) ; although (cp. *al speke he*, *al have I*, *al be it*).

Alauntz (or **Alauns**), a species of dog. They were used for hunting the boar. Sp. *alano*. Tyrwhitt says they were much esteemed in Italy in the fourteenth century. *Gualv. de la Flamma* (ap. Murator. Antiq. Med. Æ. t. ii. p. 394), commends the governors of Milan, "*quod equos emissarios equabus magnis commiscuerunt*, et *procreati* sunt *in nostro territorio* DESTRARII *nobiles, qui in magno pretio ha-bentur*. Item CANES ALANOS altæ *staturæ* et *mirabilis fortitudinis nutrire studuerunt*."

Alder, Alther, Althur, Aller, of all (gen. pl. of *al*). The older forms are *alra*, *alre*, *aller*; *oure* *althur*, of us all; *here aller*, of them all; *youre alther*, of them all; *alther-best*, best of all, &c. The insertion of *d* serves merely to strengthen the word, as in *lend*, *spend* (older forms *lene*, *spene*).

Ale-stake, a stake set up before an ale-house by way of sign; "*le moy d'une taverne*" (Palsgrave). It appears that a *bush* was often placed at the top of the ale-stake.

Algate, always. O.E. *algates*, *swagate*, thus; North Prov. Eng. *gates*, way; Eng. *gait*; Icel. *gata*, a path; Sw. *gata*, way, street.

Alighte (p.p. *alight*), alighted. Cp. the phrase 'to *light* upon.' A.S. *alihtan*, to descend, alight.

Aller. See Alder.

Alliaunce, alliance. Fr. *allier*, to ally; Lat. *ligare*, to tie; *alligare*, to write.

Als, Also, as. A.S. *alswa*; O.E. *al-se*, *ase*. These forms shew that *as* is a contraction from *all-so*. Cp. Ger. *also*, *als*; O.Fris. *alsa*, *alse*, *æsa*, *ase*.

Alther, Althur. See Alder.

Amblere, a nag.

Amiddes, amidst, in the middle.

Amorwe, on the morrow.

Amounte, to amount, signify, denote.

And = *an*, if.

Anhange, Anhonge, to hang up; p.p. *anhanged*, *anhonged*. The prefix *an* = on, up.

Anlas (or Anelace), a kind of knife or dagger, usually worn at the girdle.

Anoon, *in one* (instant), anon. O.E. *an an*.

Anoynt, anointed.

Apayd, Apayed, pleased, satisfied. Fr. *payer*, to satisfy, pay (Lat. *pacare*); whence O.E. *pay*, satisfaction, gratification, pleasure; Eng. *pay*.

Ape, metaphorically, a fool.

Apotecaries, apothecaries.

Appalled, become weak, feeble, dead; not, as Tyrwhitt thinks, made *pale*. Chaucer speaks of "an old *appalled* wight," i. e. a man enfeebled through old age. It is connected with *pall*. Welsh *paller*, to fail; *pall*, loss of energy, failure.

Apparailyng, preparation. Fr. *appareiller*, to fit, suit; *pareil*, like; Lat. *par*, equal, like. The original meaning of *appareiller* is to join like to like.

Appetyt, desire, appetite.

Aray, Array, state, situation, dress, equipage.

Araye, Arraye, to set in order, dress, adorn, equip. It. *arredare*, to prepare, get ready; O.Fr. *arroyer*, *arréer*, dispose, fit out. The root is to be found in the Teutonic dialects. Cp. Sw. *reda*, to prepare; *reda*, order; A.S. *ræd*; Ger. *bereit*, ready; Dan. *rede*, plain, straight, clear.

Arest, the support for the spear. It is sometimes written *rest*.

Aretted, ascribed, imputed, deemed. According to Cowell a person is *aretted* "that is covenanted before a judge, and charged with a crime." O.E. *rette*, to impute; O.N. *retta*. The A.S. *aretan*, signifies to correct, set right.

Arive, arrival, or perhaps disembarkation (of troops). Fr. *arriver*, to arrive, from Lat. *ad ripare*, to come to shore (*ripa* shore).

Arm-gret, as thick as a man's arm.

Armypotent, mighty in arms.

Arrerage, arrears.

Arreste, seizure, custody.

Arresten, to stop, seize. Fr. *arrester* (from Lat. *restare*, to stand still), to bring one to stand, to seize his person.

Arsmetrike, arithmetic.

Arwe, arrow. A.S. *arewa*; Icel.

ŏr (gen. *aurva*); Sw. *burra*, to whirl.

Aschen, Asschen, ashes.

Asegid, besieged. Fr. *siège;* It. *sedia, seggia,* a seat or sitting; *assedio* = Lat. *obsidium,* the sitting down before a town in a hostile way.

Aslake, to moderate, appease. O.N. *slak,* loose; Norse *slekkja,* to make slack, to *slake,* quench; *slokna,* to go out, faint; O.E. *sloke.* With this root we must connect A.S. *slacian,* relax, *slack; sleac,* slack; also *slack-*lime, *slag* of a furnace.

As-nouthe, at present. Cp. O.E. *as-swiðe,* immediately; *as-now, als-tite,* at once. *nouðe* = A.S. *nu* (now) and *ða* (then).

Aspye, to see, perceive, discover, spy. Fr. *espier;* It. *spiare.*

Assaut, assault. Fr. *assaillir,* to assail; *saillir,* to leap, *sally;* Lat. *salire,* to leap, spring.

Assise, assize. Fr. *assire,* to set (Lat. *assidere*); *assis,* set, seated; *assise,* a settled tax; *cour d'assize,* a court held on a set day. Cp. It. *assisa,* a settled pattern of dress; Eng. *size.*

Assoillyng, absolution, acquittal. O. Fr. *assoiller,* Lat. *absolvere,* to loose from.

Assuren, to make sure, confirm.

Astat, Astaat, estate, rank.

Astoneyd, astonished. Fr. *estonnir,* to astonish, amaze (Lat. *attonare,* to thunder at, stun); O.E. *stonnie,* to benumb or dull the sense; Ger. *erstaunen.*

Asur, azure.

Athamaunte, adamant.

Atrede, to surpass in counsel, out-wit; *at-* = A.S. *æt,* of, from, out. We have a remnant of this prefix in *t-wit* = O.E. *at-witen,* to reproach. For the second element see Rede.

At-renne, out-run. See Renne.

Atte, at the. O.E. *at-tham, at-than.*

Cp. *atte beste,* in the best manner, *atte laste,* at the last.

Attempre, adj. temperate, moderate.

Atteyne, to attain. Fr. *attaindre* (Lat. *tangere,* to touch, *attingere,* to reach to).

Attournynge, returning. See note on Knightes Tale, p. 144, l. 1237.

Auctorite, authority; a text of Scripture, or some respectable writer.

Auctours, authors, writers of credit.

Aughte, vb. ought.

Auter, altar.

Avantage, advantage. See Avaunce.

Avaunce, to be of advantage, be profitable. Fr. *avancer,* to push forward, *avant;* It. *avante,* before, forwards. Lat. *ab ante.*

Avaunt, to boast, *vaunt.*

Avaunter, boaster.

Aventure, adventure.

Avis, Avys, advice, consideration, opinion. O. Fr. *advis,* It. *avviso,* view, opinion, settlement; Lat. *visum,* from *videri.*

Avisioun, Avysoun, vision.

Avow, vow, promise.

Awayt, watch. This is connected with *wake.* A.S. *wæcan,* Goth. *wakan,* O.N. *vaka,* vigilant; Eng. *watch, waits,* to *await.*

Awe, fear, dread. A.S. *ege,* O.E. *eie,* Dan. *ave,* correction, fear; Icel. *agi,* discipline; Goth. *ogan,* to fear.

Axe, to ask. A.S. *acsian.*

Axyng, asking, petition.

Ay, ever, aye.

Ayein, Ayeins, Ayens, again, back, against, towards.

Ayel, a grandfather. Fr. *aïeul.*

B.

Baar, bore, carried. See Bere.

Bacheler, Bachiller, an unmarried man, *bachelor,* a knight. Welsh *bachgen*, a boy, from *bach*, little, *geni*, to be born; whence O. Fr. *bacelle, bacelote, bachellette*, a servant, apprentice; *bacelerie*, youth; *bachelage*, apprenticeship, art and study of chivalry; *bachelier*, a young man, an aspirant to knighthood.

Bacoun, bacon. O. Fr. *bacon*, O. Du. *backe*, a pig.

Bak, back.

Bake = *baken*, baked. This verb now belongs to the *weak* or regular conjugation.

Ballid, Ballyd, bald. The original meaning seems to have been (1) shining, (2) white (as in *bald*-faced stag). O.E. *bal*, a blaze; A.S. *bæl*, Icel. *bâl*, blaze, fire.

Balliff, bailiff. O.E. *baili*. "He is my ryve [= reeve] and *bayly*, Inquilinus prediorum urbicorum et rusticorum." (Horman.) Fr. *baille*, It. *balivo, bailo*, from Low Lat. *bajulus*, a bearer, with the later meanings of (1) a nurse (2) a tutor. From Fr. *bailler* (Lat. *bajulare*), to hand over, comes Eng. *bail*. In the Wicliffite versions, *baili* seems to imply the charge or office: "ȝelde rekenyng of the *baili*, for thou might not now be *baylyf*." Luc. xvi.

Bane, destruction, death. A.S. *bana, bona*, O. H. Ger. *bana*, Fris. *bona*, O.N. *bani*, destruction, a violent death, *bane*; Goth. *banja*, a blow; Icel. *bana*, to slay. It is perhaps connected with Eng. *bang*, Icel. *banga*, to strike. The O.E. *bane* sometimes signifies poison, whence *hen-bane, fly-bane*.

Baner, Banere, a banner. Mid. Lat. *banera, bannerium*; Fr. *bannière*; It. *bandiera*. Mr. Wedgwood suggests the Goth. *bandvo*, a sign or token, as the root, which is connected with Eng. *bend*, Icel. *benda*, to bend, beckon, *banda*, to make signs.

Bar, bore, conducted.

Barbour, a barber. Fr. *barbier*, from Lat. *barba*, the beard.

Bare, open, plain. See **Bere**.

Bareyn, Bareyne, barren. O. Fr. *baraigne, brebaigne*. The root, *breb*, is perhaps connected with Du. *braeck*, sterile.

Baronage, an assembly of barons. It. *barone*; Sp. *varon*; O. Fr. *ber*; Fr. *baron*. Originally ⸲man, husband. "Le *bar* non es creat per la femna mas la femna per le *barô* "—' The man was not created for the woman, but the woman for the man.' In our own law it was used for married men; *baron* and *femine*, man and wife. The root perhaps is identical with the Lat. *vir*. (Wedgwood.)

Barre, bar or bolt of a door. O. Fr. *barre*, Mid Lat. *barra*, M. H. Ger. *barre*, a beam or long pole of wood. *Barricade* and *barrier* are formed direct from the Fr. *barre*. The A.S. *sparran*, Ger. *sperren*, to bar, bolt; Sw. *sparre*, a bar, Eng. *spar*, are sibillated forms of the root *bar* or *par*, which may be referred to O.N. *barr*, a tree.

Barres, ornaments of a girdle. See note on l. 331 of Prol. p. 127.

Batail, Bataile, Bataille, Batayl, Batayle, battle. Fr. *bataille*, a battle; it also signifies, like O.E. *bataille*, a squadron, an armed host, a *battalion*. It. *battere*; Fr. *battre*, to beat. With the root *bat* are connected *battery, batter*.

Batayld, embattled. Fr. *batillé, bastillé*, built as a bastille or fortress, furnished with turrets.

Bathe, both. A.S. *begen, ba*; Goth. *bai, baioths*; Norse *batbir*. Probably the *ba* (O.E. *bo, bey*), which is seen also in Latin *ambo*, Gr. ἄμφω, is connected with A.S. *twagen, twa*, two.

Bathud, bathed.

Bawdrik, *baudrick,* or *baldrick,* belt, or girdle, worn transversely. It sometimes signified the *cingulum* or military belt. It was used in the sixteenth century for the jewelled ornament worn round the neck both by ladies and noblemen. O.Fr. *baudré,* O.H.Ger. *balderich,* Icel. *belti,* O. H. Ger. *balz,* a belt.

Be, (1) to be, (2) been.

Bede, a bead (pl. *bedes*). A.S. *bead, gebed,* O.Sax. *beda,* O.Fris. *bede,* a prayer; O.Sax. *bedon,* to pray. "*Beads* were strung on a string, and originally used for the purpose of helping the memory in reciting a certain tale of prayers or doxologies. To bid one's *bedes* or *beads* was to say one's prayers." (Wedgwood.)

Beem, Bemys, beam, rafter (pl. *beemes, beemis*). A.S. *beám,* a tree, stick, beam; Ger. *baum,* Du. *boom,* a tree. Cp. *boom* of a vessel, *beam* in horn-*beam.*

Been, (1) to be, (2) are, (3) been.

Beer, Beere, a bier.

Beest, Best, a beast.

Beete, to kindle, light. The literal meaning is to mend, repair. A.S. *bêtan,* O.Fris. *beta,* Goth. *bôtjan,* to amend, repair, expiate; whence Eng. *boot, booty, bootless, better.*

Begger, Beggere, a beggar. It signifies literally a *bag*-bearer. Cp. Flemish *beggaert,* a beggar. "It must be borne in mind that the *bag* was a universal characteristic of the beggar, at a time when all his alms were given in kind; and a beggar is hardly ever introduced in our older writers without mention being made of his *bag.*" (Wedgwood.)

Ben, (1) to be, (2) are, (3) been.

Benigne, kind.

Bent, declivity of a hill, a plain, open field. Low. Ger. *bend,* meadow.

Berd, Berde, beard.

Bere, to bear, to carry, to conduct oneself, behave. A.S. *beran,* Goth. *bairan.*

Bere, to pierce, strike, as 'to *bere* through' = to pierce through. A.S. *berian,* O.N. *berja,* to strike.

Berkyng, barking. A.S. *beorcan,* to bark; Icel. *braka,* to crash; Dan. *brag,* crack, crash; O.H.Ger. *gebreh,* A.S. *gebræc,* a boisterous wind. With the root *brak* are connected Eng. *bark, brag,* and *bray.*

Berstles, bristles. A.S. *byrst,* bristle; Du. *borstel.* Ger. *borste.*

Berye, a berry.

Beseken, to beseech. A.S. *sécan,* to seek, enquire, ask for, (we have the same root in *for-sake,*) which is connected with *secgan,* to say. Goth. *sakan,* to object, reprove; Ger. *sache,* a complaint; O.E. *sake,* strife, contention; Eng. *sake.*

Best, Beste, a beast.

Besy, busy, industrious, anxious.

Bet, better. A.S. *bet,* O.H.Ger. *baz.* See **Beete.** The O.E. *go bet* = hasten, go along quickly.

Bete, (1) to beat, (2) beaten, ornamented.

Beth, (3rd. pers. sing. of *Ben*), is; (imp. pl.), be.

Betwix, betwixt. A.S. *betwuh, betweox.* The second element *-tweox* is connected with *two,* and occurs in *be-tween.*

Bihight, promised. A.S. *bâtan* (pret. *hêht*), Goth. *haitan,* Ger. *heizan,* to call, command, promise. The Goth. perfect *haihait* shews that *hight* is a reduplicated form, like Lat. *pependi, tetendi,* from *pendere* and *tendere.* Eng. *did* is probably another example of reduplication.

Biholde, to behold (pret. *biheld,* pp. *biholde, biholden*).

Biknew, acknowledged, confessed.

Bile, bill (of a bird). A.S. *bile.*

Biloved, beloved.

Bisette, to employ, use (pret. *bi-sette*, pp. *biset*).

Biside, Bisides, beside, near, be-sides.

Bitweene, Bytweene, between. See Betwix.

Bitwix, Bitwixe, Bytwixe, be-twixt, between.

Bladde, blade (of a knife).

Blak, black (def. form and pl. *blake*). A.S. *blac, blæc,* black. With this root are connected bleak, bleach.

Blankmanger, some compound of capon minced, with cream, sugar, and flour.

Ble, colour, complexion. A.S. *bleo,* colour. It is probably connected with *blue.* O.H.Ger. *blao, blaw,* blue; Ger. *blau,* O.E. *bla, blo,* livid, blue.

Blede, to bleed (pret. *bledde,* pp. *bled* and *bleynte*).

Bleynte, blenched, started back. O.E. *blenchen,* to blench, glance. O.N. *blekkja,* to turn aside, wince, *blink.*

Blis, bliss. A.S. *blis,* joy, gladness, is formed from the adj. *blithe,* joy-ful. Cp. A.S. *blithsian,* to rejoice.

Blisful, blissful.

Blive, Blyve, quickly, forthwith. O.E. *bilife.* Cp. Dan. *oplive,* to quicken, enliven, and the two senses of our Eng. *quick.*

Boceler, Bocler, Bokeler, buck-ler. Fr. *bouclier,* a shield with a central boss, from *boucle,* pro-tuberance; Mid. Lat. *bucula scuti.* It is of course connected with Eng. *buckle,* Fr. *boucle; bouclé,* swollen; Ger. *buckel,* a stud; Dan. *bugne,* to bulge, swell.

Bok (pl. *bokes*), a book.

Bokelyng, buckling.

Boket, a bucket. O.Fr. *baquet,*

Du. *bac,* a trough, bowl; Eng. *back,* a brewer's vat.

Bole, bull; pl. *boles.*

Bond, bound = O.E. *band* (pret. of *binden*).

Boon, Boone, prayer, petition, boon. A.S. *bên,* O.N. *bôn,* prayer.

Boon, bone (pl. *boones*). The oo arises out of an earlier *ā,* as A.S. *ban* = O.E. *bon.*

Boor, boar. A.S. *bar,* Du. *beer.*

Boot, Boote, remedy. See Beete.

Boras, borax.

Bord, table. A.S. *bord,* table, margin; Du. *boord,* edge, border.

Bord, joust, tournament. O.Fr. *behourd,* M.H.Ger. *buhurt,* O.Fris. *bord.* See note on l. 52 of Prol. p. 118.

Bore, pp. born.

Born, pp. conducted.

Borwe, pledge, security. A.S. *borh,* security, pledge; *borgian,* to lend (on security). Cp. Ger. *bürge* from *beorgan,* to protect (whence *borough*), a surety; *bürgen,* to become a surety, to give bail for another. In the phrase 'a snug berth,' a *berth* on board ship, we have a derivative of the same root. Provincial *barth,* a place near a farmhouse, well-sheltered; *barth-less,* houseless.

Bothom, bottom. A.S. *botm,* O.E. *bothem,* O.Du. *bodem.* Cp. *bottom,* a small valley, and Gr. βόθρος, ditch, with βαθύς, deep.

Botiler, butler. O.E. *botelere,* Fr. *bouteillier.* It is generally con-nected with *bouteille,* a bottle; but it is more probably connected with *buttery* and *butt.* Fr. *botte,* Sp. *bota,* a wine-skin.

Botus, boots. It is probably con-nected with the preceding word. Cp. Fr. *botte,* boot; Du. *bote.* "The boot appears to have originally been, like the Irish brogue and Indian mocassin, a sort of bag of skin or leather, enveloping the foot and laced on the instep." (Wedgwood.)

Bouk, body. Icel. *bukr*, the body. Sc. *bouk*, trunk, body; Icel. *bulka*, to swell; whence Eng. *bulk*, Prov. Eng. *bulch*. Cotgrave has "*bossé*, knobby, *bulked* or bumped out." With this root are connected Eng. *billow*, *bulge*, *bilge* (Icel. *bolgna*, to swell).

Bour. A.S. *bur*, bower, inner chamber; Prov. Eng. *boor*, a parlour.

Bourdon, burden (of a song), a musical accompaniment. See note p. 135. O.Fr. *bourdon*, a drone of a bagpipe; Sp. *bordon*, the bass of a stringed instrument, or of an organ.

Bowcher, a butcher. Fr. *boucher*, from *boc*, a goat. Cp. It. *becco*, a goat; *beccaro*, a butcher; *boccino*, young beef, veal; *bocciero*, a butcher.

Bracer, armour for the arms.

Brak (the pret. of *breke*), broke.

Bras, brass.

Brast (the pret. of *bersten* or *bresten*), burst. It is sometimes written *barst*; the pp. was *brusten*, *bursten*, or *borstan*. A.S. *berstan*, O.Du. *bersten*, O.N. *bresta*, to burst.

Braun, Brawn, muscle (pl. *brawnes*). O.E. *brahun*. Cp. Eng. *brawny*, Sc. *brand*, calf of the leg; O.Fr. *braion*, *braoun*, a lump of flesh; Fris. *braeye*, Low Ger. *bråe*, a lump of flesh, calf of the leg, flesh of a leg of pork. In O.E. writers *brawne* often signifies the flesh of a boar.

Braunche, a branch. Fr. *branche*.

Brayde, started. See **Abrayde**.

Bred, Breed, bread.

Brede, breadth. A.S. *bråd*, *bréd*, Ger. *breit*, Dan. *bread*; A.S. *brædu*, O.Fris. *brêde*, breadth. With this is connected A.S. *bred*, O.Du. *berd*, a surface, board (cp. Lat.

latus, a side, and *latus*, broad; A.S. *side*, a side, and *sid*, wide); A.S. *brerd*, brink, margin; Dan. *bred*, an edge; Sw. *brad*, edge, *bred*, broad; Icel. *bard*, a lip, border, edge.

Breeme, fiercely, furiously. A.S. *brême*, loud, keen; O.E. *bream*, fierce.

Breeth, Breethe, breath. In O.E. *bræth* signifies vapour, smell, also fervour, rage.

Breke, to break (pret. *brak*, *brok*; pp. *brok*, *ibroken*).

Brem, a fresh-water fish, bream. O.Fr. *bresme*, O.H.Ger. *brahsema*.

Bren, bran. Welsh *bren*, bran; O.Fr. *bren*. Cp. Gael. *brein*, stink; Fr. *bren*, ordure.

Brend, burnished, bright.

Brende, (pret. *brente*, pp. *brent*), burnt. See **Brenne**.

Brenne, to burn. A.S. *brennan*, *bernan*, O.Du. *bernen*, Goth. *brannjan*, to burn. We have the same root in *brim*-stone, O.E. *brenstone*.

Brenningly, fiercely, ardently.

Brennyng, Brennynge, burning.

Breres, briers. A.S. *brêr*, a briar.

Brest, Breste, breast.

Brest-plat, breast-plate.

Breste, to burst (pret. *brast*, pp. *borsten*, *borsten*). See **Brast**.

Bretful, brimfull. Tyrwhitt says that the sense of this word is much clearer than the etymology. The O.E. *brurdful* = full to the brim, is connected with A.S. *brerd*, brink, brim. See **Brede**, breadth.

Brethurhede, brotherhood, brothers of a religious order.

Briddes, birds. A.S. *bridd*, a (young) bird; *brod*, a brood; O.H.Ger. *bruot*, heat; Ger. *brut*, brood; A.S. *bredan*, to nourish, keep warm; Du. *broeden*, to hatch; Low Ger. *bridde*, a chicken. We have the same root in *brew* and *broth*. Shakespeare uses *bird* in its original sense in the following passage :—

" Being fed by us, you used us so
   As that ungentle gull, the cuckoo's
     bird,
   Useth the sparrow." (Hen. IV, Pt. 1, v. 1.)

Broch, Broche, a brooch. O. Fr. *broche,* Sp. *broche,* a clasp. Cp. Lat. *brocchus,* a projecting tooth ; It. *brocco,* a stump, peg ; Fr. *broche,* a spit.

Brode. See **Brood.**

Broke, broken. See **Breke.**

Brood, Broode, Brode, broad. See **Brede.**

Broode, broadly, plainly.

Brouke, have the use of, enjoy, *brook.* A.S. *brûcan,* O. H. Ger. *brûchan,* Ger. *brauchen,* brook, use, enjoy, eat. Cp. Goth. *brukjan,* to enjoy ; and *bruks,* useful. Lat. *frui, fructus.*

Broun, brown. A.S. *brûn,* Ger. *braun,* Fr. *brun.* It is perhaps connected with *brennan,* to burn.

Browdid, braided, woven. For the etymology see **Abrayde.**

Browdyng, embroidery.

Bulde, built.

Bult, to bolt (corn), sift meal. Sw. *bulta,* to beat.

Burdoun, a humming noise, the bass in music. O. Fr. *bourdon,* a drone of a bagpipe ; Sp. *bordon,* the bass of a stringed instrument or of an organ.

Burgeys, citizen, burgess. O. Fr. *burgeois,* from Lat. *burgensis,* a citizen ; Fr. *bourg,* It. *borgo,* a city. Cp. Goth. *baurgs,* A. S. *burh, burg,* Eng. *borough.*

Burned, burnished.

Busynesse, Bysynesse, labour, care, anxiety.

But-if, unless.

By and by, separately. See note, p. 137.

Bycause, because.

Byfel, Byfil, befell.

Byfore, Byforen, Byforn, before.

Bygan, began.

Bygonne, pp. begun.

Bygynne, to begin.

Byhote, promised. See **Bihight.**

Byhynde, behind.

Byjaped, deceived, befooled. O. E. *jape,* joke, lie ; Fr. *japper,* to yelp. The root, *jap,* is connected with *gab, jab,* as in *gabble, jabber.*

Byknowe, to acknowledge.

Byloved, beloved.

Bynne, bin, chest. It is sometimes written *bing,* and seems to have signified orig nally a heap. Sw. *binge,* heap ; Icel. *bunga,* to swell. " You might have seen them throng out of the town
   Like ants, when they do spoil the
     bing of corn." (Surrey's Poems, p. 191, ed. Bell.)

Byquethe, to bequeath. A.S. *cwéthan,* to say ; whence Eng. *quoth.*

Byraft, bereft. A.S. *bereafian,* to deprive of, strip ; *reafian,* to spoil, reave.

Byside, beside, near.

Bysmoterud, spotted, smutted. A.S. *besmitan,* to defile, besmut ; Du. *smodderen,* to dirty, daub. Cp. Dan. *smuds,* Sw. *smuts,* spot, splash, dirt ; Eng. *smut, smutch, smudgy,* &c.

Byt (3rd pers. sing. of *bidden*), bids.

Bythoughte, ' am bethought,' have thought of, have called to mind.

Bytwixe, betwixt, between.

Bywreye, make known, bewray. A.S. *wregan,* Ger. *rügen,* to discover, accuse.

C.

Caas, case, condition, hap, misfortune.

Caas, case, quiver. It. *cassa,* O. Fr. *casse.*

Cacche, Cachche, to catch. It. *cacciare,* O. Fr. *cachier,* to catch ; Fr. *chasser,* to drive out, *chase.*

Caitif, Caytif, wretch, wretched. It. *cattivo* (Lat. *captivus*), a captive, a wretch; Fr. *chêtif*, poor, wretched.

Cam, came.

Can, (1) know, knows; (2) acknowledge as in the phrase ' can thank' (Fr. *savoir gré*), where *thank* is a *noun*, and not a verb. A.S. *cunnan*, to know; *cunnian*, to enquire, search into; Goth. *kunnan*, to know; Sw. *kunna*, to be able. The root is preserved in *cunning*, *ken*, ale-*conner* (an inspector of ales).

Cantel, corner, cantle. O.Fr. *chantel*, *chanteau*, a corner, a lump. Cp. Icel. *kantr*, side; Dan. *kant*, edge.

Cappe, a cap, hood.

Caraigne or Caroigne, carrion. Fr. *charogne*, It. *carogna;* from Lat. *caro.*

Care, sorrow, grief. A.S. *caru*, Goth. *kara.*

Careful, sorrowful.

Carf, carved (the pret. of *kerve*, to cut, *carve*). A.S. *ceorfan*, O.Fris. *kerva*, to cut.

Carl, a churl. A.S. *ceorl;* Icel. *karl*, a man. Cp. Sc. *carlin*, an old woman; Eng. *churl, churlish.*

Carol, a round dance. Carole, to dance. Fr. *carole* (from Lat. *corolla*, the diminutive of *corona*). Robert of Brunne calls the circuit of Druidical stones a *karole*. By some it is derived from the Lat. *chorale.*

Carpe, to talk, discourse. Cp. Portug. *carpire*, to cry, weep.

Carte, chariot, cart. O.N. *karti.*

Carter, Cartere, charioteer.

Cas, case, condition, hap, chance. See Caas.

Cas, medley, heap (of dead bodies). It is perhaps derived from Fr. *casser*, to break; It. *casciare*, to squeeze, squash; Lat. *cassus*, hollow.

Cast, casteth.

Cast, device, plot. It is connected with the vb. to *cast.* Cp. O.E. *turn*, a trick; Eng. ' an *ill turn.'*

Caste, Casten, to plan, devise, suppose.

Catapus, Catapuce, a species of spurge.

Catel, wealth, goods, valuable property of any kind, *chattels.* O.Fr. *chatel, catel*, a piece of moveable property, from Lat. *capitale*, whence *captale, catullum*, the principal sum in a loan (cp. Eng. *capital*). The Lat. *captale* was applied to beasts of the farm, *cattle.*

Caughte, took. Cp. Eng. ' caught cold.' See Cacche.

Celle, a religious house, *cell.*

Century, the name of an herb.

Cercles, circles.

Cerial, belonging to the species of oak called *Cerrus* (Lat.). It. *Cerro*, Fr. *Cerre.*

Certein, Certeyn, Certes, Certis, certain, certainly, indeed.

Certeinly, Certeynly, certainly.

Ceruce, white lead.

Chaas = *cas*, heap, medley. See Cas.

Chaffer, merchandise. O.E. *chafare, chap-fare;* A.S. *ceap*, O.S. *côp*, O.N. *kaup*, O.H.Ger. *chauf*, bargain, price (cp. Eng. *dog-cheap, dirt-cheap*); A.S. *ceapian*, O.S. *côpon*, O.N. *kaupa*, to buy; O.H.Ger. *chaufan*, to buy, sell; Eng. *chop* (as in ' *chop* and change.'

Champartye, a share of land; a partnership in power.

Champioun, a champion. A.S. *camp*, O.H.Ger. *champh*, combat, contest; A.S. *campian*, to fight; O.Fris. *kampa*, to contend; Prov. Eng. *champ*, a scuffle; *cample*, to talk, contend, argue; Ger. *kampeln*, to debate, dispute. The Lat. *campus* is probably borrowed from the Teutonic dialects.

Chanterie, Chaunterie, "An endowment for the payment of a priest to sing mass agreeably to the appointment of the founder. There were thirty-five of these Chanteries established at St. Paul's, which were served by fifty-four priests.—Dugd. Hist. pref. p. 41." (Tyrwhitt.)

Chapelleyn, a chaplain.

Chapman, a merchant. A.S. *ceapman.* See **Chaffer.**

Chare, car, chariot. Fr. *char,* Lat. *carrus;* whence Fr. *charrier,* to carry; *charger,* to load, charge.

Charge, harm, as in the phrase ' it were no *charge.*' It signifies literally (1) load, burden; (2) business of weight, matter for consideration.

Chaunce, chance, hap. Fr. *chance,* O. Fr. *chéance,* from *cheoir,* to fall; Lat. *cadere.*

Chaunge, Chaungen, to change.

Chaunterie. See **Chanterie.**

Cheef, chief. Fr. *chef,* head; Lat. *caput.*

Cheer, Cheere, Chere, countenance, appearance, entertainment, cheer. O. Fr. *chiere,* countenance; Fr. *chere,* face, look.

Cherl, churl. See **Carl.**

Ches, imp. sing. *chose;* imp. pl. *cheseth.*

Chese, to choose. A.S. *ceosan,* Du. *kieren, kiesen,* O.H. Ger. *chiusan,* to choose.

Chesteyn, a chestnut-tree. O. Fr. *chastaigne,* Lat. *castanea.*

Cheventen or **Chevetein,** a chieftain, *captain.* See **Cheef.**

Chevysaunce, Chevisance, gain, profit; also an agreement for borrowing money. Fr. *chevir,* to compass, make an end, come to an agreement with; *achever,* to bring to an end, *achieve* (from *chef,* head).

Cheyne, a chain.

Chiden, to chide (pret. *chidde,* pp. *chid*). A.S. *cidan,* to scold.

Chikne, a chicken. A.S. *cicen,* O. Du. *kieken.* The word is evidently formed in imitation of the sound made by young birds. Cp. *chuck, chuckle,* &c.

Chirkyng, sb. shrieking. The O.E. *chirke* signifies 'to make a noise like a bird,' being a parallel form with *chirp,* and imitative of the sound made by birds. Cp. A.S. *cearcian,* to creak, crash, gnash; Prov. Eng. *chirre,* to chirp.

Chivachie, a military expedition. See next word.

Chivalrie, Chyvalrye, knighthood, the manners, exercises, and valiant exploits of a knight. Fr. *chevalerie,* from *chevalier,* a knight, a horseman; *cheval;* It. *cavallo,* Lat. *caballus,* a horse; O.E. *caple, cable,* a horse.

Choys, choice. A.S. *cys.* See **Chese.**

Chronique, a chronicle.

Cite, a city. Fr. *cité,* Lat. *civitas.*

Citole, a kind of musical instrument with chords.

Clapsud, clasped. O.E. *claps,* a clasp. It is connected with O.E. *clippe,* to embrace. Cp. *gripe, grip, grasp.*

Clarioun, clarion.

Clarré, wine mixed with honey and spices, and afterwards strained till it was *clear.* It was also called *Piment.*

Clatere, Clateren, to clatter. O. Du. *klateren,* to clatter, rattle.

Cleer; Cleere, adj. clear, adv. clearly. O. Fr. *cler,* clear; Lat. *clarus.*

Clene, adj. clean, pure; adv. cleanly.

Clennesse, cleanness, purity (of life).

Clense, to cleanse.

Clepe, to call, cry, say. A.S. *cleopian, clypian,* to call; Ger. *klaffen,* to chatter, babble; Du. *klappen,* to sound, strike. Cp. Sc. *clep,* prattle, tattle; Eng. *claptrap.*

Cleped, Clept, called.

Clerk, a man of learning, a student at the University. O. Fr. *clerc*.

Cloke, a cloak. Ir. and Gael. *clôca*, *cleoca*.

Clomben, climbed, ascended.

Cloos, close, shut.

Clos, enclosure, yard.

Clothred = *clottred*, clotted. O. Du. *klotteren*, to clotter, coagulate. We have the root-syllable in *clot* and *clod*; A. S. *clot*, clod; Ger. *kloss*, a clod, a ball. Golding has a "*clottred clod* of seeds," and he uses *clodded* for *clottred*. Eng. *cloud* is evidently from the same source as *clod*. Cp. O. E. *clowdys*, clods (Coventry Mysteries).

Cloystre, a cloister.

Cofre, coffer, chest. O. Fr. *cofre*, Fr. *coffre*, Lat. *cophinus*, Gr. κοφι-νος, a basket.

Col, coal. A. S. *col*, Icel. *kol*, Ger. *kohle*.

Cole-blak, coal-black, black as a coal.

Cole fox, a crafty fox. The prefix *col*, deceitful, treacherous, occurs in O. E. *col-prophet*, a false prophet; *col-knyfe*, a treacherous knife; *colwarde*, deceitful, false; *colsipe* (= *colschipe*), deceit, treachery; *collen*, to deceive, allure.

Colers of, having collars of.

Com, pret. came, imp. come.

Comaunde, to command.

Comaundement, commandment, command.

Communes, commoners, common people.

Compaignye, company.

Companable, companionable, sociable.

Compassyng, craft, contrivance.

Comper, gossip, a near friend.

Compleint, Compleynt, complaint.

Complet, complete.

Compleynen, to complain.

Composicioun, agreement.

Comune, common; *as in comune* = as in common, commonly

Condicionel, conditional.

Condicioun, condition.

Confort, comfort.

Conforte, to comfort.

Confus, confused, confounded.

Conne, know, be able. See Can, Con.

Conscience, feeling, pity.

Conseil, Conseyl, counsel.

Conserve, to preserve.

Contek, contest. Fr. *contencer*, to strive.

" And therwithal I termed have all strife,
All quarrels, *contecks*, and all cruell *jarres*,
Oppressions, bryberes, and all greedy life,
To be (*in genere*) no bet than warres." (Gascoigne, The Fruites of Warre).

Contrarie, an opponent, adversary, foe.

Contre, Contrie, country.

Contynanunce, countenance.

Coote - armour. See Cote - armour.

Cop, top of anything. A. S. *copp*, O. Du. *kopp*, Ger. *kopf*, top, summit.

Cope, a cloak, cape. It. *cappa*, Fr. *chappe*.

Corage, heart, spirit, courage. Fr. *courage*, from Lat. *cor*, the heart.

Coroune, Corowne, a crown.

Corrumpe, to corrupt.

Corumpable, corruptible.

Corven (pp. of *kerve*), cut.

Cosin, Cosyn, a cousin, kinsman.

Cote, cottage. A. S. *cot*, O. Du. *kote*. Cp. *sheep-cote*, *dove-cote*.

Cote, coat. O. Fr. *cote*.

Cote-armour, Coote-armour, a coat worn over armour, upon which the armorial ensigns of the wearer were usually embroidered. The usage of wearing an upper garment, or surcoat, charged with armorial bearings, as a personal distinction in conflict, when the features were concealed by the aventaile, commenced possibly in the reign of John, but was not generally adopted before the time of Henry lll. Sir Thomas de la More relates that the Earl of Gloucester was slain at Bannockburn, 1314, in consequence of his neglecting to put on his insignia, termed in the Latin translation "*togam propriæ armaturæ.*" During the reign of Edward III the surcoat gave place to the jupon, and this was succeeded by the tabard, the latest fashion of a garment armorially decorated, and the prototype of that which is still worn by the heralds and pursuivants. (Way.)

Couchid, Cowched, (1) laid, (2) inlaid, trimmed. Fr. *coucher,* O. Fr. *culcher,* to lay down (Lat. *collocare*).

Counseil, counsel, advice.

Countrefete, counterfeit, imitate.

Cours, course.

Courtepy, a sort of upper coat of a coarse material. Du. *kort,* short; *pije,* a coarse cloth; Goth. *paida,* a coat. The syllable *pije* is still preserved in *pea-*jacket.

Couthe, Cowde, Cowthe, (1) could, (2) knew. See **Can.**

Covyne, *covin,* deceit; literally a deceitful agreement between two parties to the prejudice of a third. Lat. *convenire,* Fr. *convenir,* to come together.

Cowardie, cowardice. Fr. *couard,* from Lat. *cauda,* a tail; O. Fr. *couarder,* to retire, draw backwards.

Coy, quiet. Fr. *coi,* Sp. *quedo,* Lat. *quietus.*

Cracchyng, scratching. Beside *cracche,* to scratch, we have *s-cratte,* and *s-cracche.* Cp. O.E.

fette and *fecche,* to fetch; Du. *kratsen,* O.N. *krassa,* Ger. *kratzen,* to stretch, tear.

Craftesman, Craftysman, a man of skill, *craftsman.* A.S. *cræft,* power; Ger. *kraft,* strength.

Crien, Cryen, to cry (pret. *cride, cryde*); *crydestow* = criedst thou.

Crisp, Crispe, crisp, curled. It is also written *cripse.* (Lydgate has *kirspe.*) A.S. *crisp,* crisp; *cirpsian,* to curl. Cp. Fr. *crespe,* Lat. *crispus,* curled.

Croppe, top, crop (pl. *croppes*). A.S. *crop,* O. Du. *krop, kroppe,* top, summit, cross, craw; whence Eng. *crop, crop-*full, 'croppings out' (of mineral strata). Cp. Fr. *crope, croupe,* top of a hill; *croupe,* the rounded haunches of an animal, the *croup; croupière.* the strap passing over the *croup;* Eng. *crupper.* The root *crup* seems to signify a swelling out, as in Welsh *crub,* a swelling out; Gael. *crap,* a knob, knot.

Crulle, curly, curled. Du. *krol, krolle,* a curl; O. Du. *kroken,* to crook, bend; *kroke,* a bending, crook; O.N. *krokr,* a hook; Low Ger. *krükel,* a curl; *krüllen,* to curl. *Crouch* (*crutch*), crook, cross, is merely a softened form of crook. Cp. O.E. *cloke* and *clouch,* a claw, *clutch;* Sw. *kirk,* Eng. *church.*

Cryk, creek. O. Du. *kreke.* Cp. Icel. *kyrki,* angle, nook, from *krokr,* a hook. *Cryke* in O.E. signifies also a stream, a brook (as it still does in America); A.S. *crecca,* a bank, brink.

Culpons, Culpouns, shreds, bundles, logs. Fr. *coupon,* Lat. *colpo,* a shred, a portion cut off.

Cuntre, country. Fr *contrée.*

Cuppe, a cup. A.S. *cuppe.*

Curat, Curior, a curate.

Cure, care, anxiety. Lat. *cura.*

Curious, careful.

Curs, curse. A.S. *curs*.

Curteis, Curteys, courteous. O.Fr. *cortois; cort*, a court (Lat. *cohors*).

Curtesie, Curtesy. courtesy. O.Fr. *courtoisie*, civility, courtesy.

Cut, lot. "*Cut* or lote. Sors." (Promptorium Parvulorum.) W. *cwt!*, a little piece.

D.

Daliaunce, gossip. "*Dalyaunce*, confabulacio, collocacio." (Prompt. Parv.) Lat. *talus*, the ankle-bone of animals, a die to play with; whence O.E. *daly*, a sort of dice-play. Horman says that "men play with three dice, and children with four *dalies*."

Dampned, condemned, doomed.

Dan, Daun, Lord, was a title commonly given to monks. It is also prefixed to the names of persons of all sorts, e. g. *Dan Arcyte, Dan Burnel*, &c. Lat. *Dominus*.

Dar, dare (1st pers. sing. present tense). Darst (2nd sing.), Dorste, Durste (pret.).

Darreyne, Dereyne, to contest, fight out, decide by battle, *darraign*. O.Fr. *desrenir*, from Lat. Mid. Lat. *derationare*, to answer an accusation, to settle or *arrange* a controversy. Shakespeare uses the word in the sense of 'to make ready to fight.'
"Royal commanders, be in readiness;
 For, with a band of thirty thousand men,
 Comes Warwick, backing of the Duke of York;
 And in the towns, as they do march along,
 Proclaims him king, and many fly to him;
Darraign your battle, for they are at hand." (Hen. VI, pt. III, ii. 2.)

Daunce, vb. to dance, sb. a dance. "The olde daunce" = the old game.

Daunger, a dangerous situation. *In daunger* = in his jurisdiction, under his control; *with daunger* = with difficulty. O.Fr. *dangier*, dominion, subjection, difficulty (from Mid. Lat. *damnum*, (1) a legal fine, (2) territorial jurisdiction). *Estre en son danger* = to be in the danger of any one, to be in his power. Cp. 'in *danger* of the judgment.' *Danger* in the sense of *debt* is not uncommon in English:
"The wandering guest doth stand in *danger* of his hoste." (Golding's Ovid.)
"You stand within his *danger*, do you not?" (Merch. of Ven. iv. 1.)

Daungerous, difficult.

Daunsynge, dancing.

Dawen, to dawn (3rd sing. *daweth*).

Dawenynge, dawn, dawning. O.E. *dawe*, a day; A.S. *dæg, daga*, Goth. *dags*, O.H.Ger. *tag*: A.S. *dagian*, to dawn; *dagung*, dawning.

Dayerie, dairy; from O.E. *deye*, a dairy-maid. See Deye.

Dayseye, a daisy. Chaucer defines *daisy* as *the eye of the day*, i.e. day's eye.

Debate, strife, quarrel. Fr. *debattre*, to contend.

Dede (pret. of *don*), did.

Dede, a deed. A.S. *dæd*, O.Fris. *dêde*, O.H.Ger. *tât.*

Dedly, Deedly, deadly, death-like.

Deed, Deede, dead. A.S. *dead*, O.Fris. *dâd, dâth*, O.H.Ger. *tôter, tôder*, dead.

Deef, deaf. A.S. *deaf*, Goth. *daubs, daufs*, O.H.Ger. *touber*, Ger. *taub*. It is probably connected with Goth. *gadaubjan*, to harden, make insensible. Cp. Scotch *dowf*, dull, flat; O.E. and Prov. Eng. *daf*, *daffe*, fool, dastard; Prov. Eng. *daver*, to stun; *dover*, to slumber.

Deel, a part. See **Del**.

Deepe, deeply.

Deer, Deere, Dere, dear, dearly. A.S. *deor*, dear, precious; whence *darling* (O.E. *der-ling*), *dearth*.

Deeth, Deth, death. A.S. *death*, O.Fris. *dâth*, O.H.Ger. *tôd*.

Degre, Degree, (1) a step, (2) rank or station in life. Fr. *degrè*, O.Fr. *degrat*, Lat. *gradus*, a step.

Deinte, Deynte, Deyntee, sb. a dainty, rarity; adj. rare, valuable. It literally signifies *toothsome*; from W. *daint*, a tooth.

Del, part, portion, whit. *Never a del* = never a whit; *somdel*, somewhat. A.S. *dæl*, O.N. *deila*, a part; A.S. *dælan*, to divide; O.E. *dale*, Eng. *dole*.

Delen, to have dealings with.

Delit, Delyt, delight, pleasure. Lat. *deliciæ*, pleasures, delights; *delectare*, to please.

Delve, to dig (pret. *delf, dalf,* pp. *dolven*). A.S. *delfan*, Du. *delven*, to dig, bury. It is probably connected with Du. *delle*, valley, hollow; Fris. *dollen*, to dig; Eng. *dell*, dale.

Delyver, quick, active, nimble; Fr. *delivre* (Lat. *liber*, free), active, nimble.

Delyverly, quickly. Cp. O.E. *delivernesse*, agility.

Deme, Demen, to judge, decide, *doom*, suppose, *deem*. A.S. *dêman*, O.H.Ger. *tuomen*, to judge; A.S. *dôm*, O.H.Ger. *tuom*, doom, judgment, sentence, decree. Cp. O.E. *demere, demstere*, a judge.

Departe, to part, separate.

Departyng, separation.

Depeynted, painted, depicted.

Dere, dear. See **Deere**.

Dere, Deren, to hurt, injure. A.S. *derian*, O.H.Ger. *terran*, to harm, hurt, injure; A.S. *daru*, O.H.Ger.

tara, harm, injury. Shakespeare uses *tarre* in the sense of 'to provoke.'

Dereyne, Derreyne. See **Darreyne**.

Dereyned = *dereyved*, derived.

Derk, Derke, dark. A.S. *deorc*, *dearc*, dark.

Derknesse, darkness.

Derre, dearer. Cp. O.E. *berre*, higher; *ferre*, further.

Desir, Desyr, desire.

Desiryng, sb. desire.

Despit, Despite, Despyt, malicious anger, vexation. O.Fr. *despire* (Lat. *despicere*), to despise; Fr. *despit*, contempt; It. *dispetto*, Sp. *despecho*, displeasure, malice.

Despitous, Dispitious, angry to excess, cruel, merciless.

Desput, dispute.

Desputesoun, disputation.

Destene, destiny, fate.

Destreine, Destreyne, to vex, constrain. Fr. *distraindre*, Mid. Lat. *distringere* (from Lat. *stringere*, to strain), to be severe with, *distrain*. *District* and *distress* are from the same source.

Destresse, distress.

Destruie, Distruye, to destroy. Fr. *détruire*.

Deth. See **Deeth**.

Dette, a debt. Lat. *debeo, debitum*, to owe; Fr. *dette*, a debt.

Detteles, free from debt.

Devise, Devyse, (1) to direct, order; (2) to relate, describe. It. *divisare*, to think, imagine, to discourse; O.Fr. *deviser*, to plan, order, dispose of, discourse, from Lat. *visum*, It. *viso*, view, opinion.

Devise, Devys, opinion, decision, direction.

Devoir, duty. Fr. *devoir*, duty, trust; *devoir*, to owe; Lat. *debeo*.

Devynynge, divination.

Devysyng, a putting in order, preparation.

Deye, a female servant. O.N. *deigja.* See note, p. 148.

Deye, Deyen (pret. *deide, deyde*), to die. O.E. *deghen,* O.N. *deyja,* O.H.Ger. *tôwan,* to die.

Deyer, a dyer. O.E. *deye,* to dye, soak; A.S. *deagan,* to dye; Dan. *dygge,* to sprinkle with water. Cp. Prov. Eng. *dag,* to moisten; *daggy,* rainy.

Deyne, to deign.

Deyntee, Deynteth. See **Deinte.**

Deys, dais, table of state, the high table. "*Dais* or *daiz,* a cloth of estate, canopy or heaven, that stands over the heads of princes' thrones; also the whole state or seat of estate." (Cotgrave.) O.Fr. *dais, deis* (Lat. *discus*). See note, p. 129.

Deyseye, a daisy.

Diapred, Dyapred, variegated, diversified with flourishes or sundry figures. O.Fr. *diaspré, diapré,* variegated; It. *diaspro,* a jasper (Gr. *ἴασπις*), which was much used in ornamental jewellery. Chaucer speaks of a meadow *diapered* with flowers. It is now applied to linen cloth woven with a pattern of diamond-shaped figures, and to church walls when the plain stone is carved in a pattern.

Dich, a ditch. See **Dike.**

Diete, Dyete, diet, daily food. It is generally derived from Mid. Lat. *dieta,* from *dies,* a day; O.E. *diet,* an appointed day; but is more probably from the Gr. *δίατα,* mode of life, especially with reference to *food.*

Digestible, easy to be digested.

Digestives, things to help digestion.

Dight, prepared. A.S. *dihtan,* dress, dispose.

Digne, (1) worthy, (2) proud, disdainful. Fr. *digne.*

Dike, to make *dikes* or *ditches.*

A.S. *dic,* O.Fris. *dik,* M.H.Ger. *tich,* a ditch.

Dischevele, with hair hanging loose. Fr. *descheveler,* to put the hair out of order; Fr. *cheveux,* Lat. *capilla,* the hair.

Discomfiture, Discomfytyng, defeat. Fr. *déconfiture,* from *déconfire,* to nonplus.

Discomforten, to dishearten.

Discrecioun, discretion.

Discret, discreet.

Disheryte, to disinherit.

Disjoint, Disjoynt, a. difficult situation.

Dispence, expense.

Dispitously, angrily, cruelly.

Disposicioun, control, guidance.

Disport, sport, diversion. Fr. *déport,* O.Fr. *desport,* It. *disporte,* diversion, solace.

Divisioun, distinction.

Dockud, cut short. O.E. *dok,* O.N. *dockr,* a tail. Cp. 'docked of one's wages.'

Doke, a duck. O.Du. *duiken,* O.H.Ger. *tûchan,* Ger. *tauchen,* to dive, plunge.

Domb, Dombe, dumb. A.S. *dumb.*

Dome, doom, decision, judgment, opinion. See **Deme.**

Dominacioun, power, control.

Don, Doon, to do, cause, make, take (pret. *dide, dede,* pp. *do, don, doon*).

Dong, Donge, dung. **Donge,** to dung.

Dore, a door. A.S. *duru,* Ger. *thor, thüre.*

Dorste. See **Dar.**

Doseyn, a dozen.

Doun, down, downward.

Doute, doubt, fear. *Oute of doute* = without doubt, doubtless.

Douteles, doubtless, without doubt.

Dowves, doves.

Dragges, drugs. O.Fr. *dragée,* It. *treggea,* Sp. *dragea,* Gr. *τράγημα* (Mod. Gr. *τράγαλα*), sweetmeats, from τρωγάλια, raw fruits at dessert, or sweetmeats, from τρώγω, to gnaw.

Drawe, to carry, lead.

Drecched, troubled (by dreams). A.S. *dreccan*, M.H. Ger. *trecken*, to trouble, plague. "Dremyn or *dretchyn* yn slepe, sompnio." (Prompt. Parv.)

Drede, Dreden, to fear, dread, doubt ; *to drede*, to be feared.

Dredful, cautious, timid.

Dreem, Dreeme, Dreme, a dream. O. Fris. *drâm*, Ger. *traum*. Cp. Sc. *dram, drum*, dull ; *drumble* (Shakespeare), to be sluggish.

Dreme, Dremen, to dream.

Dremynges, dreams.

Dresse, to set in order. O. Fr. *dresser*, to straighten, direct, fashion ; It. *drizzare*, to address, to turn toward a place ; Lat. *dirigere*, to direct.

Dreye, dry. A.S. *dryge*.

Dreynt (pp. of *drenche*), drowned. Cp. O.E. *queynt*, quenched ; *cleynt*, clenched, &c.

Dronke, Dronken, pp. drunk.

Dronken, pl. pret. drank.

Drope, a drop. A.S. *dropa*.

Drowpud, drooped. O.N. *drûpa*, to droop.

Drugge, to drag, *drudge*, to do laborious work. Ir. *drugaire*, a slave.

Duk, a leader, duke. Fr. *duc*, Lat. *dux*, from *ducere*, to lead. See Trench, English Past and Present, p. 196.

Dure, to endure, last.

Duskyng, growing dark or dim. Sw. *dusk*, dark, dull.

Dweld, pp. dwelt.

Dwelle, to tarry.

Dyamauntez, diamonds.

Dyapred. See **Diapred**.

Dyched, diked. See **Dich, Dike**.

Dyete. See **Diete**.

Dym, dull, indistinct.

Dyvynistre, a divine.

E.

Ecclesiaste, an ecclesiastical person.

Ech, Eche, each. A.S. *ælc*, from *æ* (*æg*), ever, and *lic*, like, Cp. O.E. *iwhere*, everywhere.

Echon, Echoon, each one.

Eek, Ek, also, moreover, *eke*. A.S. *êc, eac*; Goth. *auk*, also ; A.S. *ecan*, to increase ; whence *hawker, huckster, eke*.

Eelde, Elde, age, old age. A.S. *eald*, old ; *eldo*, age.

Eeres, Eres, ears. A.S. *eare*, Goth. *auso*, an ear.

Eese, Ese, pleasure, amusement, ease. Fr. *aise*, opportunity, leisure ; Lat. *otium*, leisure.

Eet, Et, ate, did eat ; imp. eat.

Eft, again, after. Cp. O.E. *eft-sone, eftsones*, afterwards, presently ; A.S. *æft*.

Eghen, eyes. See **Ey**.

Elde. See **Eelde**.

Elles, else. A.S. *elles*, O.H. Ger. *elles, alles*. (A.S. *el-* in composition signifies other, foreign. Cp. O.Fr. *el*, Gr. ἄλλος, Lat. *alius*, other.)

Embrowdid, embroidered.

Emprise, an undertaking, enterprise. O. Fr. *emprendre*, Fr. *entreprendre*, to undertake ; *entreprise*, an enterprise.

Encombred, (1) wearied, (2) troubled, in danger. It is sometimes written *acombred*. O. Fr. *encombrer*, to hinder, trouble, grieve, annoy. Cp. Du. *kommer*, loss ; Ger. *kummer*, trouble, grief.

Encres, sb. increased.

Encresce, Encrescen, to increase.

Endelong, Endlang, lengthways, along. A.S. *andlang*, Ger. *entlang*.

Ender, one who causes the death of another.

Endite, to dictate, relate.

Enduren, to endure.
Enforce, to strengthen.
Engendred, produced.
Engyned, tortured, racked. O. Fr. *engin,* contrivance, craft, an instrument of war, torture, &c.
Enhaunsen, to raise. Lat. *ante.*
Enhorte, to encourage. We have *discourage* and *dishearten,* but *enhorte* has given way to *encourage.*
Enoynt, anointed.
Enpoysonyng, poisoning.
Ensample, example.
Enspirud, inspired, breathed into.
Entente, intention, purpose.
Entre, entry.
Entuned, tuned, intoned.
Envyned, stored with wine. See note, p. 127.
Eny, any.
Ercedeknes, archdeacon's.
Ere, to plough, *ear. Earing* is used in our Eng. Bible. A.S. *earian,* Du. *eren.*
Erely, early. A.S. *ær,* before, *ere; ærlice,* early.
Ernest, earnest. A.S. *georn,* Ger. *gern,* eager, intent; O.Du. *ernsten,* to endeavour.
Erst than, for *er than,* before that, *erst* = first; *er* = before.
Erthe, earth. A.S. *eorthe,* Ger. *erde.*
Eschange, exchange.
Eschiewe, Eschewe, to avoid, shun. Fr. *eschever,* It. *schivare,* to avoid; Dan. *skieve,* oblique, *a-skew.*
Esely, easily.
Esen, to entertain. See **Eese.**
Espye, to see, discover.
Est, east.
Estat, estate, state, condition.
Estatlich, Estately, stately, dignified.
Estres, the inward parts of a building. Fr. *estre,* state, plan.
Esud, to be entertained, accommodated.

Esy, easy.
Et. See **Eet.**
Ete, Eten, to eat.
Eterne, eternal.
Evel, evil; **Evele,** badly.
Everich, every,
Everichon, Everychon, every one.
Ew, a yew-tree.
Exemple, example.
Expouned, expounded.
Ey, an egg. A.S. *æg,* pl. *ægren* (O. E. *ayren*), Eng. *eyry.*
Eyen, Eyghen, Eyhen, eyes.

F.

Fader, Fadir, father; gen. sing. *fader, fadres.* (The gen. sing. in A.S. was *fader,* not *fadres.*)
Fair, Fayr, Faire, Fayre, adj. beautiful, fair, good; adv. gracefully, neatly.
Fairnesse, (1) beauty, (2) honesty.
Faldyng, a sort of coarse cloth. See note, p. 130.
Fals, false. Lat. *falsus.*
Falsly, falsely.
Falwe, pale. A.S. *falw,* Ger. *falb,* pale, faded, yellow.
Famulier, familiar, homely.
Fand (pret. of *fynden*), found.
Fare, proceeding, affair. A.S. *faru,* O.N. *för,* course, proceeding, movement, bustle, ado. Tyrwhitt is evidently wrong in deriving it from the Fr. *faire.*
Fare, Faren, to go. A.S. *faran,* to go.
Fare, Faren, pp. gone.
Faren, pl. pres. go.
Farsud, stuffed. O. E. *farse,* to stuff; Fr. *farcir,* Lat. *farcire, farsum,* to stuff.
Faught (O. E. *faght*), fought.
Fawe, glad. A.S. *fægen,* O. E. *fawen,* glad, fain.
Fayn, Fayne, glad, gladly.
Fedde, pret. fed.
Fee, money, reward. A. S. *fech,*

O. N. *fê*, Lat. *pecus*, cattle, property, money.

Feeld, Feelde, Feld, a field. A. S. *feld*, O. Fris. *feld*, Ger. *feld*, the open country. Horne Tooke is wrong in connecting it with the verb to *fell*.

Feend, Feende, Fend, a fiend, devil. A. S. *feond*, Ger. *feind*, an enemy, fiend; A. S. *feon*, Goth. *fian*, to hate.

Feer, Feere, fear. See **Fer.**

Feith, faith. Fr. *foi*, Lat. *fides*.

Fel, Felle, cruel, fierce. A. S. *fell*, O. Du. *fel*, O. Fr. *fel*, cruel, fierce; *felon*, cruel; *felonie*, anger, cruelty, treason; any such heinous offence committed by a vassal against his lord, whereby he is worthy to lose his estate. (Cotgrave.)

Felaw, Felawe, a fellow. O. E. *felaghe*. The syllable *fe = fee*, goods, and *law = *order, law. Cp. O. N. *félagi*, a fellow, a sharer in goods; O. N. *fé*, money, goods; and *lag*, order, society.

Felawschipe, fellowship.

Feld, felled, cut down.

Feld. See **Feeld.**

Felonie, Felonye, crime, disgraceful conduct of any kind.

Fend, Fende. See **Feend.**

Fer, far (comp. *ferre*, further; superl. *ferrest*). A. S. *feor*, far; O. Fris. *fer*.

Fer, Fere, fear, terror. A. S. *fær*, O. N. *fûr*.

Ferd, Fered, frightened, terrified. See **Aferd.**

Ferde, (1) went, proceeded; (2) acted, conducted. A. S. *féran*, to go.

Ferforth, Ferforthly, far forth, as far as.

Fermacye, a medicine, pharmacy.

Ferme, rent. Fr. *ferme*.

Ferne = *ferrene*, distant, from *fer*, far.

Ferthere, further.

Ferthing, farthing, fourth part; hence a very small portion of anything.

Fest, Feste, a feast. Lat. *festum*.

Feste, to feast.

Festne, to fasten.

Fet, fetched, brought. A. S. *fettan*, O. Du. *vatten*, to fetch.

Feteres, fetters (for the *feet* and legs).

Fether, a feather. It is probably connected with Du. *vledern*, to flutter, flap.

Fetously, Fetysly, neatly, properly.

Fetys, neat, well-made. O. Fr. *faictis* (Lat. *facticius*), well-made, neat, *feat*, from O. Fr. *faire*, Lat. *facere*.

Feyne, to feign. O. Fr. *feigner* (Lat. *fingere*, to form), Fr. *feindre*, to feign.

Fiers, fierce. Fr. *feroce*, Lat. *ferox*.

Fil (pret. of *fallen*), fell.

Fir, Fyr, fire.

Fithul, fiddle. Mid. Lat, *fidula*, *vitula*; Lat. *fidis*, It. *viola*, a fiddle; whence *violin*.

Fleigh (pret. of *fle*), flew.

Fleische, flesh.

Flete, to float, swim. A. S. *fleotan*, O. H. Ger. *fliozan*, to flow, float, swim, whence Eng. *fleet, float*.

Fletyng, floating.

Flex, flax. A. S. *fleax*. It is probably connected with A. S. *feax*, hair. Cp. *flix*, fur of a hare (Dryden); Prov. Eng. *fleck*, down of rabbits. The A. S. had *flax-fote = *web-footed, so that there must have been a verb corresponding to O. N. *flietta*, to weave.

Flikeryng, fluttering. A. S. *flycerian*, to flicker; Ger. *flackern*, to flare.

Flotery, wavy, flowing. (Tyrwhitt renders it *floating*.) *Flotery berd = *a long, flowing beard. In Early Eng. Alliterative Poems we find the phrase '*floty valez*' (vales), where *floty* has the same sense as *flotery*. Ger. *flotern*, *flutern*, to flutter.

Flough, Fleigh, flew.

Flowen, pret. pl. flew.

Flowtynge, playing on a flute. O.Fr. *flabute, flaute,* Fr. *flûte,* a flute ; O. Fr. *flagoler,* to pipe, whence *flageolet.*

Fole, a fool.

Fome, foam. A.S. *fám.*

Fomen, to foam.

Fond, found, provided.

Foo, Fo, foe, enemy. A.S. *fá,* enemy. See **Fend.**

For, (1) because, (2) '*for* al,' notwithstanding.

Forbere, to forbear.

Forby, forth by, past.

Force. '*No force*' = no matter.

Fordo, to ruin, destroy.

Forgete, to forget (pp. *forgeten, foryeten*).

Forheed, forehead.

Forncast, pre-ordained.

Forneys, furnace. Fr. *fournaise,* It. *fornace,* Lat. *furnus,* an oven.

Forpyned, was'ed away (through *pine* or torment), tormented. See **Pine.**

Forslouthe, to lose through sloth.

Forster, a forester.

Forther, Forthere, further. A.S. *furthra.* The O.E. *forthere* signifies also fore, front. The root *fore* occurs in *former, far.*

Forthere, to further, aid. A.S. *fyrthrian,* to promote, support.

Forthermore, furthermore.

Forthy, therefore. *-thy* = the ablative case of the def. article.

Fortune, to make fortunate, to give good or bad fortune.

Forward, Forwarde, covenant, agreement. A.S. *foreweard,* O.N. *forvörthr,* a compact, covenant.

Foryete. See **Forgete.**

Fothur, a load, properly a carriage-load. It is now used for a certain weight of lead. A.S. *fother,* O.Du. *voeder,* Ger. *fuder.*

Foughten, pp. fought.

Foul, Fowel, a bird, *fowl.* A.S. *fugol, flugol* (Ger. *vogel*), a bird, from *fleogan,* to fly.

Founden, pp. found.

Foundre, to founder, fall down. O.Fr. *fondrer,* to sink, fall down.

Foyne, Foynen, to make a pass in fencing, to push, *foine.* O.Fr. *foindre, foigner,* to feign, make a feint.

Fre, free, generous, willing.

Fredom, freedom, liberality.

Freend, Frend, a friend.

Freisch, Freissh, Freissche, fresh. A.S. *fersc,* O.N. *friskr.* The Eng. *frisk, frisky,* are from the same source.

Frendly, friendly.

Frendschipe, friendship.

Freknes, freckles. Prov. Eng. *frackens,* O.N. *frekna,* freckles ; Ger. *fleck, flecken,* a spot, stain.

Frere, a friar.

Frete, Freten, to eat (pp. *freten*). A.S. *fretan,* Ger. *fressen,* devour, eat ; Eng. *fret.*

Fro, Froo, from. O.N. *fra,* from. It still exists in the phrase ' to and *fro,*' and in *froward* and *forward* (bold).

Frothen, to froth, foam.

Fume, drunkenness.

Fumytere, name of a plant, *fumitory.*

Fuyr, fire ; **Fuyry,** fiery.

Fyfe, five.

Fyled, cut, formed.

Fyn, fine.

Fynde, to invent, provide.

Fyr, fire ; **Fyry,** fiery.

Fyr reed, red as fire.

G.

Gabbe, to lie. A.S. *gabban,* O.N. *gabba,* to lie, jest ; O.N. *gabb,* a jest. We have the same root in *gabble, gibberish.*

Gadere, Gadre, to gather.

Galyngale, sweet cyperus.

Game, pleasure, sport. A.S. *gamen,* O. Fris. *game,* sport, play; A.S. *gamenian,* to sport.

Gamed, verb impers. pleased.

Gan (a contraction of began) is used as a mood auxiliary, e. g. *gan singe* = did sing.

Gapeinge, Gapyng, having the mouth wide open, gaping. A.S. *geápan,* O.N. *gâpa,* Ger. *gaffen,* to stare (i. e. with open mouth). *Gasp* is a sibillated form of the same root. Cp. O. E. *galping,* gaping; O. Du. *galpen,* to yawn, gape; O. N. *glápa,* to stare; Eng. *gulp.*

Gappe (dative). A.S. *geap,* O. N. *gap,* a gap,

Garget, the throat. Fr. *gorge,* a throat; It. *gorgo,* a gurgle; Ger. *gurgel,* the gullet, throat.

Garleek, garlick; spear-plant; from A.S. *gar,* a spear, *leac,* an herb, plant, *leek.* We have the second element in many names of plants, as *hemlock* (O. E. *hemlick*), *charlock, barley,* (O. E. *berlic,* from *bere,* barley).

Gaste, to terrify. See **Agast.**

Gastly, horrible. See **Gaste.**

Gat, got, obtained.

Gattothud, having teeth far apart. Du. *ga/,* a hole. It is sometimes written *gaptoothed. Gagtoothed* = having projecting teeth.

Gaude grene, a light green colour. "Colour hit *gaude grene.*" (Ord. and Reg. p. 452.)

Gayler, a gaoler. It. *gaiola,* Sp. *gayola,* a cage.

Gayne, to avail. O. N. *gegna,* to meet, to aid; O.N. *gagn,* A. S. *gegn,* against; whence *ungainly.*

Gaytre beriis, berries of the dogwood-tree, *cornus fæmina.*

Geeres, manners, habits. See **Gere.**

Gees, geese.

Geet, jet. Fr. *jaiet,* Lat. *gagates.* Used for beads, and held in high estimation. Bp. Bale makes allusion to this in Kynge johan, p. 39:
"Holy water and bredde, shall dryve away the devyll;
Blessynges with *black bedes* will helpe in every evyll."

Gent, neat, pretty.

Gentilesse, gentleness.

Gepoun, Gypoun, a short cassock.

Ger, gear. See **Gere.**

Gerdul, girdle.

Gere, gear, all sorts of instruments, tools, utensils of armour, apparel, fashion. A.S. *gearwa,* clothing; *gearwian,* to prepare, whence Eng. *yare.*

Gerland, a garland.

Gerner, a garner. Fr. *grenier.*

Gery, changeable. Fr. *girer,* to turn round; Lat. *gyrare.*

Gesse, to deem, suppose, think. *guess.* Du. *gissen,* Sw. *gissa,* Dan *gisse,* to believe, suppose.

Get, fashion, mode. O. Fr. *get,* contrivance.

Gete, to get, obtain, pp. *geten.*

Gile, guile. O. Fr. *guille,* deceit.

Gilteles, free from guilt, guiltless.

Gipser, a pouch or purse. Fr. *gibbecière,* a pouch, from *gibbe,* a bunch.

Gir, conduct, behaviour. See **Gere.**

Gird, pp, girded.

Girful, changeable. See **Gery.**

Girt, pierced. *Thurgh-girded,* pierced through, is used also by Surrey:
"With throat ycut he roars, he lieth along,
His entrails with a lance *through-gyrded* quite." (Poems, p. 215, ed. Bell.)
The O. E. *girde,* or *gride,* signifies also to strike, and may be connected with O. E. *yard* (as in *yard*-measure), Du. *garde,* Ger. *gerte,* a rod.

Glade, to console, gladden.

Glader, sb. one who makes glad; adj. more glad.

Glaryng, staring (like the eyes of the hare). Norse *glora*, to stare.

Gleed, Gleede, a live coal, *gleed*. A.S. *glêd*, O. Du. *gloed*. Cp. O.N. *glóa*, to burn, *glow; glod*, a live coal; Ger. *glüben*, to glow; *gluth*, hot coals.

Gliteren, to glitter, shine. O.N. *glitra*, to glitter.

Glowen, to glow, shine; Gloweden, (pl. pret.) shone; Glowyng, fiery. See Gleed.

Go, Gon, Goo, (pp. *go, gon, goon*), to go, walk; Gooth, goes; Goon, (pl.) go, walk.

Gobet, piece, morsel, fragment. Prov. Eng. *gob*, Gael. *gob*, the mouth; whence *gobble, gabble*, &c.

Godhed, godhead, divinity.

Golyardeys, a buffoon. See note p. 133.

Gon. See Go.

Gonne (pl. of *gan*), began, did.

Good, property, goods.

Goost, ghost, spirit.

Goot, a goat.

Goune, Gowne, a gown. It. *gonna*, Mid. Lat. *guna, gouna*.

Governaunce, management, control; management of affairs, business matters.

Governynge, control.

Graunte, grant, permission.

Graunte, to grant, consent to.

Grauntyng, consent, permission.

Gree, the prize, *grant*. Lat. *gratus*, Fr. *gré*, will, liking, consent.

Greene, Grene, green. A.S. *gréne*.

Grees, grease.

Greet, Gret, def. form and pl. *greete, grete*, great; comp. *grettere, gretter, grettest*.

Greve, to grieve.

Greve, a grove. This form is used by many of the Elizabethan poets.

Griffoun, a griffin.

Grim, Grym, fierce. A.S. *grimm*, fierce, furious; Du. *grimmen*, to snarl; It. *grima*, wrinkled; Fr. *grimace*, a wry mouth, *grimace*.

Grisly, horrible, dreadful, from O.E. *grise, agrise*, to terrify. A.S. *agrîsan*, to dread, fear; Ger. *grausen*, to shudder at; O. Du. *grijsen*, Prov. Eng. *gryze*, to snarl, grind the teeth.

Grone, Gronen, to groan; Gronyng, groaning. A.S. *gránian*, to groan, murmur.

Grope, to try, test. It signifies originally to feel with the hands, to *grope;* hence to probe a wound, to test, put to the proof.

Grote, a groat.

Groynyng, stabbing. Tyrwhitt renders it ' discontent.'

Grucchen, to murmur, grumble, grudge. Fr. *groucher*, to murmur. Gr. γρύζειν, to murmur, mutter.

Gruf, with face flat to the ground; whence Eng. *grovelling, grovel*. O.E. *grovelinges, gruflinges*, O.N. *grufa*, to stoop down. *Liggia á grufa*, to lie with the nose to the ground.

Grys, fur of the gray rabbit.

Gulde or Golde, a flower commonly called a *turnsol*. Fr. *goude*, a *marigold*, so called from its golden colour. See note p. 143.

Gult, Gylt, guilt, conduct which has to be atoned for by a payment. A.S. *gild*, a money payment; Swiss *gült*, Dan. *gjeld*, a debt. Cp. A.S. *gildan*, Ger. *gelten*, pay, *yield*.

Gulty, guilty.

Gurles, young people, either male or female. Low Ger. *gör, göre*, a child. The O.E. *wench-el*, a boy, is our word *wench*.

Gyde, Gye, to guide. Fr. *guider, guier*.

Gylt, guilt. See Gult.

Gyngle, to jingle.

Gynne, to begin.

Gyse, guise, fashion, mode, *wise*. Fr. *guise*, Welsh *gwis*, Ger. *weise*, Eng. *wise*, mode, fashion.

H.

Haburdarsher, a seller of hats. "The *Haberdasher* heapeth wealth by *hattes*." (Gascoigne, The Fruites of Warre.) See note, p. 128.

Haburgeon, Haburgeoun, Haburgoun, a diminutive of *hauberk*, a coat of mail. O. Fr. *hauberc*, O. H. Ger. *halsberc*, A.S. *healsbeorg*, a coat of mail, from *heals*, the neck, and *beorgan*, to cover or protect.

Hadden, pl. had.

Hade = *havede*, sing. had.

Hakke, to hack. Du. *hacken*, Ger. *hacken*, to cut up, chop; Dan. *hakke*, to peck; Fr. *hacher*, to mince; whence Eng. *hash*, *hatch*, *hatchet*.

Haldyng, holding.

Halwes, saints. A.S. *hálga*, a saint (as in 'All Hallows E'en'), from *hál*, whole.

Hamer, a hammer.

Han = *haven*, to have.

Happe, to happen, befall; whence *happy*, mis-*hap*, per-*haps*, may-*hap*. O.E. *happen*, happy; O.N. *happ*, fortune.

Hardily = *hardely*, certainly.

Hardynesse, boldness.

Haried, hurried, taken as a prisoner. Fr. *harier*, to hurry, harass.

Harlot. This term was not confined to a female, nor even to a person of a bad character. It signifies (1) a young person; (2) a person of low birth; (3) a person given to low conduct; (4) a ribald. W. *herlod*, *herlawd*, a youth.

Harlotries, ribaldries.

Harnays, Harneys, Herneys, Hernoys, armour, gear, furniture, *harness*. O.Fr. *harneis*, Fr. *harnois*, all manner of harness, equipage, furniture; Ger. *harnisch*, armour.

Harneysed, equipped.

Harrow, a cry of distress. O.Fr. *harau*, *hare! Crier haro sur*, to make hue and cry after. O.H.Ger. *haren*, to cry out; Scottish *harro*, a cry for help.

Harre, a hinge. A.S. *heor*, *heorra*, a hinge.

Hauberk, a coat of mail. See Haburgeon.

Haunte, (1) a district, (2) custom, practice, skill. Breton *hent*, a way; Fr. *hanter*, to frequent.

Hede, Heed, Heede, head. A.S. *heafod*, O.Du. *hoofd*, head; Scottish *haffet*, side of the head.

Heeld, held.

Heep, heap, assembly, host. A.S. *heap*, Ger. *haufe*, heap, band, crowd. Cp. O.E. 'a *heep* of houndes;' *hep*, a band of armed men.

Heer, Heere, Here, hair. A.S. *hǽr*, *hér*.

Heere, to hear.

Heete, to promise. A.S. *hátan*, O.Sax. *hêtan*, O.N. *heita*, to call, promise.

Heeth, Heethe, a heath. A.S. *hǽth*, heath; Goth. *haithi*, the open country; O.N. *heidi*, a waste; Ger. *heide*, a heath; whence *heathen*, *hoyden* (O.Du. *heyden*, a clown, rustic).

Hegge, a hedge. A.S. *hegge*, Ger. *hag*, a bush, shrub, hedge. We have another form of the root in *haw-thorn* (A.S. *haga*, a hedge), and in the local name *Hayes*; '*Broken hayes*' (Oxford).

Heigh, Heygh, Heih, high.

Heigher, upper.

Hele, health. A.S. *hǽl*, whole; *hel*, *hælu*, health.

Helpen, to help (pret. *halp*, pp. *holpen*).

Hem, them.

Hemselve, Hemselven, themselves.

Heng (pret. of *honge*), hanged.

Henne, hence. O.E. *hennes, hens*, a more modern form is our *hence*.

Hente, to seize, take hold of (pret. *hente*, pp. *hent*). A.S. *hentan*.

Her, Here, their, of them. *Here aller* = of them all.

Heraude, Herawde, Herowde, a herald. Fr. *hérauld, héraut*, from O.H.Ger. *haren*, to shout.

Herbergage, Herbergh, lodging, inn, port, harbour. A.S. *here*, an army, and *beorgan*, to protect, defend.

Herde, a herd, keeper of cattle, a shep*herd*. A.S. *hyrde*, a keeper, guardian; Ger. *hirt*, a herdsman; O.N. *hirda*, to keep guard.

Here, hair. See Heer.

Here, to hear.

Hered, haired.

Herken, Herkene, Herkne, to hark, hearken, listen.

Hernoys. See Harnays.

Hert, a hart.

Hert, Herte, a heart.

Herte-spon. The provincial *heart-spoon* signifies the navel. Tyrwhitt explains it as " the concave part of the breast, where the lower ribs unite with the *cartilago ensiformis*."
" . . . . He that undoes him (the deer),
Doth cleave the *brisket bone*, upon the *spoon*,
Of which a little gristle grows."
(Sad Shepherd, A. 1, S. vi)

Herteles, without heart, cowardly.

Hertely, Hertily, heartily.

Hest, command, *behest*. A.S. *hæs*, from *hátan*, to command.

Hete, heat.

Hethe, heath. See Heeth.

Hethene, a heathen.

Hethenesse, the country inhabited by the heathens, in contradistinction to *Christendom*.

Heve, to heave, raise. *Heve of* = to lift off (pret. *haf, hof*, Eng. *hove*). A.S. *hebban*, O.Fris. *heva*, to heave, lift.

Heven, Hevene, heaven.

Hew, Hewe, colour, complexion, *hue*; *hewes*, colours for painting. A.S. *heow*.

Hewe, to cut. A.S. *heawian*, Ger. *hauen*.

Hey, Heye, Heygh, Heyghe, high, highly. A.S. *heh*.

Hider, hither.

Hidous, hideous; Hidously, hideously. O.Fr. *hide, hisde, hidour, hisdour*, dread.

Hiere, to hear.

Hiew, hue, colour.

Hiewed, coloured. See Hew.

Hight, Highte, was called. A.S. *héht, hét;* pret. of *hátan*, to command, promise. The proper preterite of *hátan* (Ger. *heissen*), to call, be called, was *hatte;* so two distinct verbs have been confounded.

Highte. '*In highte*' = aloud.

Hih, Hihe, high.

Hild = *hield*, held.

Hiled, hidden, kept secret. A.S. *helan*, to cover, conceal; Prov. Eng. *hele*, hill (Ger. *hüllen*, to cover, wrap); whence Eng. *hull*, cod of pease.

Himselve, Himselven, dat. and acc. of *himself*.

Hir, Hire, her.

Hirselve, Hirselven, herself.

Hit, it.

Ho, Hoo, an interjection commanding a cessation of anything. Cp. the carter's *whoa!* to his horse to stop.

Hold, 'in hold,' in possession, custody. A.S. *ge-heald*, O.N. *hald*, custody, *hold*; A.S. *healdan, haldan*, to hold, retain.

Holde, Holden, beholden, esteemed, held.

Holly, wholly. See **Hool**.

Holpen, helped. See **Helpen**.

Holt, Holte, a wood, grove. A.S. *holt*, O.H.Ger. *holz*, a wood. *Holt* is still used in some parts of England for an orchard or any place of trees, as a *cherry-holt*, an *apple-holt*. In Norfolk a plantation is called a *holt*, as *nut-holt*, *osier-holt*, *gooseberry-holt*. It occurs frequently as an element in local names, as *Holt*, a wood near Havant (Hants); *Knock-holt*, a wood near Tenterden (Kent).

Holwe, hollow. A.S. *hol*, a hole; *holb*, a ditch; Low. Ger. *holig*, hollow. The termination *-we* or *-ow* had originally a diminutival force.

Hom, home; **Homward**, homeward.

Homicides, murderers.

Hond, Honde, hand.

Honge, Hongen, to hang (pret. *heng*).

Hont, Honte, a hunter.

Honte, Honten, to hunt. *On hontyng* = a-hunting.

Honest, creditable, honourable, becoming.

Hoo. See **Ho**.

Hool, whole. A.S. *hál*, whole, sound; whence *wholesome, holy,* &c.

Hoom, home; **Hoomly**, homely. A.S. *ham*, Ger. *heim*.

Hoot, Hoote, Hote, hot. A.S. *hât*.

Hoppesteres (applied to ships), dancers. *-ster* is a termination marking the feminine gender, as in modern Eng. *spinster*.

Hors, horse; pl. *hors*, horses.

Hosteller, inn-keeper. Fr. *hôtelier*.

Hostelrie, Hostelrye, an hotel, inn. Fr. *hôtel*, O. Fr. *hostel*, Mid. Lat. *hospitale*, a hostel, inn (whence Eng. *hospital*), from Lat. *hospes*, a guest.

Hote, hot. See **Hoot**.

Hote, Hoten, to be called. See **Heete, Hight**.

Hous, Hows, house; **Houshaldere**, householder.

Howpede = *houped*, whooped. Fr. *houper*, to call out. *Hooping-cough* is properly *whooping-cough*. A.S. *wop*, outcry, *weeping;* Fris. *wopa*, to call; Goth. *wopjan*, to crow as a cock; O.N. *op*, cry, clamour.

Huld, held. The *u* represents an older *eo*, as in the O. E. *heold*.

Hunte, a hunter.

Hunteresse, a female hunter.

Hupes, hips. A.S. *hype*, Du. *heupe*, Ger. *hüfte*, the flank, hip.

Hurtle, to push. Fr. *heurter*, Du. *horten*, to dash against. *Hurt*, *hurl*, are connected with the root *hort*.

Huyre, hire, reward.

Hy, Hye, Hyhe, high, highly.

Hye, haste; *in hye*, in haste, hastily.

Hynderest, hindmost. Cp. *overest*, overmost, uppermost.

Hyne, hind, servant. A.S. *hina, hine*, a servant, domestic; *hige, hiwa*, family; whence *hive*.

Hynge (pl. pret. of *hongen*), hung.

I.

I, a prefix used to denote the past participle (like the modern German *ge*), as in the following words: *I-bete*, ornamented; *I-bore*, borne, carried; *I-born*, born; *I-bought*, bought; *I-bounden*, bound; *I-brent*, burnt; *I-caught*, caught; *I-chapud*, having *chapes* or plates of metal at the point of a sheath or scabbard, (Sp. *chapa*); *I-cleped*, called; *I-clothed*, clothed; *I-clenched*, fastened, *clinched; I-doo, I-doon*, done; *I-drawe*, drawn; *I-falle*, fallen; *I-fetered*, fettered; *I-founde*, found; *I-go, I-gon, I-goon*, gone; *I-lad*, led; *I-laft*, left; *I-knowe*, know; *I-korve*, cut; *I-logged*, lodged; *I-mad, I-maad, I-maked*, made; *I-peynted*, painted; *I-pynched*, plaited; *I-proved*, proved; *I-rad*, read;

I-ronne, run, clotted; *I-sayd*, said; *I-sayled*, sailed; *I-schadewed*, shaded; *I-schave*, shaven; *I-schreve*, shriven; *I-sent*, sent; *I-served*, deserved; *I-set*, set, appointed; *I-slaked*, slaked, appeased; *I-slawe*, *I-slayn*, slain; *I-stored*, stored; *I-storve*, died, dead; *I-styked*, pierced, stabbed; *I-swore*, sworn; *I-take*, taken; *I-taught*, taught; *I-wedded*, wedded; *I-wonne*, got, won; *I-write*, *I-writen*, written; *I-wrought*, wrought, made; *I-wrye*, covered (see **Wrye**).

Iliche, alike.

Ilk, Ilke, same. A. S. *ylc.* Cp. ' of that *ilk.*'

In, Inne, house, lodging, inn.

Inne, adv. in.

Inned, lodged, entertained.

Inough, enough.

Iwis, Iwys, indeed, truly. It is often contracted into *wis*. A. S. *gewis*.

J.

Jangle, to prate, babble.

Jangler, a prater, babbler. O. Fr. *jangler*, to prattle, jest, lie. It is perhaps connected with *jingle*.

Jape, a trick, jest.

Jape, to befool, deceive. Fr. *japper*, to yelp. It is probably connected with Eng. *gabble, gabbe*, &c.

Jolyf, joyful, pleasant. Fr. *joli*, It. *giulivo*, gay, fine, merry. Diez connects it with O. N. *jol*, Eng. *yule*, Christmas.

Jolynesse, joyfulness.

Journee, a day's journey.

Juge, Jugge, a judge. Fr. *juge*, Lat. *judex*.

Juggement, judgment.

Juste, Justne, to joust, tilt, engage in a tournament. Fr. *jouster*, to tilt; Eng. *jostle*.

Joustes = *jouste*, a tournament.

Juwyse, judgment. Fr. *juise*, judgment, from Lat. *judicium*.

K.

Kaytives, prisoners, wretches. See **Caytif**.

Keep, Keepe, Kepe, care, attention, heed; *take keep*, take care.

Keepe, Kepe (pret. *kepte*, ſp. *kept, kepud*), to guard, preserve to care, as in *I kepe nat* = I care not. A. S. *cépan*.

Kempe, shaggy, literally crooked. Cp. the phrase ' clean cam.' See note, pp. 144, 145.

Kempt, (pp. of *kembe*); combed, neatly trimmed.

Kerver, a carver.

Kerving, Kervyng, cutting, carving. See **Carf**.

Keverchef, a kerchief.

Kind, Kynd, Kynde, nature; *by kynde* = by nature, naturally. Cp. ' the kindly (natural) fruits of the earth.' A. S. *cynd*, nature.

Knarre, a knotted, thick-set fellow. Cp. O. E. *gnarr*, a knot; *gnarled*, knotted; Swed. *knorla*, to twist.

Knarry, full of *gnarrs* or knots.

Knave, a boy, a servant. A. S. *cnapa*, Ger. *knabe*, a boy, youth, servant; O. E. *knave*-child, a male-child.

Knobbe, a pimple.

Knyf, a knife.

Kowthe, known. See **Couthe**.

Kyn, kine.

Kynled, kindled. O. N. *kynda*, to set fire to; *kynnel*, a torch; whence Eng. *cannel* coal.

Kynrede, kindred (A.S. *ræden*). The affix *-rede* is equivalent to *-ship*, and occurs in *hat-red*. The O. E. has *frend-reden*, friendship; *fo-reden*, enmity.

L.

Laas, a lace, belt. Fr. *lacqs*, Prov. Fr. *laz* (Lat. *laqueus*), a lace, snare.

Lacert, a fleshy muscle, so called from being shaped like a lizard (Lat. *lacerta*).

Lad (pp.), Ladde (pret.), led, carried.

Lafte (pret. sing.), Laften (pret. pl.), left, ceased. Cp. the phrase 'left off.'

Lak, want, lack. Du. *lack*, fault, want.

Lakke, to lack, be wanting.

Lang, Lange, long.

Langage, language.

Large, adj. free; adv. largely. Chaucer says 'at *his large*,' where we should say 'at large.'

Lasyng, lacing, fastening. See Laas.

Lat, imp. let; *lat be*, cease.

Late, lately, recently; *late* comen; '*late* ischave.'

Latoun, a kind of brass, or tinned iron, *latten*. Fr. *laiton*, brass; It. *latta*, tin plate.

Launde, a plain surrounded by trees, hunting-grounds. Cotgrave has "*lande*, a land or *launde*, a wild untilled shrubberie or bushy plaine." It seems to be, with a difference of meaning, our modern word *lawn*. Welsh *llan*, a clear space. Shakespeare uses the word in Hen. VI, pt. III, iii. 1:
"Under this thick-grown brake we'll shroud ourselves;
For through this *laund* anon the deer will come."

Laurer, a laurel.

Lawghe, to laugh.

Laxatif, Laxatyf, a purging medicine.

Laynere, a lanner or whiplash. Fr. *lanière*, a thong, *laniard*; *lanier*, lash of a whip.

Lazar, Lazer, a leper.

Lechecraft, the skill of a physician, from *leche*, a physician. A.S. *læce*, a leech, physician.

Leede (dat.), a cauldron, copper. It also signifies a kettle. Gael. *luchd*, a pot, kettle.
"Mow haulm to burn,
To serve thy turn,
To bake thy bread
To burn under *lead*." (Tusser.)

Leef (pl. *leeves, leves*), leaf.

Leef (def. form voc. case *leeve*), dear, beloved, pleasing. 'Be him loth or *leef*' = be it displeasing or pleasing to him. A.S. *leof*, dear; Eng. *lief, liefer*.

Leere, Lere, to learn. A.S. *læran*, to teach; *lár*, doctrine, *lore*.

Leese, Lese, to lose. A.S *leósan* (pret. *leas;* O.E. *les*, pp. *loren*). The old past participle occurs in *for-lorn*.

Leesyng, loss.

Leet, pret. let. A.S. *lætan* (pret. *lét*, pp. *læten*). *Leet brynge* = caused to be brought.

Lef, imp. leave.

Lene, to lend, give. A.S. *lænan*, to give, lend; *læn*, a loan; Ger. *leben*, to lend.

Lene, Leene, lean, poor. A.S. *blæne*, from *blinian*, to lean, bend.

Leng, Lenger, Lengere, longer.

Lepart, a leopard.

Lere. See Leere.

Lese, to lose. See Leese.

Lest, List, Lust, pleasure, delight, joy. A.S. *lyst, lust*, desire, love; *lystan. lustan*, to wish, will, desire; Eng. *list, listless, lust, lusty*.

Lest, Leste, least.

Leste, Liste, Lyste, Luste, vb. impers. it pleases (pret. *leste, liste*). 'Me *list*' = it pleases me; 'him *luste*' = it pleased him; 'hem *leste*' = it pleased them; 'us *leste*' = it pleased us.

Lesten, lost. See Leese.

Lesynges, leasing, lies. A.S. *leas*, false, loose; *leasung*, falseness; Goth. *laus*, empty, vain; whence the affix *-less*.

Lete. Lette, to leave; '*letten of*' = refrain from. See Leet.

Lette, to hinder, delay, tarry, put off (pret. *lette*). A.S. *lettan*, to hinder; Goth. *latjan*, to delay; O.N. *latr*, lazy, slow. Cp. Eng. *late, lazy*.

Lette, delay, hindrance. See previous word.

Letuaries, electuaries.

Lever, rather (comp. of *leef* or *lief*). ' Him was *lever* ' = it was more agreeable to him, he would rather.

Lewed, Lewid, ignorant, unlearned ; *lewed-man,* a layman. A.S. *læwed,* pertaining to the laity ; A. S. *leod,* people ; Du. *læte,* a peasant ; Ger. *leute,* people. (Eng. *lad, lout,* belong to this family of words.)

Leye, to lay (imp. *ley,* pret. *leyde,* pp. *leyd*).

Leysir, leisure. Fr. *loisir,* from Lat. *licere.*

Licenciat, one licensed by the Pope to hear confessions in all places, and to administer penance independently of the local ordinaries.

Liche-wake, the vigil, *watch,* or *wake* held over the body of the dead. A.S. *lic,* Ger. *leiche,* Goth. *leik,* a corpse ; whence *lich-gate,* the gate where the corpse is set down on entering a churchyard to await the arrival of the minister.

Licour, liquor.

Lief, beloved. See **Leef.**

Lif, Lyf, life.

Liggyng, lying. O.E. *ligge, legge,* to lie, lay ; A.S. *licgan,* to lie, from *lecgan,* to lay.

Lightly, (1) easily, (2) joyfully.

Lik, Lyk, like.

Like, vb. impers. to please.

Liken, Likne, to compare.

Lipsede, lisped. Du. *lispen.*

Liste. See **Leste.**

Listes, Lystes, lists, a place enclosed for combats or tournaments.

Litarge, white lead.

Lite, Lyte, Litel, little. A.S. *lyt, lytel,* Goth. *leitils,* Du. *luttik.*

Lith, lies.

Lith, a limb, any members of the body. A.S. *lith,* Ger. *g-lied,* a joint, limb ; Norse *lide,* to bend

the limbs, whence Eng. *lithe, lissome.*

Live, dat. of *lif,* life ; *on live,* in life, alive. Cp. O.E. *on slepe* = asleep.

Lodemenage, pilotage. Used in this sense in 3 Geo. 1, c. 13. Courts of *Lodemanage* are held at Dover for the appointment of the Cinque Port pilots. See **Loodesterre.**

Logge, Loge, to lodge, sb. a lodging, inn. **Loggyng,** lodging. Fr. *loge,* a hut or small apartment ; *loger,* to sojourn.

Loke, to see, look upon.

Loken, locked, enclosed.

Lokkes, locks (of hair), curls.

Lokyng, appearance, sight.

Lond, Londe, land.

Longe, Longen, to belong.

Longe, Longen, to desire, long for.

Loode, a load.

Loodesterre, a loadstar, the polestar. The first element is the A.S. *lád,* away, from *lædan,* to lead, conduct. It occurs again in *load-stone ; lode,* a vein of metal ore ; O. E. *lode-men, loders,* carriers, pilots ; *lode-ship,* a kind of fishing-vessel mentioned in early statutes ; Prov. Eng. *loads,* ditches for draining away the water from the fens ; *loadstone,* a leading stone for drains.

Loor, Loore, Lore, precept, doctrine, learning. See **Leere.**

Lordynges, Lordlynges (a diminutive of *lord*), sirs, my masters.

Lorn, lost. See **Leese.**

Los, loss.

Losingour, a flatterer, liar, O. Fr. *losengier.*

Loth, odious, hateful, disagreeable, displeasing, *loath.*

Lounges, lungs.

Lovyer, a lover.

Lowde, loud, loudly.

Luce, a pike.

Lust, pleaseth. See **Leste.**

Lusty, pleasant. Lustily, Lustely, merrily, joyfully.

Lustynes, Lystynesse, pleasure.

Lyfly, lifelike.

Lyk, like, alike.

Lymytour, a friar licensed to ask alms within a certain limit.

Lynage, Lyne, lineage.

Lystes. See Listes.

Lyve. See Live.

Lyvere, livery. See note, pp. 128, 129.

M.

Maad, Mad, pp. made.

Maat, dejected, downcast. Fr. *mat*, faded, quelled; Sp. *matar*, to quench, kill; cp. Du. *mat*, exhausted; Ger. *matt*, feeble, faint.

Magik, magic.

Maist, mayest; Maistow, mayest thou.

Maister, Mayster, a master, chief, a skilful artist; *maister streete* = the chief street.

Maistre, skill, power, superiority.

Make, a companion or mate. A.S. *maca*, a companion; O.N. *maki*, a spouse; Eng. *match*.

Maked, Makid, made.

Male, a portmanteau, bag, *mail*. O. Fr. *male*, a great budget. Fr. *malle*.

Malencolie, Malencolye, sb. melancholy; adj. Malencolyk,

Manace, Manasyng, a threat, menace. Fr. *menace*, Lat. *minae, minaciae*, threats.

Mancioun, a mansion.

Maner, Manere, manner, kind, sort. 'A *maner* dey' = a sort of dey, or farm servant.

Manhede, manhood, manliness.

Manne, of men.

Mantelet, a little mantle, a short mantle.

Marchal, marshal. Mid. Lat. *marescalcus*, Fr. *marechal*, the master of the horse; O. Ger.

mähre, a horse, and *schalk*, a servant. "The *marshal of the hall*, was the person who, at public festivals, placed every person according to his rank. It was his duty also to preserve peace and order. The *marshal of the field* presided over any out-door games." (Halliwell.)

Marchaunt, a merchant.

Martirdam, torment, martyrdom.

Martyre, to torment.

Mary, marrow. A.S. *mearh*, marrow; Dan. *marg, marv*, Prov. Eng. *merowe*, tender; A.S. *mearu*, soft, tender.

Mase, a wild fancy. O. N. *masa*, to jabber, chatter; Norse *masast*, to drop asleep, to begin to dream; Prov. Eng. *mazle*, to wander, as if stupefied. Cp. the phrase 'to be in a *maze*.'

Mateere, Mater, Matere, Matier, Matiere, matter.

Matrimoyn, matrimony.

Maugre, Mawgre, in spite of. Fr. *malgré*, against the will of, in spite of; *mal*, ill, and *gré*, will, pleasure.

Maunciple, an officer who has the care of purchasing victuals for an Inn of Court or College. Lat. *manceps*, a purchaser, contractor.

Maydenhode, maidenhood.

Mayne, domestics, servants. See Meyné.

Mayntene, Maynteyne, to maintain.

Mayst, mayest.

Med, Meed, Mede, Meede, a reward, *meed*. A.S. *méd*, Ger. *miethe*, hire; whence Eng *midwife*, O. E. *meedful*, meritorious.

Mede, a mead or meadow, hay-land. A.S. *mæd, mædewe*, a meadow: Fris. *made*, a low, swampy piece of ground; O. Du. *mad*, a marshy plot of ground. *Mud, moist*, belong to the same family of words.

Medled, of a mixed colour. Fr. *medler, mesler,* to mix,

Meel, a meal. A.S. *mæl,* what is marked out, a separate part, a meal, a mark, spot. Cp. O.E. *cup-mele,* cup by cup; *stound-mele,* at intervals; Eng. *piece-meal,* Ger. *ein-mal,* once.

Meke, meek.

Mellere, a miller.

Men, one; used like the Fr. *on.*

Mencioun, mention.

Mene, to mean, intend (pret. *mente*).

Menstralcy, minstrelsy.

Mere, a mare. A.S. *mære,* a mare, O.N. *mar,* a horse.

Meremayd, a mermaid. A.S. *mere,* a lake, sea; Ger. *meer,* the sea.

Merie, Mery, Merye, Murye, pleasant, joyful, merry. A.S. *myrg,* pleasure; *myrðð,* pleasure, joy, mirth.

Meriely, pleasantly.

Merthe, Myrthe, pleasure, amusement.

Mervaille, Mervayle, marvel. Fr. *merveille,* Lat. *mirabilia,* wonderful things.

Meschaunce, mischance, misfortune.

Mescheef, Meschief, misfortune, what turns out ill. Fr. *meschef* (*mes = minus,* less; *chef = caput,* head).

Messager, a messenger.

Meste, most.

Mester, Mestir, trade, business, occupation; *mestir men =* sort of men. Lat. *ministerium,* Fr. *ministère, mestier,* occupation, art. O.Fr. *menestrel,* a workman, artist.

Mesurable, moderate.

Met, pp. dreamed. See **Mete**.

Mete, meat, food. Cp. Goth. *mats,* food; *matjan,* to take food; O.H. Ger. *maz,* food, dish; Eng. *mess.*

Mete, to meet.

Mete, to dream, pret. *mette.* (*Met* for *mette* before a word commencing with a vowel.) It is used impersonally as *me mette,* I dreamed; A.S. *mætan.*

Meth, mead, a drink made of honey.

Mewe, a *mue* or coop where fowls were fattened. *Mew* also signified a place where *hawks* were confined while moulting. Fr. *muer,* to change; It. *muta,* a change; Lat. *mutare,* to change. We have a similar root in Du. *muiten,* O.E. *moute,* to moult.

Meyné, household, attendants, suite. O.Fr. *mesnée, maisgnée;* Mid. Lat. *maisnada* (from Lat. *minores natu;* cp. O.Fr. *mainsné,* a younger son), a family, household, suite.

Middes, middle, midst.

Minister, Mynistre, an office of justice.

Misboden (pp. of *misbede*), insulted, injured. The root *bede,* A.S. *beódan, =* to offer, as in our phrase ' to *bid* the banns;' *bid* for a thing.

Mischaunce. See **Meschaunce**.

Mo, Moo, more. A.S. *má.*

Moche, Mochel, Mochil, adj. much, great; adv. greatly. *Moche and lite =* great and small. A.S. *mycel,* great, *mickle.*

Moder, mother.

Moevere, mover, first cause.

Mone, Moone, the moon.

Moneth, a month.

Mood, anger. A.S. *mod,* Ger. *muth,* mind, courage, passion. Cp. Eng. *moody.*

Moone, a moan, lamentation. A.S. *mænan,* to moan.

Moot, Moote, may (pret. must, ought; pl. pres. *mooten, moste*). A.S. *mót,* 1st and 3rd pers. sing.; *móst,* 2nd pers.; *móton,* pl.; *moste,* pret.

Mor, More, greater, more.

Morder, Mordre, sb. murder; vb. to murder.

Mordrer, a murderer.

Mormal, a cancer, sore, or gangrene. See note, p. 130.

Morn, morning, morrow; **To-morn**, to-morrow.

Morne, adj. morning.

Morning, mourning.

Morthre, vb. to murder; sb. murder.

Mortreux, a kind of soup or pottage. See note, p. 130.

Morwe, **Morwenynge**, morning, morrow.

Mosel, Fr. *museau*, muzzle, nose of an animal. It. *musolare*, to muzzle.

Moste, must. See **Moot.**

Moste, greatest, most.

Mot may, must. See **Moot.**

Motheleye, motley.

Mountaunce, amount, value.

Mourdre, **Murdre**, vb. to murder; sb. murder.

Mous, **Mows**, a mouse.

Moyste, supple.

Murtheryng, murdering.

Murye, pleasant, merry.

Mynde, remembrance.

Mynour, a miner.

Mynstralcye, minstrelsy. See **Mester.**

Myrour, a mirror.

Myselven, myself.

Myshappe, to mishap, turn out badly, befall amiss.

N.

Nacioun, nation.

Naker, a kettle-drum.

Nam = *ne + am*, am not.

Namely, especially.

Narwe, close, narrow, narrowly.

Nas = *ne + was*, was not.

Nat, not.

Nath = *ne + hath*, hath not,

Natheles, nevertheless.

Naught, nothing, not.

Nay, sb. denial. ' It is no nay' = there is no denial, it is not to be denied.

Ne, adv. not; conj. nor. *Ne . . . ne*, neither . . . nor.

Neede, needful.

Needely, **Needily**, of necessity.

Needes, **Nedes**, of necessity; *needes-cost* = *needes-ways*, of necessity.

Neer, **Ner**, near, nearer.

Neigh, **Neighe**, **Neih**, **Neyh**, nigh, near. *As neigh as* = as near as.

Nekke, neck; *nekke-boon*, bone of the neck.

Nere = *ne + were*, were not.

Newe, newly, recently. *Al newe* = recently, lately; *of newe* = anew.

Nexte, nearest.

Nice, **Nyce**, foolish.

Night, pl. nights.

Nightertale, the night-time. *-tale* = reckoning, period.

Nis, **Nys** = *ne + is*, is not.

Nolde = *ne + wolde*, would not.

Nombre, number.

Non, **Noon**, none.

Nones, nonce.

Nonne, a nun.

Noot, **Not** = *ne + wot*, knows not. See **Wot.**

Noote, a note (in music).

Norice, nurse.

Norisching, **Norischynge**, nutriment, nurture.

Nos-thurles, nostrils. See **Thirle.**

Not = *ne + wot*, knows not.

Notabilite, a thing worthy to be known.

Not-heed, a nut-head, round head.

Nother, neither.

Nothing, adv. not at all.

Nought, not.

Nouthe = *non + the* = *now + then*, just now, at present. *As nouthe* = at present. A.S *tha*, then.

Nygard, a niggard. O.E. *nig*, *niggon*, a niggard; Norse *nyggja*, to gnaw, scrape; Sw. *njugga*, to scrape up (money); *njugg*, sparing.

O.

Obeissance, Obeisaunce, obedience.

Observance, Observaunce, respect.

Of, off, from.

Offende, to hurt, injure, attack.

Offensioun, offence, hurt, damage.

Offertorie, a sentence of Scripture said or sung after the Nicene Creed in the Liturgy of the Western Church.

Offryng, the alms collected at the Offertory.

Ofte sithes, oftentimes.

Ok, Ook, an oak.

On, Oo, Oon, one. **Oones,** once.

Oonely, Oonly, only.

Oost, army, host.

Oost, Ooste, Ost, a host, keeper of an inn.

Ooth, an oath. **Oothe,** of oaths.

Opye, opium.

Or, ere, before. So Ps. xc. 2. '*Or ever*' = ere ever.

Oratory, a closet set apart for prayers or study.

Ordeyne, to ordain.

Ordynaunce, plan, orderly disposition.

Orisoun, prayer, orison.

Orlogge, a clock.

Ost, (1) host, inn-keeper; (2) army, host.

Osteller, an inn-keeper.

Ostelrie, inn. See **Hostelrye.**

Oth, an oath.

Oughne, own.

Outehees, outcry, alarm. Mid. Lat. *butesium.*

Outrely, utterly, wholly.

Over, upper. **Overest,** uppermost.

Overal, everywhere. Cp. Ger. *überal.*

Over gon, passed over.

Over lippe, upper lip.

Over-ryden, ridden over.

Overspradde, pret. spread over.

Over-thward, overthwart, athwart, across. A.S. *thweor,* crooked, oblique. (Eng. *queer* = O.E. *quer,* Ger. *quer,* athwart.)

Owen, Owne, own.

Owher, anywhere.

Oynement, ointment, unguent.

Oynouns, onions.

P.

Paas, Pass, a foot-pace. Fr. *pace,* Lat. *passus.*

Pace, to pass, pass on, or away, to surpass.

Paleys, palace.

Palfrey, a horse for the road. Fr. *palefroi,* Mid. Lat. *para veredus, palafridus,* an easy-going horse for riding; *veredus,* a post-horse. Cp. Ger. *pferd,* Du. *paard,* a horse.

Pan, the skull, brain-pan. Cp. O.E. *hern-pan,* brain-pan.

Paramentz, ornamental furniture or clothes.

Paramour, by way of love; a lover of either sex.

Parde, Pardee = *par Dieu,* a common oath.

Pardoner, a seller of indulgences.

Parfyt, perfect.

Parischen, Parisschen, a parishioner.

Part, party, company.

Partrich, a partridge.

Party, partly; **Partye,** a part, party; adj. partial.

Parvys. See note, p. 126.

Pas, foot-pace. See **Paas.**

Passe, to surpass; **Passant, Passyng,** surpassing.

Payen, pagan. Fr. *paien,* a pagan.

Peere, equal, as in *peerless.*

Pees, peace.

Penaunce, penance, pain, sorrow.

Perce, to pierce. Fr. *percer.*

Perchaunce, perchance.

Perfight, Perfyt, perfect.

Perrye, jewelry. Fr. *perré.*

Pers, of a sky-blue colour.

Persone, a person.

Persoun, a parson or parish priest.

Pertourben, to disturb.

Pestilens, pestilence, plague.

Peyne, sb. pain, grief.

Peyne, Peynen, to take pains, endeavour.

Peynte, to paint.

Peyre, a pair.

Pight = *pighte*, pitched.

Pike, to pick, prune, trim. A.S. *pycan*, to pick, pull; Du. *picken*, to pick.

Piked, adj. trimmed. "*Pykyd* or *purgyd*, fro fylthe or other thynge grevous, *purgatus*." (Promptorium Parv.)

Pikepurs, a pick-purse.

Piled, stripped of hair, bald. Norse *pila*, to pluck; Low. Ger. *pulen*, to pluck, pick; Eng. *peel*, Fr. *piller*, to rob.

Piler, a pillar.

Pilour, a plunderer. See Piled.

Pilwe beer, a pillow-case. Dan. *vaar*, cover, case. Cp. Ger. *küssen-biere*, a cushion-cover.

Pitance, a mess of victuals; properly an additional allowance served to the inmates of religious houses; a high festival.

Pitous, compassionate, piteous.

Pitously, piteously.

Playnen, to complain.

Plein, Pleyn, Pleyne, full, fully, openly. *Pleyn bataile* = open battle.

Pleinly, Pleynly, fully.

Plentyvous, plentiful.

Plesance, Plesaunce, Pleasaunce, pleasure.

Plesant, Plesaunt, pleasant.

Pley, Pleye, play, pleasure.

Pleye, Pleyen, to play, take one's pleasure; Pleyynge, playing, amusement.

Pleyne, to complain.

Pocock, peacock. It is also written *pacock*. Fr. *paon*, Lat. *pavo*.

Poeple, people.

Pollax, a halbert, pole-axe. O.N.

pál, a pick-axe. Some connect it with *poll*, Du. *pol*, head.

Pomel, top of the head.

Pomele, marked with round spots like an apple, dappled. *Pomely gray* = apple-gray. Fr. *pomme*, Lat. *pomum*.

Poplexie, apoplexy.

Poraile, the poor.

Pore, poor. See Povre.

Port, carriage, behaviour.

Portraiture, Pourtraiture, a picture.

Portreyour, a painter. Fr. *pourtraire*, to draw, from *traire*, Lat. *trahere*, to draw.

Post, pillar, support.

Potecary, an apothecary.

Poudre marchaunt, a kind of spice.

Povre, poor; Povrely, poorly. Fr. *pauvre*, Prov. Fr. *poure*, Lat. *pauper*.

Powpe, to make a noise with a horn.

Powre, to pore, to look close and long.

Poynant, Poynaunt, pungent.

Poynt, particle, particular.

Practisour, practitioner.

Preche, to preach. Fr. *prêcher*, Lat. *predicare*.

Preest, Prest, a priest.

Preisen, Praysen, to praise. Fr. *prix*, price; It. *pretio*, price, worth; Sp. *prez*, honour, glory.

Prelat, a prelate.

Prese, to press.

Prest, ready. Lat. *præsto*, in readiness; O.E. *in prest* = in hand; *press money* = *prest-money*, money given in hand, earnest money received by a soldier at impressment; hence 'to *press*' (= to *prest*), to engage soldiers.

Preve, sb. *proof*; vb. to prove.

Preye, to pray. Fr. *prier*, It. *pregare*, Lat. *precari*.

Pricasour, a hard rider.

Prik, Prikke (dat.), a point. Du. *prik*, a stab; Sw. *prick*, a point.

Prike, (1) to prick, wound; (2) to spur a horse, to ride hard; (3) to excite, spur on. Low Ger. *prikken*, to pick, stick; *an prikken*, to stimulate, set on. See previous word.

Prikyng, riding.

Prime, Pryme, the first quarter of the artificial day.

Pris, Prys, price, praise, estimation. See **Preisen**.

Prise = *prese*, press, crowd.

Privily, Pryvyly, secretly.

Propre, peculiar, own.

Prow, advantage, profit (cp. Eng. *prowess*, Fr. *prouesse*). Prov. Fr. *pros*, good (for its purpose); O.Fr. *preux*, valiant, loyal; *prou*, much, enough; Lat. *probus*, good, sound.

Prys, price, prize, fame. See **Preisen.**

Pryvyte, privity, privacy, private business.

Pulled, plucked. See note, p. 123.

Pultrie, poultry. Fr. *poule*, a hen; Lat. *pullus*, young of an animal.

Purchase, anything acquired (honestly or dishonestly); proceeds of begging. Fr. *pourchasser*, It. *procacciare*, to hunt after, *chase*, *catch*.

Purchasour, prosecutor.

Pure, mere, very.

Purfiled, embroidered, fringed. It. *porfilo*,. a border in armoury, a worked edge, a *profile*; *porfilare*, to overcast with gold or silver lace. Fr. *pourfiler*, to tinsel or overcast with gold or silver lace. (Cotgrave.) Bailey has the contracted form *purl*, a kind of edging for bone lace.

Purpos, purpose, design. Fr. *proposer*, which has supplanted O. Fr. *pourpenser*, to bethink himself; *pourpens*, purpose.

Purs, purse. Fr. *bourse*, Lat. *bursa*, hide, skin.

Purtreture, painting, picture.

Purveans, Purveaunce, Purvey- ans, foresight, providence, plan. O. Fr. *pourveoir*, Lat. *providere*.

Pynche, to find fault with.

Pyne, sb. torment, pain, grief.

Pyne, Pynen, to torment, grieve. A. S. *pin*, pain, torment (Du. *pigne*); *pinian*, to torment; Eng. *pine*, to languish (as one does who suffers pain).

Pynoun, a pennant or ensign (borne at the end of a lance). Fr. *pennon*, Lat. *penna, pinna*, a feather, wing, fin.

Q.

Qualme, sickness, pestilence. A.S. *cwealm, cwylm*, destruction, pestilence, death; Dan. *quæle*, to choke; Sw. *qual*, torment; *qualm*, hot, stifling weather; Ger. *qualm*, vapour.

Quelle, to kill. A.S. *cwellan*, to kill. See **Qualme**.

Queynt, pp. *queynte*, pret. *quenched*. Cp. *dreynte* = drenched. A. S. *cwincan*, O. Fris. *kwinka*, to waste away; A.S. *cwencan*, to quench; Du. *quijnen*, to moan, languish; Eng. *whine*.

Queynte, strange, quaint, uncouth. Fr. *coint*, Lat. *cognitus*, known, acquainted with.

Quok, quaked, trembled. A.S. *cwacian*, to quake, tremble; Ger. *quackeln*, to waver. To this family of words belong *quag*, *quaver, wag, wave*.

Quyen, a queen.

Quyk, alive, quick. A.S. *cwic*, alive. Cp. 'the *quick* and the dead;' 'cut to the *quick*;' couchgrass (=*quitch*-grass), called in Norfolk *quicken*.

Quyte. free. as in our phrase 'to get *quit* of.' Lat. *quietus*, at rest, free from all claims; It. *quieto*, a discharge from legal claims; whence *acquit, requite*.

Quyte, to set free.

Quytely, free, at liberty.

R.

Rad (pp. of *rede*, to read), read.

Rage, vb. to play, toy wantonly; sb. a rabble. Fr. *rage*, Lat. *rabies*.

Ransake, to search (for plunder), ransack. The O.E. *ransake* also signifies to search. try, probe. Sw. *ransaka*, to search; *ran* (= O.N. *rannr*, A.S. *ern*), house; *saka* (= Sw. *súka*), to seek.

Rasour, a razor. Fr. *ras*, shaven, cut close by the ground; Lat. *radere*, *rasum*, to shave; whence ' to *raze* ' = to lay even with the ground.

Rather, sooner. Milton uses *rathe* in the sense of ' early.' A.S. *hræð*, swift, quick; O.N. *hradr*, quick.

Raughte, **Raught**, (pret. of *reche*), reached. A.S. *ræcan*, pret. *ræhte;* Ger. *reichen*, reach, extend; whence *rack*, an instrument of torture.

Raunceoun, **Raunsoun**, ransom. Fr. *rançon*, O. Fr. *raention*, *raençon*, Lat. *re-emptio*, a purchase back, *redemption*.

Rayhing, by some explained as grinding, but more probably *arraying*, putting in order, but see note, p. 146.

Real, **Rial**, **Ryal**, royal, kingly; **Really**, royally.

Rebel, rebellious; **Rebellyng**, rebellion.

Recche, **Rekke** (pret. *roghte*, *roughte*), to care, take heed to, *reck*. A.S. *réccan*, to care for, regard.

Recheles, reckless.

Recomforte, to comfort.

Récorde, to remember, remind.

Red (imp. of *rede*), read.

Red, **Rede**, **Reed**, counsel, advice, plan, line of conduct.

Rede, to advise, explain, interpret. A.S. *rædan*, to advise, explain; Sw. *rede*, to explain; Ger. *rathen*, to conjecture, ' to *read* a riddle.'

Rede, to read. A.S. *redan*, O.N. *rætha*, Ger. *reden*, to talk, discourse, read.

Redoutyng, reverence. O.E. *redoute*, to fear.

Reed, plan. See **Red**.

Reed, **Reede**, red.

Reeve, steward, bailiff. A.S. *gerefa*, Du. *graef*, Ger. *graf*, a count. In composition, *shire-reeve = sheriff*, *port-reeve*, *borough-reeve*, &c.

Refreische, to refresh.

Regne, a kingdom, reign.

Reherce, to rehearse. Fr. *rebercer*, to go over again, like a harrow (Fr. *herce*) over a ploughed field. Cp. our phrase to ' *rake up* old grievances.'

Rehersyng, rehearsal.

Reken, **Rekene**, **Rekne**, to reckon. A.S. *recan*, to say, tell, number; Ger. *rechnen*, to reckon.

Rekkenynges, reckonings.

Reme (pl. *remis*), realm. O.Fr. *realme*, It. *reame*, a kingdom, according to Diez, from Lat. *regalis*.

Remenant, **Remenaunt**, a remnant.

Rendyng, tearing (of hair). A.S. *brendan*, to tear; O.E. *renne*, to rend; O. N. *ræna*, to seize (by violence).

Renges, ranks. Fr. *renge*, *reng;* Sc. *raing*, a row, line, *range*.

Renne (pret. *ron*, *ran;* pret. pl. *ronne;* pp. *ironne*, *ironnen*, *ronne*, *ronnen*), to run. We have this form in *rennet*, or *runnet*, that which makes milk *run* or curdle.

Rennyng, running.

Rente, revenue, income, profits. Fr. *rendre*, It. *rendere*, Lat *reddere*, to give up, yield; Fr. *rente*, income, revenue.

Repentaunce, penitence.

Repentaunt, penitent.

Repplicacion, a reply.

Rescous, rescued. O. Fr. *rescourre,* to deliver, *rescous,* recovered; It. *riscuotere,* (Lat. *re-excutere*), to fetch a thing out of pawn; Lat. *excutere,* to tear from, take by force; Fr. *escourre,* to beat corn from the chaff.

Resons, opinions, reasons.

Resoun, reason.

Resowne, to resound.

Respite, delay. Lat. *respectus,* It. *rispetto,* Fr. *respit,* regard, consideration, delay, respite.

Rethor, a rhetorician.

Rette, to ascribe, impute. See **Aretted.**

Reule, sb. rule; vb. to rule. Fr. *règle,* Lat. *regula.*

Revel, feasting, merry-making, O. Fr. *revel,* noise, gaiety.

Reverence, respect.

Revers, the reverse, contrary.

Rew, imp. have pity upon.

Rewe, Rewen, to be sorry for, to have compassion or pity on, to *rue.* ' *Me reweth* ' = I am sorry, grieved. A.S. *breowan,* to be sorry for, grieve; Ger. *reue,* mourning.

Rewe, a row, line. A.S. *ræwa,* a line; Fr. *rue,* a row of houses, or street.

Rewle, to rule. See **Reule.**

Reyce, to make an inroad or military expedition. O.E. *race,* to dash, tear; A.S. *ræsan,* to rush, attack; Ger. *reissen,* to rage, tear; A.S. *ræs,* a stream, race; O. N. *rás,* a rapid course. Cp. *race,* a violent current of water; the *Race* of Alderney.

Reyne, sb. rain; vb. to rain.

Rial, royal; **Rially,** royally.

Richesse, riches. This word, as well as *alms* (O.E. *elmesse*), is a singular form derived immediately from the French.

Ride, Ryde, pret. *rood;* pret. pl. *riden, ridden;* pp. *riden, ryden.*

Right, rite, ceremony.

Rightes, rightly. *At alle rightes* = rightly in all respects.

Rikne, to reckon, calculate.

Rome, to walk, roam. A.S. *rúm,* Ger. *raum,* space, *room.*

Romyng, walking.

Ronne, Ronnen, pret. pl. *ran.*

Rood, rode.

Roos, rose.

Roote, rote. *By roote* = by rote. O. E. *rote,* to hum a tune; *route,* to snore; A.S. *brutan,* Sc. *rout,* to roar, bellow; O. Fr. *rote,* a hurdy-gurdy; *roterie,* a song.

Rore, to roar. A. S. *raran.*

Roste, to roast. Fr. *roster,* to roast; It. *rosta,* a frying-pan; Ger. *rost,* a grate.

Rote, a hurdy-gurdy. Rocquefort supposes it to be a fiddle with three strings. See **Roote.**

Roughte, cared for. See **Reeche.**

Rouke, to lie close, cower down, to *ruck.* Low Ger. *burken,* to squat down.

Rouncy, a hackney. Fr. *roncin.*

Route, Rowte, a company, assembly. O. Fr. *route.*

Routhe, Rowthe, pity, compassion, sorrow. See **Rewen.**

Rubeus, rubies.

Ruggy, rugged (lit. torn, broken, uneven). O.E. *rogge,* to shake, tear; Norse *rugga,* to rock, shake. Shakespeare uses *ragged* for *rugged,* rough, harsh.

Ryal, royal.

Ryngede, rung, resounded.

Ryt, rides. Cp. *byt* = bids; *sent* = sends.

S.

Sadly, firmly. O.E. *sad,* firm.

Salue, to salute.

Saluyng, salutation.

Sangwin, of a blood-red colour.

Sauf, save, except.

Saufly, safely.

Saugh, Sawgh, Sauh (pret. of *se*), saw.

Save, the herb sage or *salvia*. Fr. *saulge*.

Sawe, a saying, word, proverb, discourse. A.S. *sagu*, a saying; from *secgan*, to say.

Sawceflem, pimpled. See note, p. 134.

Saws, sauce. Fr. *sauce*, It. *salsa*; from Lat. *sal*, salt; *salsa*, salted things, salted food.

Sawtrie, a psaltery, a musical instrument something like a harp.

Say (pret. of *se*), saw.

Sayn, seen.

Saynd (pp. of *senge*), singed, toasted.

Scape, to escape. Fr. *eschapper*, It. *scappare*.

Scarsly, parsimoniously.

Schaft, an arrow, shaft. A.S. *sceaft*, an arrow, pole (Du. *schaft*, a reed, rod, pole); A.S. *scafan*, to shave.

Schake, pp. shaken.

Schamefast, modest; **Schamfastnesse,** modesty.

Schap, form, shape.

Schape, Schapen, pp. destined, planned.

Schape, Schapen, Schappe, to plan, purpose, ordain (pret. *schop*, *schoop*). A.S. *scapan*, to form, create; *ge-sceap*, creation, form; O.N. *skap*, form, shape.

Schaply, fit, likely.

Sche. O.E. *scæ*, *sco*, A.S. *seo*, *sio*.

Scheeld, Scheld, a shield.

Scheeldes, coins called crowns. Fr. *écus*.

Scheene, Schene, bright, fair, beautiful. A.S. *scyne*, bright, clear; Ger. *schön*, beautiful.

Schente (pret. of *schende*; pp. *schent*), hurt, destroy. A.S. *scendan*, to confound, shame.

Schep, sing. and pl. sheep.

Schere, pl. shears. A.S. *scéran*, to cut, divide, *shear*; Du. *schoren*, to tear; O.N. *skera*, to cut. To this root belong *shear, share, shire, shore, plough-share*, a *sheard*, or *sherd* (as in *pot-sherd*), *short, skirt, shirt*.

Scherte, a shirt.

Schipman, a sailor.

Schipne, stables. A.S. *scypen*, a stall (for sheep), a stable.

Schirreve, the governor (reeve) of a shire or county. See **Reeve**.

Schitt, pp. shut. A.S. *scittan*, to shut. It is connected with *shoot*; for to *shut* is to close the door by means of a *bolt* or *bar* driven forwards.

Schode, the temple (of the head), properly the parting of the hair of a man's head, *not*, as Tyrwhitt and others say, the hair itself. "*Schodynge* or *departynge*. Separacio, divisio." (Prompt. Parv.) "*Schodynge* of the heede, discrimen." (Ibid.) A.S. *sceàddan*, *scàddan*, Ger. *scheiden*, to separate, divide. To this family of words belong *shide*, a board, lath; O.E. *shider*, a shiver; *shider*, to shiver to pieces; Eng. *shudder, sheath, scuttle*, wain-*scot*.

Scholde, Schulde, should.

Scholne, Schollen, pl. should.

Schon (pret. of *schine*), shone.

Schoo, a shoe.

Schorte, to shorten. See **Shere**.

Schowte, to shout.

Schrewe, to curse, beshrew; hence *shrewd*. Originally O.E. *shrewed* = wicked, and hence crafty, sharp, intelligent, clear-sighted. A horse-keeper calls a vicious horse a *screw*. The *shrew-mouse* was so called because its bite was supposed to be fatal.

Schrighte, Schryked, shrieked. Sw. *skrika*, to cry, *screech*, *shriek*.

Schul, pl. shall.

Schuld, Schulde, should.

Schulder, a shoulder; **Schuldered,** shouldered, having shoulders. A.S.

sculder, Ger. *schulter*, a shoulder; O.E. *scheeld*, the shoulder of a wild boar; Prov. Eng. *shield-bones*, blade-bones; A.S. *scylan*, Norse *skilja*, to divide; whence *scale*, *skill*, *shell*, *shield*, *shale*, *sill*.

Schullen, pl. shall.

Sclender, slender. O. Du. *slinder*, thin. It is probably only a sibbilant form of *lean*.

Soclaye, to attend school, to study.

Scole, a school, Scoler, a scholar.

Scyne, shin, leg. A.S. *scyne*, the shin; Ger. *schiene*, Dan. *skinne*, a splint; O.N. *skamta*, to divide; Du. *schinden*, to skin. To this family of words belong *skin*, *scant*, *scantling*, *shank*, *shinder*, *shingle*.

Seche, Seke, to seek, as in be*seech*.

Secre, secret.

Seek, Seeke, sick; Seeknesse, sickness. A.S. *seoc*, sick. It is perhaps connected with *sigh*, O.E. *sike*.

Seene, to be seen.

Seet (pl. *seeten*), sat.

Sege, a siege. Fr. *siège*, It. *sedia*, *seggia*, a seat or sitting; Lat. *sedes*, a seat; *obsidium*, the sitting down before a town in an hostile way.

Seide (pret. of *seye*), said.

Seie, Seye, to say. A.S. *secgan*.

Seigh (pret. of *se*), saw.

Seint, Seinte, saint.

Seistow, sayest thou.

Seith, saith, says.

Seke, to seek. See Seche.

Seke, pl. sick. See Seek.

Seknesse, sickness.

Selle, house, cell.

Selve, same. Cp. 'the *self-same* day,' &c. A.S. *seolf*, Ger. *selb*.

Sely, simple, happy. A S. *sælig*, Ger. *selig*, blessed, happy; whence Eng. *silly*.

Semeley, seemly, comely, elegantly, what is beseeming. O.N. *sama*, to fit, adorn; Norse *sams*, like; A.S. *sama*, the same.

Semycope, a short cope.

Sen, Seen, Seene, Sene, to see, to be seen.

Sendal, a thin silk. See note, p. 131.

Sende, pret. sent.

Senful, sinful. O.E. *senne*, sin; O.N. *sunta*, Ger. *sünde*, sin; probably connected with Eng. *sunder*.

Sentence, sense, meaning, judgment, matter of a story. 'Tales of *sentence* and *solas*' = instructive and amusing tales.

Sergeant (or Sergeaunt) of law = *serviens ad legem*, a servant of the sovereign for his law business. The king had formerly a sergeant in every county. Fr. *sergent*, It. *sergente*.

Sermonyng, preaching. O.E. *sermounen*, to preach, discourse.

Servaunt, a servant.

Servysable, willing to be of service.

Serye, series.

Sesouns, seasons.

Seten (pp. of *sette*), sat.

Sethe, to boil, seethe. A.S. *seóthan*, to boil, cook; Eng. *sodden*, *suds*.

Seththen, since. See Sith.

Seurete, security, surety.

Sewed, followed. O.Fr. *sewir*, Lat. *sequi*, Eng. *sue*, to follow; whence *suite*, *suit* (at law), *suit* (of clothes).

Sey, saw.

Sey, Seye, Seyn, to say (pret. *seyde*).

Seye, pp. seen.

Seyh, saw.

Seyl, a sail.

Seynt, Seynte, holy, a saint.

Seynt, a girdle. "*Ceinct*, a girdle." (Cotgrave.) Lat. *cinctus*.

Shef, a sheaf. A.S. *sceaf*, Du. *schoof*, Ger. *schob*.

Shortelich, shortly, briefly.

Shright. See Schrighte.

Sicurly. See Sikerly.

Sight, providence.

Sik (pl. *sike*), sick. See Seek.

Sike, sb. a sigh; vb. to sigh. A.S. *sican*, to sigh. See Swough.

Siker, Syker, sure, certain; comp. *sikerer,* Ger. *sicher.*

Sikerly, Sikurly, surely, certainly, truly.

Sistren, sisters.

Sith, Sithe, Sithes, time, times. *Ofte-sithe* = oft-times.

Sith, Siththen, since, afterwards. A.S. *sith,* time; *sithan,* times; *sith-tha, sith-than,* after, afterwards. Eng. *since* = *sinn-es.* Cp. Du. *sinds,* Ger. *seit,* since.

Skalled, having the *scall, scale* or *scab,* scurfy. Cp. 'a *scald* head.'

Skape, to escape. See **Scape.**

Skathe, loss, misfortune. It still exists in *scatheless, scathing.* A.S. *sceathan,* Goth. *skathjan,* Ger. *schaden,* to harm, injure.

Sklendre, slender. O. Du. *slinder* (probably connected with *lean*).

Slake, slow. See **Aslake.**

Slaught, a slaughter.

Slawe (pp. of *sle*), slain.

Sle, Slee, Slen, to slay. A.S. *slagan, slean,* to strike, slay (Ger. *schlagen,* to strike); whence *slaughter, sledge,* which are connected with *slap, slash, f-log.*

Sleep (pret. of *slepe*), slept.

Sleer, a slayer.

Sleeth, slays.

Sleighly, prudently, wisely. It is not used in a bad sense.

Sleight, contrivance, craft. O.N. *slægr,* crafty, *sly; slægd,* contrivance, cunning. The O.E. *slegh* = wise; *sleight* = wisdom, prudence.

Slep, sleep, slept.

Slepy, causing sleep.

Slepyng, sleeping.

Slider, slippery. Du. *slidderen,* to slide, fall. With the root *slide* are connected *sledge* (O.E. *sled*), *slade, glide, glade,* &c.

Sloggardye, sloth. O.E. *slogge,* to be sluggish; whence *slug, slug-gish.* "I *slogge,* I waxe slowe or drawe behynde." (Palsgrave.) Cp. Du. *log,* heavy; Eng. to *lug, luggard.*

Slough, Slowh (pret. of *sle*), slew.

Smal, Smale, small.

Smerte, adj. smarting, sharp, grievous; adv. sharply, smartly.

Smerte (pret. *smerte*), to pain, hurt, displease. A.S. *smeortan,* to smart; Du. *smart,* Ger. *schmerz,* pain, ache.

Smokyng, perfuming.

Smoot, Smot (pret. of **Smite**), smote.

Smothe, smooth, smoothly.

Snewed, swarmed, abounded. Prov. Eng. *snee, snie, snive, snew,* to swarm.

Snybbe, to reprove, snub. Fris. *snubbe,* to reprove; O.N. *snubba,* to cut short; *snoppa,* a snout; Dan. *snubbed,* stumpy (cp. *snub-nose*). Cp. O.E. *snub,* a jag, knot; Prov. Eng. *snoup,* a blow on the head. To this class of words belong *snipe, snap, snape, sneap,* to nip with cold.

Soburly, sad, solemn.

Sodein, Sodeyn, sudden.

Sodeinly, Sodeynliche, Sodeyn-ly, suddenly. O. Fr. *soubdain, soudain,* Lat. *subitus, subitaneus,* sudden.

Solaas, Solas, solace, mirth.

Solempne, festive, important, pomp-ous.

Solempnely, pompously.

Solempnite, feast, festivity.

Somdel, somewhat.

Somer, summer.

Sompnour, an officer employed to summon delinquents to appear in ecclesiastical courts, now called an apparitor.

Sond, sand.

Sondry, sundry, various.

Sone, soon.

Sone, a son.

Song, pret. sang; **Songe,** pp. sung.

Sonne, the sun.

Soot, Soote, sweet. A.S. *swót,* Du. *zoet.*

Sop (in wyne). See note, p. 121.

Soper, supper.

Sore, sb. grief; adv. sorely.

Sort, destiny, chance.

Sorwe, sb. sorrow; **Sorwen,** vb. to be sorrowful, grieve.

Sorwful, sorrowful.

Sory, sorrowful. '*Sory* comfort' = discomfort; '*sory* grace' = misfortune.

Soth, Sooth, Sothe, sb. truth; adj. true. It still exists in *forsooth, soothsayer.* A.S. *sóth,* truth; *sóth,* true; *sóthe,* truly.

Sothely, Sothly, truly.

Sothfastnesse, truth.

Sotil, Sotyl, subtle, fine wrought.

Soun, Sown, sound.

Souper, supper.

Souple, supple, pliant.

Soveraignly, surpassingly.

Soverayn, Sovereyn, high, supreme, sovereign.

Sowle, soul. A.S. *sawel.*

Sowne, vb. to sound; sb. sound.

Sownynge in, tending to. Chaucer uses *sownen into goode* = tending to good.

Spak, spake.

Spare, to refrain, abstain.

Sparre, bar, bolt (Eng. *spar*). O.E. *sparre,* to bolt; A.S. *sparran,* Ger. *sperren,* to shut, bolt, Du. *sperre, sparre,* a rod, bar; Dan. *sparre,* Ger. *sparren,* a rafter. Cp. Norse *barr,* a tree, with Eng. *bar, barricade.*

Sparth, a battle-axe, or halberd.

Speede, to speed, succeed (pret. *spedde*).

Speken, to speak (pret. *spak*).

Spende, spent.

Spere, a spear.

Spiced, sophisticated, or scrupulous. See note, p. 133.

Spicerie, spices.

Spices, species, kinds. Fr. *épices,* Lat. *species.* Cp. the phrase 'a general dealer.' Sp. *generos,* kinds.

Spores, spurs. A.S. *spura, spora,* Ger. *sporn;* whence Eng. *spurn.*

Sprenge, to spring. A.S. *sprengan;* Sw. *springa, spricka,* to burst, spring; Ger. *sprengen,* to scatter, burst open; Eng. *sprig, spray, sprinkle, spruce,* belong to this family of words.

Spronge (pp. of *springe*), sprung.

Squyer, a squire.

Stalke, to step slowly and stealthily. A.S. *stælcan,* to step; Dan. *stalke,* to go with long steps. Cp. O.E. *stalker,* a goer upon stilts.

Starf (pret. of *sterve*), died. See **Sterve.**

Steep, Stepe. O.E. *steap,* bright, glittering; not deep or sunken, as it is generally explained. See note, p. 124.

Stele, to steal (pret. *stal,* pp. *stole, stolen*).

Stemed, shone. O.E. *stem, steem,* a gleam of light. "*Steem* or lowe of fyre, *flamma.*" (Prompt. Parv.)

Stente (pret. *stente,* pp. *stent*), to stop, cease. A.S. *stintan,* to be blunt; *stunt,* blunt, blockish; O.N. *stuttr,* short; O.Sw. *stunt,* short; Ger. *stutzen,* to crop, dock. Cp. Eng. *stunted* and *stinted.*

Stere, a yearling, bullock, a *steer* or stirk. A.S. *styrc,* a heifer; Prov. Ger. *ster, sterch,* the male sheep; *stier,* an ox-calf; O.H.Ger. *stero,* a ram; Ger. *stier, stierchen,* a bull.

Sterre, a star. O.E. *stare,* to glitter, shine; A.S. *steorra,* a star; Du. *sterren,* to twinkle.

Stert. *At a stert* = in a moment, immediately.

Sterte, to start, leap, escape (pret. *sterte,* pp. *stert*). Prov. Eng. *startle,* to fall, scatter, sparkle; Du. *storten,* to tumble, fall.

Sterve (pret. *starf,* pp. *i-storve.*

storven). A.S. *steorfan,* Du. *sterven,* Ger. *sterben,* to die.

Steven, Stevene, (1)voice, sound; (2) a time appointed by previous agreement. A.S. *stefen,* (1) voice, message; (2) agreement.

Stewe, a fish-pond. O.E. *steeve,* Low Ger. *stau,* a dam.

Stille, quietly, secretly.

Stith, an anvil. A.S. *stith,* a post, pillar; O.N. *stethi,* an anvil; whence Eng. *stithy.*

Stiward, a steward. A.S. *stiward,* a steward; O.N. *stivardr,* the person whose business it is to look to the daily work of an establishment; *stjá,* domestic occupation; Norse *stia,* to be busy about the house; O.N. *stia,* a sheep-house (Eng. *sty*). The syllable *-ward =* keeper.

Stoke = *steke,* to stick.

Stomble, to stumble. O.E. *stumpe,* O.N. *stumpa,* to totter, fall. It is connected with *stammer, stump, stub.*

Stonde, Stonden, to stand (pret. *stod,* pp. *stonde, stonden*).

Stonge, Stongen, pp. stung.

Stoon, stone. A.S. *stán.*

Stoor, Store, stock (of a farm). O.Fr. *estorer,* to erect, build; garnish (Lat. *instaurare*). *Telle no store* = set no value upon, set no store by.

Stope (pp. of *steppe,* to step), advance. A.S. *steppan* (pret. *stop,* pp. *ge-stopen*), to step, advance.

Stot, a stallion, a *stoat* (which also signifies a weasel). A.S. *stod* (in composition), a stallion; Du. *stuyte.* The Promptorium Parvulorum has "*stot,* a horse, caballus."

Stounde, a moment, a short space of time. A.S. *stund,* a short space, space of time; O.H.Ger. *stunt,* a moment; Ger. *stund,* an hour.

Stoute, Stowte, strong, brave.

Straughte (pret. of Strecche), stretched.

Straunge, foreign. Fr. *estrange,* Lat. *extraneus,* from *extra,* without.

Stre, Stree, straw. A.S. *streow,* Norse *strá;* A.S. *streowian,* Ger. *streuen,* to *strew.*

Strecche, to stretch. O.E. *streke,* to stretch; A.S. *streccan,* to stretch; *strec,* rigid, violent; with which are connected *streak, strike, stroke, stark,* &c.

Streem, stream, river.

Streepe, to strip. We have the other form of this root in *strip, stripe, strap.*

Streigne, Streyne, to constrain.

Streite, outstretched.

Streyt, close, narrow, stinted, strict.

Streyte, closely. O.Fr. *estroit,* It. *stretto,* strait, narrow; Lat. *stringere, strictum,* to strain.

Strif, Stryf, strife, contest. O.Fr. *estrif,* strife; *estriver,* Ger. *streben,* to strive.

Strike (of flax), a hank.

Strof (pret. of *strive*), strove, disputed, vied with.

Strond, Stronde, strand.

Strook, a stroke.

Stubbes, stumps, trunks. A.S. *styb,* Du. *stobbe,* stump; whence *stubborn, stubble,*

Stynt, 3rd. pers. sing. stops, and imp. sing. stop.

Stynte, Stynten, to stop. See Stente.

Sufficaunt = *suffisaunt,* sufficient.

Suffisance, sufficiency.

Sunge, Sungen, pp. sung.

Surcote, an upper coat.

Suspecte, suspected.

Susteene, to sustain.

Suster, Sustir, Sustyr (pl. *sustres*), a sister.

Swelde = *swelte,* fainted. A.S. *sweltan,* to die, perish (through heat). The O.E. *swelte,* to faint (through heat). The Prompt. Parv. has "Sweltrynge or swalterynge or swownynge (sincopa)." "Swalteryn for hete or febylnesse, or other cawsys (or swonyn) exalo, sincopizo." Cp. A.S. *swælan*, to be hot; Prov. Eng. *sweal*, Eng. *sultry* (= *sweltry*), 'sweltering heat.'

Swerd, a sword. A.S. *sweord.*

Swere (pret. *swor, swoor;* pp. *i-swore, i-sworen*), to swear. We have the same root in an-*swer.*

Swet, Swete, sweet. A.S. *swet.*

Sweven, a dream. A.S. *swefen,* from *swefan,* O.N. *sofa,* to sleep.

Swich, such = *swich sorwe,* so great. A.S. *swilc,* such = *swa,* so, and *lic,* like.

Swinke, Swynke, to labour, toil. A.S. *swinc,* labour; *swincan,* to toil.

Swinker, a labourer.

Swoot, Swoote, Swote, sweet.

Swor, Swore. See **Swere.**

Swough, the raging of the elements, a storm. Cp. Sc. *souch, swouch, sough,* the sound of the wind. A.S. *swég,* a sound; *swógan,* to sound; whence Eng. *sigh.*

Swowne, to swoon. The O.E. *swoghe* shows that *swoon* is connected with *sigh, sough,* &c.

Swymbul, a moaning, sighing sort of noise, caused by the wind. *Swymbul = swymel,* is a diminutive of O.E. *swim* or *sweem,* mourning, sighing. O.E. *sweamen,* to disturb; O.N. *sweima,* to move to and fro. (Cp. 'a *swimming* in the head.')

Swyn (sing. and pl.), swine.

Swynk, sb. labour, toil.

Syk, Syke, sick.

Syke, sb. a sigh; vb. to sigh. See **Sike.**

Syn, since. See **Sith.**

Sythnes, since. See **Sith.**

T.

Tabard, Tabbard, the sleeveless coat on which arms were embroidered; a herald's coat of arms. It was the old dress of the labourer, and Chaucer applies it to the loose frock of the ploughman. It. *tabarro,* overcoat.

Taille, a tally, an account scored in a notched piece of wood. Fr. *tailler,* to cut.

Take, pp. taken.

Takel, an arrow. It seems to have signified (like *loom,* O.E. *lome*) any sort of implement or utensil, whether used as a tool or weapon. Welsh *taclau,* implements; *taclu,* to dress, deck.

Tale, speech, discourse. *Telle tale* = take account of, estimate; 'litel *tale* hath he told' = little heed has he paid; 'telle no *tale*' = take no notice of, make no account of.

Tallege = to allege.

Tapicer, an upholsterer. Fr. *tapis,* a carpet.

Tapstere, a female tapster.

Targe, a target or shield. Fr. *targe.*

Tathenes = to Athens.

Teche, to teach.

Teene, vexation, annoyance. A.S. *teón, teóna,* injury, wrong; A.S. *teonan, tynan,* to anger, incense. It is probably connected with A.S. *tyndan,* Du. *teenen,* O.E. *teene,* to kindle; Eng. *tinder.*

Testers, head-pieces, or helmets. O.Fr. *teste,* Fr. *tête,* the head.

Thankes, the genitive of *thank;* used adverbially with the personal pronouns (possessive): *his thankes,* he being willing; *here thankes,* they being willing; like the Fr. *son gré, leur gré,* with his or their good-will.

Thanne, then.

Tharme, the arms.

Tharray, the array.

Thasse, the ass.

Thavys, the advice.

The, to thrive, prosper.　A.S. *théon,* to flourish, grow.

Theffect, the effect.

Thei, they.　The Northern form is *tha* or *thai.*

Thencens, Thensens, the incense.

Thenke, (1) to think; (2) to seem. *Thank* is another form of the root. See **Thinke.**

Thentre = the entrance.

Ther, there, where.

Thestat, the state or rank.

Thider, thither.

Thilke, the same, this same.　A.S. *thillíc, thylc,* the like.

Thinke, Thynke, to seem.　It is used impersonally, as 'me *thinketh*' =:it seems to me; 'hem *thoughte*.' =:it appeared to them.　A.S. *þin-can,* Ger. *dünken.*

Thirle, to pierce.　A.S. *þirel,* a hole; *þirlian,* to pierce, *drill;* whence *nostrils* (O.E. *nose-thirles*), *thrill, trill.*　The A.S. *þirel* seems to be a diminutive, and a simpler form is found in Goth. *thairko,* a hole; with which we may compare O. H. Ger. *durchel,* O.E. *thorruck,* a door; *thurruk,* of a ship (sentina).　Prov. Eng. *thurruck,* a drain.

This, pl. these.　A.S. *thæs.*

Tho, pl. the, those.　A.S. *tha.*

Tho, then.　A.S. *tha.*

Thoffice, the office.

Thondur, thunder.　A.S. *thunor,* Ger. *donner.*　With this class of words are connected *din, dun, stun.*

Thopynyouns, the opinions.

Thorisoun, the orison or prayer.

Thorugh, Thoruh, through.　See **Thurgh.**

Thral, slave, serf.　A.S. *thrall,* a servant.　By some it is connected with *thirlian,* to pierce; but it is probably a diminutive

from A.S. *threagan,* to chide, vex, torment.　Grim connects it with A.S. *thrægan,* Goth. *thragjan,* to run.

Thred, thread; **Thredbare,** threadbare.

Threisshe, to thrash.　A.S. *therscan,* O.N. *threskja; threshold* = O. E. *threish-wold,* from A.S. *therscan,* to beat; and *wold* (=A.S. *wald*), wood; so that it signifies, not the threshing-floor, but the part beaten by the foot.

Threste, to thrust, press.　A.S. *thræst-ian,* to rack, twist, torture, which seems to be a derivative of *þreatian,* to urge, press, threaten.

Thridde, third.

Thries, thrice.

Thurgh.　A. S. *thurh,* through.

Thurgh-fare, a *thorough*-fare.　Cp. Goth. *thair,* Ger. *durch,* Eng. *through* and *thorough.*　Horne Tooke has been censured for connecting this root with *door* (which originally, like *gate,* signified *way*), but compare Lat. *fores* with *forare,* and the forms collected under **Thirle.**

Til, to.　O. N. *til,* to.

To, as a verbal prefix = Ger. *zu,* Lat. *dis.*

To-breste, burst asunder.　See **Breste.**

To-broken, broken in pieces.

To-hewen, hewed or cut in pieces.

Tollen, to take toll or payment. A.S. *tól,* tax.　It seems connected with A.S. *dal,* a part; Ger. *theil,* Eng. *dole, deal,* &c.　The Romance form of the root is seen in *tally, tailor, entail, retail, tallage.*

To-morn, to-morrow.　The *to* (as in *to-yere* = this year) was originally a demonstrative word, connected with *the, that, this,* &c.

Tonne-greet, having the circumference as great as a tun.

Toon, toes.

Torne, to turn.　Fr. *tourner.*　The

root *tor*, turn, twist, is seen in the Lat. *tornus*, a lathe ; *torquere*, to twist ; *turben*, a whirlwind,

To-schrede, cut in shreds. See **Schere**.

Trace, track, path. " Trace, of a wey over a felde, trames." (Prompt. Parv.) Fr. *trace*.

Trapped, having trappings.

Trappures, trappings of a horse.

Traunce, a trance.

Trays, the traces by which horses draw, horse-harness.

Treccherie, treachery. Fr. *tricherie*, trickery ; *tricher*, to trick.

Trede, to tread.

Tresoun, treason.

Tresse, a tress, plait. Fr. *tresse*.

Treté, treaty.

Trewe, true ; **Trewely**, truly. In O.E. we have a form *trye*, corresponding to Goth. *triggws*.

Trompe, **Trumpe**, a trumpet, a trumpeter.

Tronchoun, a headless spear or truncheon. Fr. *tronçon*, from Lat. *truncus*.

Trouthe, truth.

Trowe, to believe, *trow* = I think it to be true. This is just the reverse of what Horne Tooke affirms —that *truth* is what we *trow* or believe. Cp. A. S. *treow*, true ; *treowe*, a pledge (Eng. *tru-ce*), *treowian*, to trust, believe.

Trussud up, packed up. O. Fr. *trousser*, *torser*, to pack up. Cp. Eng. *truss*, a bundle.

Tukkud, tucked, coated. A.S. *tucian*, to clothe ; O.E. *tuck*, cloth.

Tunge, a tongue.

Turneying, **Turneynge**, a tournament. See **Torne**.

Tway, **Twayn**, **Twayne**, **Twey**, **Tweye**, **Twoo**, **Tuo**, two, twain, A.S. *twegen* (m.), *twa* (f. n.); Goth. *twai* (m.), *twos* (f.), *twa* (n.); O. N. *tveir* (m.), *tvær* (f.), *tvau* (n.). With this root we must connect *twin*, *twine*, *twill*, *twig*. (Tusser calls ewes that bear twins by the name of *twiggers*.) It appears also in *twelve* (= 2 + 10), and *twenty* (2 × 10).

Twynne, to depart, separate. See **Tway**.

Tyde, time. A.S. *tíd*, time ; whence *tidy*, *tides*.

Typtoon, tiptoes. See **Toon**.

U.

Unce, a small portion (Eng. *ounce*).

Uncouth, **Uncouthe**, **Uncowth**, **Unkouthe**, unknown, rare, *uncouth*. See **Couthe**.

Undergrowe, undergrown.

Undern, the time of the mid-day meal. A. S. *undern*, the third hour of the day. It signifies literally the intervening period, and hence a part of the forenoon, a meal taken at that time.

Undertake, to affirm.

Unknowe, unknown.

Unknowyng, not *cunning* (knowing), ignorant. In our English Bible the word *cunning* is used in a good sense.

Unset, not at a set time, not appointed.

Unwist, unknown. See **Wite**.

Unyolden, not having yielded. See **Yolden**.

Uphaf (pret. of *upheve*), upheaved, uplifted. See **Heve**.

Upper hond, higher hand.

Upright, flat on the back.

Upstert, **Upsterte**, upstarted. See **Sterte**.

Upyaf, gave up.

V.

Vasselage, valour, courage (displayed in the service rendered by a *vassal*).

Vavaser. O. F. *vavaseur*. This term is explained in various ways : Tyrwhitt says it means a middle class landholder; Blount explains it as one next in dignity to a baron. A *Vavaser* was most probably a sub-vassal holding a small fief, a sort of esquire.

Venery, Venerye, hunting. Lat. *venari*, to hunt, chase; whence venison.

Vengance, vengeance.

Ventusyng, cupping, a surgical term.

Venym, poison, venom.

Verdite, verdict, judgment, sentence.

Vernicle. See note, p. 135.

Verray, Verrey, true, very; **Verraily,** truly.

Vestimenz, vestments.

Veyne blood, blood of the veins.

Viage, voyage.

Victoire, victory.

Vilonye, Vylonye, sb. unbecoming conduct, disgrace.

Vitaille, victuals.

Vouchesauf, to vouchsafe, grant.

Voyde, to expel.

W.

Waar, aware, wary. See **War.**

Wake-pleyes, ceremonies attending the vigils for the dead. A. S. *wæcan, wacian,* to watch, keep watch; Eng. *waits, watch.*

Walet, a wallet.

Wan, won, conquered. See **Winne.**

Wane, to decrease, diminish. A. S. *wanian,* to diminish; *wan* a deficiency. To the root *wan* belong A. S. *wan,* pale; whence *wan, s-wan.*

Wanhope, despair. See **Wane.**

Wantoun, wanton, free, unrestrained. The prefix *wan = -un; -toun = -togen,* trained, from A. S. *teon* (to lead, educate, pp. *getogen*).

Wantounesse, wantonness.

War, aware, cautious, prudent. A. S. *wær, war,* caution.

Ware, to warn, to cause one to beware. A. S. *warian,* to be ware, be cautious. With this root are connected *ward, warder, warn.*

Wastel-breed, bread-cake. O. Fr. *gasteau,* a cake. See note, p. 121.

Watirles, without water.

Wawes, waves. A. S. *wæg,* a wave; *wagian,* to wave, *wag.*

Wayke, weak. O. E. *woc,* A. S. *wác,* weak, mean, worthless.

Wayleway, alas! well-a-way! welladay!

Waymentyng, Weymentyng, a lamentation, wailing. O. Fr. *waimenter,* to lament; literally to cry *wai!* or *woe.* Cp. Ital. *guaiolare,* to cry *guai!*

Wayte, to be on the look out for, to look for.

Webbe, a weaver. Cp. O. E. *hunt-e,* a hunter; *tromp-e,* a trumpeter; *prison-e,* a prisoner.

Wedde, pledge, security. 'To wedde' = for a pledge. A. S. *wæd,* agreement; whence Eng. *wed, wedding, wedlock.*

Wede, clothing. A. S. *wæd,* clothing, attire of men and women. It is still retained in 'widow's *weeds.*'

Weel, well.

Weep, wept. Cp. O. E. *crep, lep* = crept, leapt.

Wel, adv. full, very.

Wele, weal, prosperity, wealth.

Wende, weened, thought.

Wende, Wenden, to go, pass away. The Eng. *went* is the past tence of *wende.* Cp. the phrase 'to *wend* one's way.'

Wene, to ween, think. A. S. *wén,* hope; *wenan,* hope, suppose. It is preserved in E. *ween, over-weening,* &c.

Wenged, winged.

Wep, wept.

Wepe, Wepen (pret. *weep, wep;* pp. *wepen*), to weep.

Wepen, Wepne, a weapon.

Werche, Wirche, Werke, to work.

Were, to defend, guard. A. S. *werian,* to defend.

Wered, Werud (O.E. *wer*), wore.

Werre, war. Du. *werre*, strife, war; Fr. *guerre*.

Werreye, Werreyen, to make war against.

Werte, a wart. A.S. *weart* (*wear*, a knot, wart), O.N. *varta*, Ger. *warze.* Some etymologists connect *wart* with *fret*, others with *wear*.

Wessch (pret. of *wasche*), washed.

Wete, wet, moist.

Wex, sb. wax.

Wex, increase, became.

Wexe, to increase, grow, become. A.S. *weaxan*, to increase. Chaucer has 'a man of *wax*' = an adult, a man of full growth.

Wexyng, growing, increasing.

Wey, Weye, a way.

Weyle, to wail; to cry *wei*! or *woe*.

Weymentynge. See **Waymentynge.**

Whan, Whanne, when.

What, lo! wherefore, why.

Whelkes, pimples, blotches. Ger. *welkèn*, to wither, fade, dry.

Wher, where, whereas.

Whether, whether, which of two.

Which, what; *which a* = what a.

While, time. A.S. *hwíle*, Norse *hvíla*, to rest. It is retained in *awhile*; 'to *while* away the time' = to pass the time away in rest or recreation.

Whilom, formerly, once. A.S. *hwilum.* The *-um* was an old adverbial ending, as seen in O.E. *ferrom*, afar; Eng. *seldom*.

Whit, white; comp. *whitter.*

Widewe, a widow.

Wif, Wyf, wife, woman.

Wight, any living creature; a person, male or female. A.S. *wiht.*

Wight, Wighte, weight. A.S. *wiht.*

Wikke, Wikked, wicked, bad, untoward. O.E. *wikke*, poor, mean, weak; A.S. *wícan*, to be weak.

Wil, Wile, vb. will.

Wilfully, willingly.

Wilne, to desire. A.S. *wiln*, wish; *wilnian*, to desire.

Wiltou, wilt thou.

Winne, Wynne (pret. *wan, won;* pp. *wonne, wonnen*), to win, obtain, gain.

Wirche, to work.

Wis, Wys, wise.

Wis = *iwis*, certainly. 'As *wis*' = as certainly, as truly. See **Iwis.**

Wise, Wyse, mode, manner. See **Gyse.**

Wisly, Wysly, truly. See **Iwis.**

Wit, understanding, judgment, wisdom.

Wite, Wyte, to know, learn; 1st. and 3rd. pers. sing. indic. *wot, woot;* 2nd. pers. *wost;* pl. *witen, wyten;* pret. *wiste.* A.S. *witan*, to know; whence *wit*, to wit, witty, &c.

Withholde, maintained.

Withouten, without.

Withsayn, Withseie, to gainsay.

Wityng, knowledge. See **Wite.**

Wive, Wyve, dat. of *wif, wyf.*

Wlatsome, loathsome, hateful. A.S. *wlatian*, to nauseate, loathe.

Wo, Woo, sb. sorrow, woe; adj. sorrowful, grieved, displeased.

Wode. See **Wood.**

Wodly, madly. See **Wood.**

Wofullere, the more sorrowful.

Wol, Wole, vb. will.

Wold, Wolde, would, wouldest, wouldst.

Wolle (pl. of *wole*), will.

Wolt, wilt; **Woltow,** wilt thou.

Wonder, Wondur, wonderful.

Wondurly, wonderfully.

Wone, custom, usage. A.S. *wune.*

Wone, to dwell. A.S. *wunian*, Ger. *wohnen*, to dwell, inhabit, rest.

Wonne (pp. of *winne*), conquered, obtained.

Wonyng, a dwelling, habitation.

Wood, Wode, mad. A.S. *wód*, mad; *wódnes*, madness.

Woodewynde, a woodbind.

Woodnes, madness.

Wook, awoke.

Woot. See Wite.

Worschipe, to honour, to pay proper respect to another's *worth.*

Worschipful, honourable.

Wortes, herbs. A.S. *weort, wyrt.* It still exists in *cole-wort, orchard* (= *wort-yerd,* herb-garden).

Worthi, Worthy, brave; Worthinesse, bravery.

Wost, knowest, Wot, Wote, knows. See Wite.

Wrastlynge, wrestling.

Wrecche, a wretch; Wrecched, wretched.

Wreke, to revenge, avenge, *wreak.*

Wrethe, a wreath, a derivative from the vb. to *writhe.*

Wright, a carpenter (literally a workman). Cp. *wheel-wright, play-wright.*

Writ, wrote.

Wroth, Wrothe, angry.

Wyf. See Wif.

Wyke, a week. A.S. *wice,* O.N. *vika.*

Wymple, a covering for the neck; Wymplid, decked with a *wymple.* Fr. *guimple.* O. Du. *wimpelen,* to wrap; *wimpel,* a veil, flag. See p. 122.

Wyn, wine.

Wynnynge, gain, profit.

Wypyltre, the cornel-tree.

Wys, wise; Wysly, wisely.

Wyte, Wyten, know. See Wite.

Y.

Yaf (pret. of *yeve* or *yive*), gave; Yave, pret. pl.

Yalwe. See Yelwe.

Yate, a gate. This old pronunciation still survives in some parts of England.

Ybrought, brought.

Yburied, buried.

Yclepud, called. See Clepe.

Ydon, done.

Ydrawe, drawn.

Ydropped, bedropped, covered with drops.

Ydryve, driven.

Ye, yea, the answer to a question asked in the affirmative form; *yis, yes,* being the affirmative answer to a question asked in the negative form.

Ye, eye. Prov. Eng. *ee;* A.S. *eage.*

Yeddynges, songs, properly the gleeman's songs. Norse *gidda,* to shake; whence *giddy.* A.S. *gydd,* a song; *gyddian,* to sing. The Prompt. Parv. has " *Yeddynge,* or *geest, idem quod geest* (a romaunce)." See note, p. 125.

Yeeldyng, yielding, return, produce.

Yeer, Yer, year. A.S. *ger.*

Yeldehalle = *geldehall,* a guildhall.

Yelle, to yell; Yelleden (pl. pret.) yelled.

Yelpe, to boast (Eng. *yelp*). A.S. *gelpan.*

Yelwe, Yolw, Yolwe, yellow. A.S. *geale;* whence *gall, gold, yolk.*

Yeman (pl. *yemen*), a yeoman, commoner, a feudal retainer. See note, p. 120. Some etymologists connect it with the A.S. *gemæne,* common (Ger. *gemeiner,* a commoner). Tyrwhitt refers it to (and rightly, I think) *yeongeman,* a young man, a vassal. The A.S. *geongra* = a vassal, and *geongorscipe* = service. (Cædmon.) It is the latter etymology that explains the modern form *yeoman.*

Yen, eyes.

Yer, Yere, a year.

Yerd, Yerde, rod, as in *yard*-measure. A.S. *gerd, gyrd,* twig, rod, stick.

Yerd, enclosure, yard. A.S. *geard,* hedge, enclosure, garden; Eng. *yard, orchard, wear, garden.*

Yeve, Yeven, Yive, to give.

Yeve, Yeven, pp. given.

Yghe (pl. *yghen*), eye.

Ygrounde, pp. ground, sharpened.

Yholde, pp. esteemed, held.

Yif, if. A. S. *gif.*

Yift, gift.

Yit, yet. *Yit now* = just now.

Yive, Yiven, to give.

Ymaked, pp. made.

Ymet, pp. met.

Ymeynd (pp. of *menge*), mingled, mixed. A. S. *mengian*, to mix.

Ynned, lodged, entertained.

Ynough, Ynowgh, enough.

Yolden, pp. yielded, repaid. A.S. *gyldan*, to repay, give up.

Yolle, to yell. Prov. Eng. *goul, youl.*

Yollyng, yelling.

Yolw, Yolwe, yellow. A.S. *geoluwe*, Ger. *gelb*. It is connected with *gold, gall, yolk*, &c.

Yong, Yonge, young.

Yore, of a long time. *Yore ago* = a long time ago; *of yore*, in olden time. A. S. *geara*, from *gear*, a year.

Yow, you.

Ypassed, pp. passed.

Yronne, pp. run, coagulated.

Yserved, pp. served, deserved.

Yslayn, slain.

Yspreynd (pp. of *sprenge*), to sprinkle, scatter. A. S. *springan*, to spring; Ger. *sprengen*, to scatter, burst open; Sw. *springa*, to split. Cp. phrase 'to spring a leak.'

Ystert, Ysterte, started, escaped.

Ytorned, pp. turned.

Ywis, Ywys, certain, sure. See **Iwis.**

Ywont, wont, accustomed.

Yyve, to give.

CONTRACTIONS.

A. S.	..	Anglo-Saxon.
Dan.	..	Danish.
Du.	..	Dutch.
Ger.	..	German.
O. E.	..	Old English.
O. H. Ger.	..	Old High German.
O. N.	..	Old Norse.
Prov. Eng.	..	Provincial English.
Sw.	..	Swedish.

CORRECTIONS.

Page 65, line 1211, *for* fothermore *read* forthermore.

  „ 72, „ 1459, „ and sende „ as sende.

  „ 77, „ 1635, „ courses „ coursers.

UNIVERSITY OF OXFORD.

Clarendon Press Series.

THE DELEGATES of the Oxford Press understand from eminent Schoolmasters and others who are authorities upon education, that there is still great need of good School Books and Manuals.

They are told that Editions with good English notes of many of the Greek and Latin Classics read in the higher classes of the Public Schools are required; that text-books, both English and Foreign, are much needed for the use of Schools, especially with reference to the Local Examinations held by the Universities; that good English and other Grammars, and Exercise-books adapted to them and with a copious supply of Examples, are much needed, and that there is a great and urgent want of Delectuses, Analecta, and generally of books of Selections from Authors, for use in Schools;—

That the Histories now read in Schools are greatly below present requirements, and in some cases there are absolute deficiencies; and that the want of good books on History is much felt in the Law and Modern History School in the University;—

That English Treatises on Physical Science, written with clearness and precision of language, and adapted for use in the higher classes of Schools, and in the Natural Science School of the University, do not exist.

They believe that the University may with propriety and efficiency do much towards remedying the defect. They have therefore determined to issue a series of Educational Works, hoping to supply some existing wants, and to help in improving methods of teaching.

The departments of Education which they propose to deal with at present are the following :—

I. CLASSICS. The Delegates hope to issue
    1. Works suitable for the Universities and the highest forms of Schools; or
    2. Books for School-work generally, beginning from the very rudiments.

II. MENTAL AND MORAL PHILOSOPHY.

III. MATHEMATICAL WORKS; both for University Students, and also with especial regard to the needs of Middle Class Schools.

IV. HISTORY. Here again there will be two classes of books :—
    1. Short Histories, such as may be useful for the History School, or for general reading ;
    2. School Histories, with all the necessary appliances for education.

V. LAW.

VI. PHYSICAL SCIENCE. The experience of teachers in the University and elsewhere has already pointed out several desirable works, and has also gone some way towards providing the books required.

VII. ENGLISH LANGUAGE AND LITERATURE, which will comprise a carefully compiled series of Reading Books, Exercise Books, and Grammars.

VIII. MODERN LANGUAGES.

IX. ART; including Handbooks on Music, Painting, and the like.

X. ENGLISH CLASSICS, a series of reprints of some of the masterpieces in our language, chiefly for the use of Schools.

The DELEGATES OF THE PRESS *invite suggestions and advice from all persons interested in sound education; and will be thankful for hints, &c. addressed to the*

Rev. G. W. KITCHIN, *Oxford.*

Now Ready.

1. A Treatise on Natural Philosophy. Volume I.

By Sir W. THOMSON, LL.D., D.C.L., F.R.S., Professor of Natural Philosophy in the University of Glasgow, and P. G. TAIT, M.A., Professor of Natural Philosophy in the University of Edinburgh; formerly Fellows of St. Peter's College, Cambridge. (Demy 8vo., cloth, price 25s.)

" Our object is twofold : to give a tolerably complete account of what is now known of Natural Philosophy, in language adapted to the non-mathematical reader; and to furnish, to those who have the privilege which high mathematical acquirements confer, a connected outline of the analytical process by which the greater part of that knowledge has been extended into regions as yet unexplored by experiment. . . . .

" We commence with a chapter on *Motion*, a subject totally independent of the existence of *Matter* and *Force*. In this we are naturally led to the consideration of the curvature and tortuosity of curves, the curvature of surfaces, and various other purely geometrical subjects. ...

" Chapter II. gives NEWTON'S Laws of Motion in his own words, and with some of his own commentaries; every attempt that has yet been made to supersede them having ended in utter failure.

" Chapter III. briefly treats of Observation and Experiment as the basis of Natural Philosophy.

" Chapter IV. deals with the fundamental Units, and the chief instruments used for the measurement of Time, Space, and Force.

" Thus closes the First Division of the Work, which is strictly preliminary.

" The Second Division is devoted to Abstract Dynamics, (commonly of late years, but not well, called Mechanics). Its object is briefly explained in the introductory (fifth) Chapter, and the rest of the present volume is devoted to Statics.

" Chapter VI., after a short notice of the Statics of a Particle, enters into considerable detail on the important subject of Attraction.

" In Chapter VII. the Statics of Solids and Fluids are treated with special detail in various important branches, such as the Deformation of Elastic Solids and the Figure of the Earth."—*Authors' Preface.*

" The attentive student will gather from its careful perusal more insight into true scientific principles, more excellent precept, bettered by still more excellent example respecting the method of modern physics, than from any other with which we are acquainted."—*Educational Times.*

. " The Delegates of the Clarendon Press are accomplishing a great work in a noble manner. They have undertaken to furnish the student with a series of text books in the different departments of science and literature written by men whose names are eminent in these departments. Already they have produced a goodly list of volumes, which they have now crowned by the excellent and profound treatise which is before us."

"We recommend the study of this *magnum opus* to the attention of high-class students; let them study it, and when they have thoroughly mastered the first volume let us hope that another may be at their service."—*Engineer.*

2. An Elementary Treatise on Quaternions.

By P. G. TAIT, M.A., Professor of Natural Philosophy in the University of Edinburgh; formerly Fellow of St. Peter's College, Cambridge. (Demy 8vo., price 12s. 6d.)

" We are of opinion that Professor Tait has succeeded in producing a really simple exposition of the principles and application of Quaternions. The Delegates of the Oxford Press are, we think, doing a great service to mathematical students by the publication of such works as this."—*Educational Times.*

3. Descriptive Astronomy. A Handbook for

the General Reader, and also for practical Observatory work. With 224 illustrations and numerous tables. By G. F. CHAMBERS, F.R.A.S., Barrister-at-Law. (Demy 8vo., cloth, 856 pp., price 21s.)

The aim of this work, briefly expressed, is general usefulness, whether in the hands of the student, the general reader, or the professional observer. Great pains have been taken to present the latest information on all branches of the science. The development of Astronomy is now so rapid that unless an author exercises constant vigilance his book must fall behindhand : and it is believed that this volume not only contains the most recent discoveries and deductions, but that in it will also be found information hitherto to be met with only in the publications of learned Societies, difficult of access and inconvenient for reference even to the Astronomer, and absolutely out of the reach of the general reader.

" A bulky, but very interesting book. * * * We gladly welcome it, and only regret that even more information could not be squeezed into its pages—though it is by no means one of those unreadable treatises which bristle with an array of scientific facts so dense as to be indigestible by an ordinary reader. * * * * The engravings are an admirable feature of this manual, and contribute much to the esteem in which we are disposed to hold it."—*John Bull.*

4. Chemistry for Students. By A. W. WILLIAMSON,

Phil. Doc., F.R.S., Professor of Chemistry, University College, London. (Ext. fcap. 8vo., cloth, price 7s. 6d.)

[*New edition in the Press.*

Also : Solutions of the Problems in " Chemistry for

Students." By the same Author. (Ext. fcap. 8vo., sewed, price 6d.)

"Within less than four hundred pages of a handy little volume, in type not fatiguing to the eye, Professor Williamson here gives to the student an outline of the leading facts and principles of inorganic and organic chemistry. * * * * This volume is really a too rare example of what a good elementary text-book in any science ought to be : the language brief, simple, exact; the arrangement logical, developing in lucid order principles from facts, and keeping theory always dependent upon observation ; a book that keeps the reason of the student active while he strives to master details difficult but never without interest, and that furnishes him with means for practising himself in the right management of each new tool of knowledge that is given to him for his use."—*Examiner.*

5. An Elementary Treatise on Heat, with numerous Woodcuts and Diagrams. By Balfour Stewart, LL.D., F.R.S., Director of the Observatory at Kew. (Ext. fcap. 8vo., cloth, price 7s. 6d.)

"All persons engaged in the teaching or study of experimental philosophy will be glad to have a manual from the pen of a gentleman competent to treat the subject, and bringing his information in it up to the science of the present day. Whilst the book is thoroughly practical and adapted for use in the class-room, Dr. Stewart has not neglected to discuss the interesting relations of heat to other forms of force, and the bearing of the phenomena of heat on the theories of 'conservation of energy' and 'dissipation of energy' in the universe."—*Athenæum.*

"The highest praise we can give this volume is to say that it is entitled to its place in the remarkable series which is now in the course of issue from the Clarendon Press, and that it follows not unworthily the *Chemistry* of Professor Williamson and the *Greek Verbs* of Mr. Veitch. Such manuals, so admirable in matter, arrangement, and type, were never before given to the world at the same moderate price. Our ideas of the nature of heat, as the author observes, have recently undergone a great change. Heat is now regarded, not as a species of matter, but as a species of motion ; and the relation between it and the other forms of motion, involving the principles of the science of energy, constitutes, perhaps, the most exciting study of the day, being just in the stage which keeps everybody on tiptoe of expectation. The publication of this manual is exceedingly well timed ; it includes within narrow limits the leading facts and principles of this youngest-born of the Sciences, and for the mastery of the greater portion of its contents only requires ordinary intelligence on the part of the reader."—*Spectator.*

"In contrasting this volume with other text-books of similar pretensions, we are struck with its superiority in point of arrangement, and in the manner in which it presents the results of the most recent researches on the subject. It has been successful, too, in mastering another difficulty which besets the writers of text-books, and that is in drawing the line between the merely popular treatise and the dry compendium."—*London Review.*

"This compact little treatise is commendable both as an elementary exposition of the chief phenomena of heat and their practical applications, and also as a brief exposition of the philosophical theories which have recently given a new interest to the phenomena. The structure of the work is also excellent."—*Fortnightly Review.*

"As a scientific essay Dr. Stewart's second book on 'Radiant Heat,' has a peculiar value ; and his third may be regarded as a new treatise on a new subject. * * * * This book is well indexed and beautifully printed, and even as a record of some results of those silent and important labours which within the memory of most readers have occupied men of science we commend the volume to those who may be disposed to regard the subject in itself as unpromising and somewhat dry."—*Pall Mall Gazette.*

6. Greek Verbs, Irregular and Defective; their
forms, meaning, and quantity ; embracing all the Tenses used by Greek writers, with references to the passages in which they are found. By W. VEITCH. New and revised edition. (Ext. fcap. 8vo., cloth, 616 pp., price 8*s.* 6*d.*)

"Mr. Veitch's work on the *Irregular and Defective Greek Verbs* is as signal a proof as could be furnished that a book designed to assist the learner or the advanced student may be convenient in size and yet exhaustive in treatment, may be quite original in investigation and yet fall readily into the educational channel, may confine itself to the strictest exposition of phenomena, and yet be fresh with the force of character and lively with the humour that belong more or less to all inquiring and independent minds.

"We shall not pretend to review the treatise of an author who stands very nearly, if not altogether, alone in knowledge of his subject. Mr. Veitch is indeed as independent of the praise or the censure of critics as any author need care to be. It is one of his claims to the gratitude of scholars that, in spite of the premature and almost universal desertion of the field of rigid, textual scholarship, for the easier, showier, and pleasanter field of aesthetic or literary disquisition, he has persevered in his forsaken and solitary path, and has produced a work unique of its kind, full of fresh and lasting contributions to our knowledge of the Greek language, and intellectually vivacious and incisive on nearly every page. Open the book anywhere, and instances of erroneous doctrines corrected, of omissions (common to all our lexicons) supplemented, of new theories propounded and vindicated, occur at once. We congratulate Mr. Veitch on the completion, and the Clarendon Press on the publication, of a work which will reinstate our scholarship in that esteem which the Germans have almost ceased to entertain for it since the days of Porson and Elmsley, and which will have the merit not only of purifying the fountain-heads of classical education, but of affording the youthful scholar an example of that moral singleness of purpose and undeviating search for truth which are even rarer than the intellectual gifts that have been lavished on its execution."—*Spectator.*

"The book before us by Mr. William Veitch is quite a wonderful contribution to critical knowledge of Greek, and has been selected by the Delegates of the Clarendon Press to lead off a new series of educational works. Its great distinction, in the first place, is that it is all derived from original reading. Mr. Veitch has gone with a careful finger through the Greek texts, and the Greek texts in their latest recensions, marking every noticeable form, and checking by his own personal examination the *dicta* of other critics. * * * * The book is useful, indeed we may say indispensable, to scholars, in the widest sense of the word. It takes a larger range than its mere title would imply; and besides being a supplement to our best Lexicons, such as that of Liddell and Scott, contains touches of fine philology which would have delighted Porson and Elmsley."—*Pall Mall Gazette.*

"Mr. Veitch has produced a book which is simply marvellous as a result of most extensive reading and scrupulous accuracy, combined with keen scholarship. For the Clarendon Press to head its series with this remarkable little book may be taken as a good omen for the classics in the University, which bears the reputation of upholding a style of scholarship that is rather broad than refined."—*London Review.*

"Je puis affirmer hardiment qu'il serait impossible de nommer un écrit mieux rédigé sous tous les rapports et témoignant de plus de science. M. Veitch a lu et annoté tous les auteurs grecs. Les verbes, rangés par ordre alphabétique, sont disséqués pour ainsi dire, et l'emploi de chaque temps est justifié par les prosateurs aussi bien que les poëtes. A chaque moment l'occasion se présente de contrôler les récensions des critiques modernes, d'expliquer quelque point de philologie, ou de rectifier quelque erreur. C'est ce que M. Veitch fait admirablement."—*Courrier Anglais.*

7. The Golden Treasury of Ancient Greek

Poetry; being a Collection of the finest passages in the Greek Classic Poets, with Introductory Notices and Notes. By R. S. WRIGHT, M.A., Fellow of Oriel College, Oxford. (Ext. fcap. 8vo., cloth, price 8s. 6d.)

"The introductions to the various periods of Greek literature are short essays full of spirit; condensed, yet clear; and a novelty which seems really useful, is a brief marginal analysis where the train of thought is obscure. The notes are a scholar's work, and shew a scholar's interest in his subject. The analyses of the specimen choruses from Æschylus and Sophocles, and the notes thereon, are excellent examples of short and pithy commentary."—*London Review.*

"One of the prettiest of the convenient 'Clarendon Press Series' is the 'Golden Treasury of Ancient Greek Poetry.' It is intended to bring together the choicest passages of all the Greek poets in a form convenient to the scholarly man who occasionally amuses his leisure hours with the classics. It is also fit for school use. The account of lyric poetry and of the gradual transition of the metres is excellent. Each poet has his date prefixed to the extracts, and every extract is headed by a short argument to show its connection, where such is at all needed. There are, besides, about two hundred pages of annotations, mainly very good. The selections are admirably made, and include many beautiful fragments and passages (among others the 'Swallow Song') that, being scattered through such authors as Athenæus, are unfamiliar to ordinary readers."—*Nation (American).*

"Les remarques présentées par notre commentateur sur les chœurs des poëtes tragiques et sur l'histoire et le développement de la poésie lyrique méritent une attention sérieuse. Somme toute, le *Golden treasury of ancient Greek poetry* est un livre extrêmement distingué et qu'on ne saurait trop recommander."—*Courrier Anglais.*

8. The Elements of Greek Accentuation (for Schools): abridged from his larger work by H. W. CHANDLER, M.A., Waynflete Professor of Moral and Metaphysical Philosophy, Oxford. (Ext. fcap. 8vo., cloth, price 2s. 6d.)

9. Sophocles. Oedipus Rex, Dindorf's Text, with English Notes by the Ven. Archdeacon BASIL JONES, M.A., formerly Fellow of University College. (Ext. fcap. 8vo., cloth, price 1s. 6d.)

10. Passages for Translation into Latin. For the use of Passmen and others. Selected by J. Y. SARGENT, M.A., Tutor, and formerly Fellow of Magdalen College. *Second Edition.* (Ext. fcap. 8vo., cloth, price 2s. 6d.)

11. The Elements of Deductive Logic, designed mainly for the use of Junior Students in the Universities. By the Rev. T. FOWLER, M.A., Fellow and Tutor of Lincoln College, Oxford. *Second Edition*, with a Collection of Examination Papers on the subject. (Ext. fcap. 8vo., cloth, price 3s. 6d.)

"We think such a manual is very opportune. Oxford requires the study of a certain amount of logic in the academical course, but hitherto, Aldrich's Manual, in its strange Latin and with its inconsistent terminology, has been the only text-book upon which students commence their acquaintance with the science of logic. Mr. Fowler's little work is not intended to be a substitute for more advanced treatises, but rather to put the general reader in possession of an outline of the science of logic, which will enable him to pursue the subject intelligently for himself on a more complete scale. It is a great thing to say of a manual of logic that it is not repulsive on first perusal, and a still higher praise to be able to describe it as not unattractive. Now, setting aside the necessary technicalities and mechanical details that must occur in every work on logic, we think this short treatise will be read with pleasure; partly owing to a judicious arrangement of the subject into short chapters and paragraphs, and not less from the clearness and freshness of the style. It is a novel plan to add at the end of the chapters, in the form of a note, a brief statement of opinions differing from the views given in the text, with references to the various works where these opinions may be examined. In a science like logic, in which doctors have agreed to disagree, there is a pleasant honesty in this which gives us confidence in our guide."—*London Review.*

"Books like Mr. Fowler's will do much to popularise the study of logic."—*Scotsman.*

12. **Specimens of Early English; being a Series of**
Extracts from the most important English Authors, Chronologically arranged, illustrative of the progress of the English Language and its Dialectic varieties, from A.D. 1250 to A.D. 1400. With Grammatical Introduction, Notes, and Glossary. By R. MORRIS. Esq., Editor of "The Story of Genesis and Exodus," &c. (Ext. fcap. 8vo., cloth, price 7s. 6d.)

"Few have done so much with such success as Mr. Morris, whose volume is not only a grammar, but a collection of well-selected reading and a dictionary, all in one. It will surprise some, perhaps, if we say that they who cannot read this book are ignorant of English, but the fact is incontrovertible nevertheless, and the task of mastering their own language is rendered easy by the clearness, good taste, and judgment of this accomplished author."—*Athenæum.*

"A book of this kind has long been needed for our colleges and higher schools, and even advanced students have never before had the results of late study on the earlier English writers thus compactly set forth. Mr. Morris has noted and classified with great care the specialties of the early dialects, arranging them under the three heads of Northern, Midland, and Southern. The outlines of the Early English grammar are, however, based on the Southern dialect only. To each declension and conjugation is added the Anglo-Saxon one from which it was degraded, so that its origin is clearly seen. Mr. Morris' . specimens include passages from every important work of the period, and are very fully and correctly annotated, with a complete glossary."—*Nation (American).*

"Anything like an acquaintance with what has been called the 'Old English period' of our literature was impossible to ordinary readers. The present volume is meant to supply this defect, and it could not have been better adapted to the object in view. Instead of the necessarily brief extracts in books of criticism, the student of the English language is here supplied with specimens extending from 9 to 42 pages of all the important English authors of the period; and these cannot fail to familiarize him with the grammar, dialects, and vocabulary of the early stages of our language in a manner which no amount of descriptive criticism can equal. The grammatical introduction—a valuable treatise of itself—and the carefully compiled notes and glossary contain everything necessary to enable the student 'to read the most difficult passages with pleasure and profit.' On many grounds we think the Oxford press has done a great service to the cause of education by the issue of this volume—of such education as may be advantageously pursued by young and old of every class, who may thus spend many a pleasant half hour in learning what Englishmen talked about and how they did it nearly six hundred years ago."—*Times of India.*

13. Spenser's Faery Queene. Book I. Designed
chiefly for the use of Schools. With Introduction, Notes, and
Glossary. By the Rev. G. W. KITCHIN, M.A., Whitehall
Preacher; formerly Censor of Christ Church. (Ext. fcap. 8vo.,
cloth, price 2s. 6d.)

"The present editor has done his work, such as it is, in the most
commendable manner, and we can even say that his numerous, though
concise, notes may be found very interesting and instructive by those
of us who have already grown familiar with the *Faery Queene* by any
ordinary and somewhat irregular course of reading. His etymological
inquiries are often completed and verified by all the resources that
modern scholarship supplies, though we must deem him to have reposed
too much confidence in Horne Tooke's system, where he has treated
the pronoun 'it' as a contraction of 'hight,' connected with the Ger-
man 'heissen.' Otherwise he is well informed on most of the needful
points, and skilful in condensing his information, and his literary refer-
ences and parallels are ample and, in general, very striking,"—*Spectator.*

" Le Spencer vient de paraître ; *Faery Queene.* Il eût été impossible
de confier ce travail à un critique plus capable. Dans une préface
très-intéressante et très-bien écrite, M. Kitchin explique pourquoi
jusqu'à ces derniers temps Spencer a été comparativement négligé."—
Courrier Anglais.

" May we be allowed to press upon our readers this admirable edu-
cational edition? * * * * Through Spenser, properly worked upon the
principles indicated by the philological notes, boys would get quickly a
large insight into language, as language."—*Literary Churchman.*

14. Chaucer. The Prologue to the Canterbury
Tales ; The Knightes Tale ; The Nonne Prest his Tale.
Edited by R. MORRIS, Editor for the Early English Text So-
ciety, &c. &c. (Ext. fcap. 8vo., cloth, price 2s. 6d.)

15. Hooker. Ecclesiastical Polity, Book I.
Edited by the Rev. R. W. CHURCH, M.A., Rector of Whatley;
formerly Fellow of Oriel College. (Ext. fcap. 8vo., cloth,
price 2s.)

16. French Classics: Vol. I. containing Cor-
neille's Cinna, and Molière's Les Femmes Savantes. Edited,
with Notes and Introduction, by GUSTAVE MASSON, B.A., Univ.
Gallic., Assistant Master in Harrow School. (Ext. fcap. 8vo.,
cloth, price 2s. 6d.)

" We can speak highly of this little volume."—*Educational Times.*
" This little work is a model of a text-book."—*The Museum.*

17. Selections from the Correspondence of
Madame de Sévigné and her chief contemporaries. Intended
more especially for girls' schools. (Ext. fcap. 8vo., cloth, price 3s.)

In course of Preparation.

I. CLASSICS.

1. Selections from the less known Latin Poets. By the Rev. NORTH PINDER, M.A., formerly Fellow of Trinity College, Oxford. [*In the Press.*

2. Ovid. Selections for the use of Schools. Being a new edition of the Selection made by the late Professor Ramsay. Edited by G. G. RAMSAY, M.A., The College, Glasgow. [*Nearly ready.*

3. Livy I–X. By J. R. SEELEY, M.A., Fellow of Christ's College, Cambridge; Professor of Latin, University College, London. Also a small edition for Schools. [*In the Press.*

4. Cicero. The Philippic Orations. By the Rev. J. R. KING, M.A., formerly Fellow and Tutor of Merton College, Oxford. [*In the Press.*

5. Cornelius Nepos (for Schools). With English Notes, by OSCAR BROWNING, M.A., Fellow of King's College, Cambridge, and Assistant Master at Eton College. [*In the Press.*

---

6. Sophocles. By the Rev. LEWIS CAMPBELL, M.A., Professor of Greek at St. Andrews, formerly Fellow of Queen's College, Oxford.

7. Homer, Iliad. By D. B. MONRO, M.A., Fellow and Tutor of Oriel College, Oxford.

8. Homer, Odyssey I–XII. By the Rev. W. W. MERRY, Fellow and Lecturer of Lincoln College, Oxford; and the late Rev. J. RIDDELL, M.A., Fellow of Balliol College.

9. ————— XIII–XXIV. By ROBINSON ELLIS, M.A., Fellow of Trinity College, Oxford.

10. A Golden Treasury of Greek Prose, being a collection of the finest passages in the principal Greek Prose Writers, with Introductory Notices and Notes. By R. S. WRIGHT, M.A., Fellow of Oriel College, Oxford, and J. E. L. SHADWELL, B.A., Student of Christ Church.

11. **Horace. With English Notes and Introduction.**
By the Rev. E. WICKHAM, M.A., Fellow and Tutor of New College, Oxford. Also a small Edition for Schools.

12. **Cicero. Select Letters. By the Rev. A. WATSON,**
M.A., Fellow and Tutor of Brasenose College, Oxford.

13. **Aristotle's Politics. By W. L. NEWMAN, M.A.,**
Fellow and Lecturer of Balliol College, Oxford.

---

14. **Selections from Xenophon (for Schools). With**
English Notes and Maps, by J. S. PHILLPOTTS, B.C.L., Fellow of New College, Oxford; Assistant Master in Rugby School.

15. **The Commentaries of C. Jul. Caesar (for Schools).**
Part I. The Gallic War, with English Notes, &c., by CHARLES E. MOBERLY, M.A., Assistant Master in Rugby School; formerly Scholar of Balliol.

Also, to follow: Part II. The Civil War: by the same Editor.

16. **Select Epistles of Cicero and Pliny (for Schools).**
With English Notes, by the Rev. C. E. PRICHARD, M.A., formerly Fellow of Balliol.

17. **Selections from Plato (for Schools). With English**
Notes, by the Rev. B. JOWETT, M.A., Regius Professor of Greek, and J. PURVES, M.A., Fellow and Lecturer of Balliol College.

18. **Theocritus (for Schools). With English Notes, by**
the Rev. H. SNOW, M.A., Fellow of King's College, Cambridge, and Assistant Master at Eton College.

II. PHILOSOPHY.

1. **The Elements of Deductive Logic, designed mainly**
for the use of Junior Students in the Universities. By the Rev. T. FOWLER, M.A., Fellow and Tutor of Lincoln College, Oxford. *Second Edition*, with a Collection of Examination Papers on the subject. (Ext. fcap. 8vo., cloth, price 3s. 6d.)

2. **A Handbook of Political Economy, for the use of**
Schools. By the Rev. J. E. THOROLD ROGERS, M.A., formerly Professor of Political Economy, Oxford. *[In the Press.*

III. Mathematics.

1. A Course of Lectures on Pure Geometry. By H. J. STEPHEN SMITH, M.A., F.R.S., Fellow of Balliol College, and Savilian Professor of Geometry in the University of Oxford.

2. A Work on Book-keeping. By R. G. C. HAMILTON, Esq., Accountant to the Education Committee of the Privy Council, and JOHN BALL, Esq. (of the Firm of Messrs. Quilter, Ball, & Co.), Examiners in Book-keeping for the Society of Arts' Examination. [*In the Press.*

A Series of Elementary Works is being arranged, and will shortly be announced.

IV. History.

1. A History of Germany and of the Empire, down to the close of the Middle Ages. By J. BRYCE, M.A., Fellow of Oriel College, Oxford.

2. A History of British India. By S. OWEN, M.A., Lee's Reader in Law and History, Christ Church; and Reader in Indian Law in the University of Oxford.

3. A History of Greece. By E. A. FREEMAN, M.A., formerly Fellow of Trinity College, Oxford.

4. A Constitutional History of England. By the Rev. W. STUBBS, M.A., formerly Fellow of Trinity College, Oxford, and Regius Professor of Modern History in the University of Oxford.

5. A History of Germany, from the Reformation. By ADOLPHUS W. WARD, M.A., Fellow of St. Peter's College, Cambridge; Professor of History, Owen's College, Manchester.

V. Law.

Commentaries on Roman Law; from the original and the best modern sources. In Two Volumes, demy 8vo. By H. J. ROBY, M.A., formerly Fellow of St. John's College, Cambridge; Professor of Law at University College, London..

VI. Physical Science.

1. Natural Philosophy. In four Volumes. By Sir W. Thomson, LL.D., D.C.L., F.R.S., Professor of Natural Philosophy, Glasgow, and P. G. Tait, M.A., Professor of Natural Philosophy, Edinburgh; formerly Fellows of St. Peter's College, Cambridge. [*Vol. I. now ready.*

2. By the same Authors, a smaller Work on the same subject, forming a complete Introduction to it, so far as it can be carried out with Elementary Geometry and Algebra. [*In the Press.*

3. Forms of Animal Life. By G. Rolleston, M.D., F.R.S., Linacre Professor of Physiology, Oxford. Illustrated by Descriptions and Drawings of Dissections. [*In the Press.*

4. On Laboratory Practice. By A. Vernon Harcourt, M.A., Lee's Reader in Chemistry at Christ Church, and H. G. Madan, M.A., Fellow of Queen's College, Oxford.

5. Geology. By J. Phillips, M.A., D.C.L., LL.D., F.R.S., Professor of Geology, Oxford.

6. Mechanics. By the Rev. B. Price, M.A., F.R.S., F.R.A.S., Fellow of Pembroke College, Oxford, and Sedleian Professor of Natural Philosophy.

7. Acoustics. By W. F. Donkin, M.A., F.R.S., Savilian Professor of Astronomy, Oxford.

8. Optics. By R. B. Clifton, M.A., F.R.A.S., Professor of Experimental Philosophy, Oxford; formerly Fellow of St. John's College, Cambridge.

9. Electricity. By W. Esson, M.A., Fellow and Mathematical Lecturer of Merton College, Oxford.

10. Crystallography. By M. H. N. Story-Maskelyne, M.A., Professor of Mineralogy, Oxford; and Deputy Keeper, British Museum.

11. Mineralogy. By the same Author.

12. Physiological Physics. By G. Griffith, M.A., Secretary to the British Association, and Natural Science Master at Harrow School.

13. Magnetism.

VII. English Language and Literature.

1. On the Principles of Grammar. By the Rev. E. Thring, M.A., Head Master of Uppingham School.
[*In the Press.*

2. Also, by the same Author, a Manual of Analysis, designed to serve as an Exercise and Composition Book in the English Language. [*In the Press.*

3. The Philology of the English Tongue. By the Rev. J. Earle, M.A., formerly Fellow of Oriel College, Oxford, and Professor of Anglo-Saxon.

4. Specimens of the Scottish Language; being a Series of Annotated Extracts illustrative of the Literature and Philology of the Lowland Tongue from the fourteenth to the nineteenth century. With Introduction and Glossary. By A. H. Burgess, A.M.

5. Typical Selections from the best English Authors from the Sixteenth to the Nineteenth Century, (to serve as a higher Reading-book,) with Introductory Notices and Notes, being a Contribution towards a History of English Literature.

VIII. French. By Mons. Jules Bué,

Honorary M.A. of Oxford; Taylorian Teacher of French; Examiner in the Oxford Local Examinations from 1858.

1. A French Grammar. A complete theory of the French language, with the rules in French and English, and numerous Examples to serve as first Exercises in the language.

2. A French Grammar Test. A book of Exercises on French Grammar; each Exercise being preceded by Grammatical Questions.

3. Exercises in Translation No. 1, from French into English, with general rules on Translation; and containing Notes, Hints, and Cautions, founded on a comparison of the Grammar and Genius of the two languages.

4. Exercises in Translation No. 2, from English into French, on the same plan as the preceding book.

FRENCH CLASSICS.

By GUSTAVE MASSON, B.A., Univ. Gallic.,

Assistant Master in Harrow School.

1. Vol. I. Corneille: Cinna. Molière: Les Femmes
Savantes. With Fontenelle's Life of Corneille and Notes.
[*Just published, price 2s. 6d.*

2. Vol. II. Racine: Athalie. Corneille: Le Menteur.
With Louis Racine's Life of his Father.

3. Vol. III. Molière: Les Fourberies de Scapin.
Racine: Andromaque. With Voltaire's Life of Molière.

4. Selections from the Correspondence of Madame de
Sévigné, &c. (Intended more especially for girls' schools.)
[*Just published, price 3s.*

5. Selections from modern French Authors: About, and
·Töpfer. [*In course of preparation.*

IX. GERMAN CLASSICS. By Dr. BUCHHEIM,

Professor of the German Language and Literature in King's College,
London; and Examiner in German to the University of London.

1. Schiller's Wilhelm Tell. With a Life of Schiller;
an historical and critical Introduction, Arguments, and a com-
plete Commentary. [*In the Press.*

2. Goethe's Egmont. With a Life of Goethe, &c.

3. Lessing's Minna von Barnhelm. A Comedy. With
a Life of Lessing, Critical Commentary, &c.

X. ART.

1. A Treatise on Harmony. By the Rev. Sir F. A.
GORE OUSELEY, Bart., M.A., Mus. Doc., Professor of Music,
Oxford. [*Nearly ready.*

2. A Treatise on Counterpoint, Canon, and Fugue, based
upon that of Cherubini. By the same Author.

3. A Handbook of Pictorial Art, with numerous Illustra-
tions, and Practical Advice. By the Rev. R. ST. J. TYRWHITT,
M.A., formerly Tutor of Christ Church. [*In the Press.*

A System of Physical Education: Theoretical and
Practical. By ARCHIBALD MACLAREN, The Gymnasium, Oxford.
[*In the Press.*

XI. English Classics.

Designed to meet the wants of Students in English Literature: under the superintendence of the Rev. J. S. Brewer, M.A., *of Queen's College, Oxford, and Professor of English Literature at King's College, London.*

There are two dangers to which the student of English literature is exposed at the outset of his task;—his reading is apt to be too narrow or too diffuse.

Out of the vast number of authors set before him in books professing to deal with this subject he knows not which to select: he thinks he must read a little of all; he soon abandons so hopeless an attempt; he ends by contenting himself with second-hand information; and professing to study English literature, he fails to master a single English author. On the other hand, by confining his attention to one or two writers, or to one special period of English literature, the student narrows his view of it; he fails to grasp the subject as a whole; and in so doing misses one of the chief objects of his study.

How may these errors be avoided? How may minute reading be combined with comprehensiveness of view?

In the hope of furnishing an answer to these questions the Delegates of the Press, acting upon the advice and experience of Professor Brewer, have determined to issue a series of small volumes, which shall embrace, in a convenient form and at a low price, the general extent of English Literature, as represented in its masterpieces at successive epochs. It is thought that the student, by confining himself, in the first instance, to those authors who are most worthy of his attention, will be saved from the dangers of hasty and indiscriminate reading. By adopting the course thus marked out for him he will become familiar with the productions of the greatest minds in English Literature; and should he never be able to pursue the subject beyond the limits here prescribed, he will have laid the foundation of accurate habits of thought and judgment, which cannot fail of being serviceable to him hereafter.

The authors and works selected are such as will best serve to illustrate English literature in its *historical* aspect. As "the eye of history," without which history cannot be understood, the literature of a nation is the clearest and most intelligible record of its life. Its thoughts and its emotions, its graver and its less serious modes, its progress, or its degeneracy, are told by its best authors in their best words. This view of the subject will suggest the safest rules for the study of it.

With one exception all writers before the Reformation are excluded from the Series. However great may be the value of literature before that epoch, it is not completely national. For it had no common organ of language; it addressed itself to special classes; it dealt mainly with special subjects. Again ; of writers who flourished after the Reformation, who were popular in their day, and reflected the manners and sentiments of their age, the larger part by far must be excluded from our list. Common sense tells us that if young persons, who have but a limited time at their disposal, read Marlowe or Greene, Burton, Hakewill or Du Bartas, Shakspeare, Bacon, and Milton will be comparatively neglected.

Keeping, then, to the best authors in each epoch—and here popular estimation is a safe guide—the student will find the following list of writers amply sufficient for his purpose: Chaucer, Spenser, Hooker, Shakspeare, Bacon, Milton, Dryden, Bunyan, Pope, Johnson, Burke, and Cowper. In other words, Chaucer is the exponent of the Middle Ages in England; Spenser of the Reformation and the Tudors; Hooker of the latter years of Elizabeth; Shakspeare and Bacon of the transition from Tudor to Stuart; Milton of Charles I and the Commonwealth; Dryden and Bunyan of the Restoration; Pope of Anne and the House of Hanover; Johnson, Burke, and Cowper of the reign of George III to the close of the last century.

The list could be easily enlarged; the names of Jeremy Taylor, Clarendon, Hobbes, Locke, Swift, Addison, Goldsmith, and others are omitted. But in so wide a field, the difficulty is to keep the series from becoming unwieldly, without diminishing its comprehensiveness. Hereafter, should the plan prove to be useful, some of the masterpieces of the authors just mentioned may be added to the list.

The task of selection is not yet finished. For purposes of education, it would neither be possible, nor, if possible, desirable, to place in the hands of students the whole of the works of the authors we have chosen. We must set before them only the masterpieces of literature, and their studies must be directed, not only to the greatest minds, but to their choicest productions. These are to be read again and again, separately and in combination. Their purport, form, language, bearing on the times, must be minutely studied, till the student begins to recognise the full value of each work both in itself and in its relations to those that go before and those that follow it.

It is especially hoped that this Series may prove useful to Ladies' Schools and Middle Class Schools; in which English Literature must always be a leading subject of instruction.

A General Introduction to the Series. By the Rev. PROFESSOR BREWER, M.A.

1. **Chaucer.** The Prologue to the Canterbury Tales; The Knightes Tale; The Nonne Prest his Tale. Edited by R. MORRIS, Editor for the Early English Text Society, &c. &c. Ext. fcap. 8vo., cloth, price 2s. 6d. [*Just Published.*

2. **Spenser.** Faery Queene, Book I. Edited by the Rev. G. W. KITCHIN, M.A., Examining Chaplain to the Bishop of Chester. Ext. fcap. 8vo., cloth, price 2s. 6d. [*Just Published.*

   Book II. By the same Editor. [*In the Press.*

3. **Hooker.** Ecclesiastical Polity, Book I. Edited by the Rev. R. W. CHURCH, M.A., Rec̃ ᴼf Whatley; formerly Fellow of Oriel College. Ext. fcap. 8vo.; ᴄ ˋ price 2s. [*Just Published.*

4. **Shakspeare.** Select Plays. Edited by the Rev. W. G. CLARK, M.A., Fellow of Trinity College, Cambridge, and Public Orator; and W. ALDIS WRIGHT, M.A., Librarian of Trinity College, Cambridge.

5. **Bacon.** Advancement of Learning. Edited by
W. ALDIS WRIGHT, M.A. [*In the Press.*

6. **Milton.** Allegro and Penseroso; Comus; Lycidas;
Paradise Lost; Samson Agonistes. Edited by R. C. BROWNE,
M.A., King's College, Cambridge.

7. **Dryden.** Stanzas on the Death of Oliver Cromwell;
Astraea Redux; Annus Mirabilis; Absalom and Achitophel:
Religio Laici; The Hind and Panther.

8. **Bunyan.** Grace Abounding; The Pilgrim's Progress.
Edited by the Rev. E. VENABLES, M.A., Precentor of Lincoln.

9. **Pope.** Essay on Man, with the Epistles and Satires.
Edited by the Rev. M. PATTISON, M.A., Rector of Lincoln
College, Oxford.

10. **Johnson.** Rasselas; Lives of Pope and Dryden.
Edited by the Rev. C. H. O. DANIEL, M.A., Fellow and Tutor
of Worcester College, Oxford.

11. **Burke.** Thoughts on the Present Discontents; the
two Speeches on America; Reflections on the French Revolution.
Edited by GOLDWIN SMITH, M.A., Fellow of University College,
Oxford; formerly Regius Professor of Modern History.

12. **Cowper.** The Task, and some of his minor Poems.
Edited by PROFESSOR SHAIRP, M.A., St. Andrews.

These volumes will be (as nearly as possible) uniform in shape and
size. There will be a brief preface, biographical and literary, to each;
and each will have such short notes only as are needed to elucidate
the text.

Published for the University of Oxford, by MACMILLAN and CO.,
London and Cambridge.

Clarendon Press Series.

ENGLISH CLASSICS.

Designed to meet the wants of Students in English Literature: under the superintendence of the Rev. J. S. BREWER, M.A., *of Queen's College, Oxford, and Professor of English Literature at King's College, London.*

It is especially hoped that this Series may prove useful to Ladies' Schools and Middle Class Schools; in which English Literature must always be a leading subject of instruction.

A General Introduction to the Series. By the Rev. PROFESSOR BREWER, M.A.

1. **Chaucer.** The Prologue to the Canterbury Tales; The Knightes Tale; The Nonne Prest his Tale. Edited by R. MORRIS, Editor for the Early English Text Society, &c. &c. Ext. fcap. 8vo., cloth, 2s. 6d. [*Just Published.*

2. **Spenser.** Faery Queene, Book I. Ext. fcap. 8vo., cloth, 2s. 6d. [*Just Published.*

3. **Hooker.** Ecclesiastical Polity, Book I. Edited by the Rev. R. W. CHURCH, M.A., Rector of Whatley; formerly Fellow of Oriel College. [*Nearly ready.*

4. **Shakspeare.** Select Plays. Edited by the Rev. W. G. CLARK, M.A., Fellow of Trinity College, Cambridge, and Public Orator; and W. ALDIS WRIGHT, M.A., Librarian of Trinity College, Cambridge.

5. **Bacon.** Advancement of Learning. Edited by
   W. ALDIS WRIGHT, M.A. [*In the Press.*

6. **Milton.** Allegro and Penseroso; Comus; Lycidas;
   Paradise Lost; Samson Agonistes. Edited by R. C. BROWNE,
   M.A., King's College, Cambridge.

7. **Dryden.** Stanzas on the Death of Oliver Cromwell;
   Astraea Redux; Annus Mirabilis; Absalom and Achitophel;
   Religio Laici; The Hind and Panther.

8. **Bunyan.** Grace Abounding; The Pilgrim's Progress.
   Edited by the Rev. E. VENABLES, M.A., Precentor of Lincoln.

9. **Pope.** Essay on Man, with the Epistles and Satires.
   Edited by the Rev. M. PATTISON, M.A., Rector of Lincoln
   College, Oxford.

10. **Johnson.** Rasselas; Lives of Pope and Dryden.
    Edited by the Rev. C. H. O. DANIEL, M.A., Fellow and Tutor
    of Worcester College, Oxford.

11. **Burke.** Thoughts on the Present Discontents; the
    two Speeches on America; Reflections on the French Revolution.
    Edited by GOLDWIN SMITH, M.A., Fellow of University College,
    Oxford; formerly Regius Professor of Modern History.

12. **Cowper.** The Task, and some of his minor Poems.
    Edited by PROFESSOR SHAIRP, M.A., St. Andrews.

These volumes will be (as nearly as possible) uniform in shape and
size. There will be a brief preface, biographical and literary, to each;
and each will have such short notes only as are needed to elucidate
the text.

Published for the University of Oxford, by MACMILLAN and CO.,
London and Cambridge.